The Democratic Constitution

The Democratic Constitution

Experimentalism and Interpretation

BRIAN E. BUTLER

THE UNIVERSITY OF CHICAGO PRESS   CHICAGO AND LONDON

The University of Chicago Press, Chicago 60637
The University of Chicago Press, Ltd., London
© 2017 by The University of Chicago
All rights reserved. Published 2017
Printed in the United States of America

26 25 24 23 22 21 20 19 18 17   1 2 3 4 5

ISBN-13: 978-0-226-47450-2 (cloth)
ISBN-13: 978-0-226-47464-9 (e-book)
DOI: 10.7208/chicago/9780226474649.001.0001

Library of Congress Cataloging-in-Publication Data

Names: Butler, Brian E., author.
Title: The democratic constitution : experimentalism and interpretation /
    Brian E. Butler.
Description: Chicago ; London : The University of Chicago Press, 2017. |
    Includes bibliographical references and index.
Identifiers: LCCN 2016049360 | ISBN 9780226474502 (cloth : alk. paper) |
    ISBN 9780226474649 (e-book)
Subjects: LCSH: Constitutional history—United States. | Democracy—Philosophy.
Classification: LCC KF4541 .B985 2017 | DDC 342.7302/9—dc23 LC record available at
    https://lccn.loc.gov/2016049360

♾ This paper meets the requirements of ANSI/NISO Z39.48-1992 (Permanence of Paper).

Contents

Introduction   1

CHAPTER 1:   The Democratic Challenge to Constitutional Law   4

CHAPTER 2:   Democratic Aims and Experimentalist Procedure   22

CHAPTER 3:   Information-Rich Jurisprudence   49

CHAPTER 4:   Epstein, Holmes, and Regulatory Takings
Jurisprudence   77

CHAPTER 5:   Lochnering   105

CHAPTER 6:   *Citizens United*   128

CHAPTER 7:   *Brown* and *Obergefell*: Two Positive Precedents?   151

CHAPTER 8:   From Social Contract Theory to Sociable Contract
Theory   182

Conclusion   200

Acknowledgments   205

Notes   207

Bibliography   235

Index   245

Introduction

This is a book centered upon constitutional law and cases decided by the United States Supreme Court. Its argument, somewhat paradoxically it might seem, is that a fixation upon the Supreme Court and United States constitutional law as it currently functions and is theoretically justified is very problematic. What I attempt in the pages that follow is a reconstruction of legal theory with the prime aim of making it more democratic in both concept and practice. This explains why I have called the title *The Democratic Constitution*. Assuming that a healthy democracy is the aim, and that John Dewey's requirement that democracy cannot properly be furthered by non-democratic means is valid, then what is needed is to offer a democratic conception of constitutional law that can satisfy this demand. This reconstructed conception of law must be attractive enough to be seen as a viable option to the dominant picture of constitutional law in contemporary thought and practice—that of constitutional law as a foundational set of ground or game rules prior to and constitutive of democratic processes.

Using pragmatic ideals, as characterized by Charles Sanders Peirce and John Dewey, in this treatise I critique and reconstruct the reasoning and the results of Supreme Court cases such as *Brown v. Board of Education*, *Citizens United*, *Lochner*, *Lucas*, *Mahon*, and *Obergefell*. As opposed to the traditional tools of legal analysis, and various conceptions of law that, along with slogans like "the rule of law as a law of rules," see law as a formally unique and separate type of practice, I instead offer a jurisprudence of "democratic experimentalism."

Further, as opposed to a conception of law as only accepting some type of particularly "legal" reasons, I present a conception of constitutional law as factually grounded, as indeed forcing the creation of necessary knowledge of whatever type that is necessary in order to make a properly informed decision.

Not only are the reasons demanded within this conception of law expected to be broader and more empirically informed than standard conceptions of constitutional law, but the type of decisions demanded from the Court changes under democratic experimentalism. Most importantly, decisions are decentered away from the Court as much as possible in order to emphasize local rule and democratic choice. Furthermore, decisions of constitutional law, when made by the Court, are not expected to be final and irrevocable but rather are to always be considered revisable in light of further investigation into options in governance and growing knowledge of empirical facts. A jurisprudence of democratic experimentalism aims at making the best available choice as is demanded at the time with the understanding that further knowledge, further social developments, or further experiments in governance may overturn what was thought incontrovertible at any given moment.

This is not a work of descriptive analysis—indeed this treatise is premised upon the idea that law is always a project under experimental construction rather than an institution that has an a priori essence or has arrived at a finalized point of perfection. Law, that is, is seen not as a "natural type" to be identified and perfectly defined but rather is conceived of as a constructed set of social practices. That is not to say that anything I argue for within this book is an example of "ideal" or "utopian" theory. This treatise is not arguing for a legal revolution. Indeed, most if not all aspects of a jurisprudence of democratic experimentalism will be seen to already be available and even sometimes advocated for in piecemeal fashion within the legal profession.

Further, this is not a book that takes sides on the issue of more or less government. Instead, in this work that issue is seen as one that ultimately should be decided on a case by case method in light of the best evidence and vigorous democratic deliberation. In this sense this treatise resides in a position uncomfortable to both the liberal and conservative political stances most prevalent today. But this is actually a quite positive aspect of the theory offered—it offers a conception of constitutional law and legal reasoning that resists entrenchment in the doctrinaire and emphasizes the discipline of empirical investigation.

Why has such a program not been attempted more wholeheartedly? The concern that motivated this book is that it is through a combination of lack of nerve, failure of imagination, and protection of professional territory through ritualized initiation into "thinking like a lawyer" that other possibilities have been ignored.[1] Hopefully this treatise will raise questions as to why there is more effort put into policing the boundaries of law "proper" than finding the best answers possible on issues important enough to find implicated and litigated in constitutional law.

In his 1930 treatise *The Bramble Bush*, Karl N. Llewellyn claimed that part of his intent for writing it was to give some counterweight to "the touching faith that the current rationalizations of an institution, first, fit the facts, second, exhaust the subject, third, negate other, negate better possibilities. Nowhere more than in law do you need armor against that type of ethnocentric and chronocentric snobbery—the smugness of your own tribe and your own time. We are the Greeks; all others are barbarians."[2] The construction of "the democratic constitution" in this treatise is offered in the same spirit. Hopefully in the process of counterweighing this tendency, this book can give also some positive weight to democratic aims.

CHAPTER ONE

The Democratic Challenge to Constitutional Law

This chapter begins by outlining one dominant explanation for judicial supremacy in interpretation of constitutional law. This explanation, the "protection from the tyranny of the majority" story, will then be critiqued through the work of contemporary theorists that are skeptical of this rationale not only due to its being empirically questionable but also and more important because of its incompatibility with democratic self-government. These critiques of Supreme Court supremacy point toward the necessity of a more democratic conception of constitutional law.

In this book the aim of a more democratic conception of constitutional law is not only accepted but is adopted in a very rigorous form. The democratic requirements accepted in this book are based upon the tenants of pragmatism as initiated by Charles Sanders Peirce and, most centrally, elaborated and championed by John Dewey. As will be shown, Deweyan democracy is very demanding. This chapter will end by noting and accepting one central implication of Dewey's demanding conception of democracy: that a democratic society can only be built upon democratic means. In the remaining chapters I construct a conception of "law as a democratic means" in order to render it plausible and desirable that constitutional law could be implemented in a more democratic manner. This conception, inspired by the 1930s work of Thurman W. Arnold and Edward Steven Robinson, and the contemporary work of Charles Sabel, Michael Dorf, and William Simon, among others, is then offered under the name of "democratic experimentalism."

Saving the People from Themselves

In his book, *The Case Against the Supreme Court*, Erwin Chemerinsky leads off with the story of *Buck v. Bell*, Oliver Wendell Holmes Jr's properly infamous opinion for the United States Supreme Court.[1] The state of Virginia had enacted a eugenics law that legalized the involuntary sterilization of persons found to be of low intelligence. The state moved to sterilize Carrie Buck under this law. A hearing was held where testimony was offered that she was "retarded." (Evidence of her later life raises great doubt as to this conclusion.) Sterilization was ordered and executed without her consent. Carrie Buck's guardian, R. G. Shelton, filed suit challenging the constitutionality of the Virginia law. Buck's attorney argued that forced sterilization was a violation of her fundamental right to bodily integrity and cruel and unusual punishment. In an eight-to-one opinion, the Supreme Court ruled against Buck arguing that, among other things, the sterilization wasn't punishment at all because she had not been convicted of a crime. Holmes wrote in the opinion that the law was reasonable because "three generations of imbeciles are enough." After offering this frightening result, Chemerinsky then continues on to tell a book-length story detailing and lamenting the many other terrible decisions made by the United States Supreme Court.[2]

The ensuing discussion of Supreme Court antiprecedent decisions that, according to Chemerinsky, in various ways set social progress back and thwarted justice, encompasses 225 of the 344 pages of his book. And the list of what he considered judicial failures is substantial. There were failures in decisions on matters of slavery and race that included *Prigg v. Pennsylvania* and *Dred Scott v. Sandford.* There was the Supreme Court's narrowing of the protections of the Equal Protection Clause through the *Slaughter-House Cases, Plessy v. Ferguson, Cumming v. Board of Education, Berea College v. Kentucky,* and *Gong Lum v. Rice.* There was the modern Court's failure in discrimination cases as seen in, among other cases, *Washington v. Davis, Mobile v. Bolden, McClesky v. Kemp, Parents Involved in Community Schools v. Seattle School District No. 1, J. A. Croson v. City of Richmond, Fisher v. University of Texas at Austin.* Then there were failures to act constitutionally in times of crisis as seen in *Korematsu v. United States, Schenk v. United States, Frohwerk v. United States, Debs v. United States, Dennis v. United States, Holder v. Humanitarian Law Project,* and *Hamdi v. Rumsfeld.* Also problematic was the way the Court has protected property and states' rights to the determinant of individual citizens seen in *Hammer v. Dagenhart, Lochner v. New York, Allgeyer v. Louisiana, Adair v. United States, Coppage v. Kansas, United States v. E. C. Knight Co., Carter v. Carter Coal Company, A.L.A. Schecter Poultry Corp. v. United States, Railroad Retirement Board v. Alton R. Co., United States v. Lopez, United States v. Morrison, National Federation of Independent Business v. Sebelius, New York v. United States,* and *Prinz v. United States.* Then there were specific failures of the Roberts Court seen in, for example, *United States v. Apel, Pliva, Inc. v. Mensing, Mutual Pharmaceutical v. Bartlett, American Express v. Italian Colors Restaurant, Circuit City v. Adams, Wal-Mart Stores v. Dukes, AT&T Mobility v. Conception,* and *Ledbetter v. Goodyear Tire and Rubber Co., Inc.* Also identified were consistent failures in protection from abuses of government power such as *Van de Kamp v. Goldstein, Mireles v. Waco, Imbler v. Pachtman, Bogan v. Scott-Harris, Briscoe v. LaHue, Hope v. Pelzer, Ashcroft v. al-Kidd, Florida Prepaid v. College Savings Bank, Kimel v. Florida Board of Regents, Board of Trustees of University of Alabama v. Garrett, Alden v. Maine, Bryan County, Oklahoma v. Brown, Citizens United, Bush v. Gore, Garcetti v. Ceballos, Arizona Free Enterprise Club's Freedom Club PAC v. Bennett,* and *Shelby County, Alabama v. Holder.*

The failures turn out, therefore, to be an impressive-sized group indeed. And Chemerinsky's list is not meant to be exhaustive of either substantive areas of law (for instance, gender is not really covered) or cases in those areas actually analyzed (there are in the area of race, as an example, many other antiprecedents that could be identified given his criteria). But there must have been successes? In fact, Chemerinsky identifies only a fifteen-year period—the Warren Court—that according to him lived up to the proper function of the Court. And in his opinion even the Warren Court did not fully fulfil the Court's proper function because it did not show a full moral commitment to its central mission. So, even in the best case scenario of a decision like *Brown v. Board of Education* (a case he deems a success) the Court, though partially living up to its job, still ultimately failed as to its essential purpose. The section of the book devoted to Supreme Court success—however limited and qualified—lasts only thirty-six pages. And many of those few pages explain why this most successful of Supreme Court eras also failed.

One conclusion Chemerinsky derives from this investigation is not surprising: "The Court has frequently failed, throughout American history, at its most important tasks, at its most important moments."[3] Furthermore, the Court has lost because "the Court usually has been on the side of the powerful—government and business—at the expense of individuals whom the Constitution was designed to protect."[4] That is, the Court consistently neglects to protect racial minorities, fails to stand up for rights in times of crisis, and has championed the strong, such as big business and states, at expense of individual rights. For Chemerinsky the Roberts Court is one of the worst disappointments in all of these areas.

Of course to know that the Supreme Court is failing at its job is to have some kind of idea of its function so as to be able to measure both its failures and its success. And some might think many of the above cases were not failures at all, though not many would find *Buck v. Bell* a success. That he sees protecting business and states at the expense of individual rights a failure gives a start at understanding what standards Chemerinsky is using to evaluate the Court. But what would be a success? To his credit, it is very clear as to what he thinks the Constitution, and the Court's relationship to the Constitution, is supposed to be when functioning properly. First, the Constitution "creates a framework for American government, but it also limits the exercise of governing authority by protecting individual rights."[5] Further, the Constitution's defining characteristic designed expressly to help in this project is that it is difficult to alter. The reason for this unchanging and foundational quality is to prevent the tyranny of the majority. Therefore, Chemerinsky concludes, the Constitution's great overriding purpose is to protect minorities because "it is minorities—political, racial, social, economic—that need protection that democracy often cannot and will not provide."[6] This purpose, in turn, explains what the Supreme Court's primary role is: "Therefore, I believe that the two preeminent purposes of the Court are to protect the rights of minorities who cannot rely on the political process and to uphold the Constitution in the face of any repressive desires of political majorities."[7] So, for Chemerinsky, to judge the Court's performance properly is to look at it in light of its success in protecting political minorities from the tyranny of the majority. And in light of this purpose he thinks the Court has been a universal and consistent failure as represented by the crushing list of antiprecedent cases above.

Contrary to Chemerinsky one might think the Constitution has a different purpose or quite possibly multiple purposes. For instance, it might have been designed not to protect minorities but rather just to slow down democratic processes so they would be more deliberate and not so volatile. Indeed, this is one of the offered Madisonian justifications for representation. And certainly the worry of faction is not just a worry of rogue majorities. Minorities are factions too. Some minorities can be very powerful. But even if the constitution was designed to protect minorities from the tyranny of the majority, there is also room for disagreement over which minorities were meant to be protected. For example, it might be outlier states that were to be protected against the majority. Or it might be the elite property owners as a minority class that were to be protected. (This last possibility is the thesis offered in Charles A. Beard's *An Economic Interpretation of the Constitution of the United States*.[8]) Protecting these last two minorities cannot be Chemerisky's stance, though, because cases that do exactly this are identified as failures in his list. Clearly he thinks it is racial minorities and things like progressive social legislation for workers that the Court should protect. But this, of course, is a contested picture of the Court's constitutional purpose. Though, admittedly, it is a picture of constitutional law that is quite popular.

Another possibility would be to use the above list as evidence to support an argument to the effect that the tyranny of the majority is not so bad and, instead of the Court, democratic process would better protect constitutional and individual rights. Maybe, that is, this is evidence for some type of constitutional populism. Indeed, a huge majority of the antiprecedents listed previously are examples where the Court gets in the way of legislation Chemerinsky approves of. So not only does the Court fail to protect minority rights in these cases, but it fails in a very destructive way because quite often its inadequacy is an impediment to legislation where more purportedly democratic branches had, in his opinion, succeeded.[9] But Chemerinsky condescendingly rejects this populist constitutionalism option as naive and its serious consideration as just a "product of academic detachment."[10] The only evidence he offers for this rejection other than the strength of his own intuitions, though, is a couple of hypothetical questions:—"Who will be participating, and what will they be doing?" and "A populist constitutional law, almost by definition, would reflect popular attitudes. But why believe that this would be better than the courts in enforcing the Constitution?"[11] These two hypothetical questions, it seems, are reason enough to eliminate any recourse to democratic means. Indeed, the questions seem to carry enough weight to eliminate any inquiry into the mere possibility of more democratic options.

But what if Chemerinsky's picture of the purpose of the United States Constitution and the Court is accepted? This leaves us with an important purpose that is being radically underserved by the institution he believes is specifically designed to further it. Normally if a tool's success rate in relation to the ends it was designed for had an easily identifiable failure rate of such magnitude it would be time to change tools. But this is not what he proposes to do. Startlingly, in the face of his own evidence of all of the Court failures he documented he argues rather that if only the justices would properly interpret the Constitution the Court could be "a moral leader."[12] So, without any empirical evidence of success other than the brief and seemingly unrepresentative moment of the Warren Court and presumably the recent isolated example of *Obergefell* (a decision that came after his book was published), and indeed much evidence of failure, even recurring evidence of the Court getting in the way of democratic successes, he argues the Court's power of judicial review is necessary because of "the need to enforce the limits of the Constitution." Indeed, he claims that "those without political power have nowhere to turn except the judiciary for the protection of their constitutional rights."[13]

He does, in service of his hope for this missing moral leadership from the Court, offer minor structural changes that would—it is assumed—help insure the that justices on the Supreme Court would have the legal knowledge, wisdom, and moral courage to ensure success. These changes are things such as making justices present a type of mission statement articulating the role of Court in enforcing the Constitution against the will of majority, picking justices on a merit system, rotating term limits, and changing the confirmation process so nominees would have to answer substantive questions honestly during hearings rather than hide behind neutral umpire rhetoric.[14]

Belief in the Court's role as protector of minorities from popular prejudice and discrimination is, admittedly, a popular and ubiquitous one in United States legal theory. It is found in Alexander M. Bickel's belief that the Court does this as protector of principle and John Hart Ely's alternate claim that it does this through, alternately, protection of process.[15] It is found in Richard Epstein's conservative theory of constitutional "classical" liberalism and Ronald Dworkin's morality-driven jurisprudential theory. It is, indeed, virtually an unquestioned assumption in legal thought relating to judicial review and judicial supremacy when it comes to the constitution.

On top of this characteristic legal claim, Chemerinsky's constitutional analysis exemplifies another recurring pattern in constitutional law theory and jurisprudence. This pattern goes as follows in Chemerinsky's text. He is both enamored by the Supreme Court and judicial supremacy in constitutional interpretation, sure of its necessity, and yet frustrated by its seemingly incessant failures. He then tries to identify the source of the failures without questioning the core constitutive assumptions behind judicial review and supremacy in the realm of constitutional law. The source of the failure is then identified as that in some manner or other the Court is not living up to its essential mission. That is, he finds one purpose or interpretive stance necessary and is somewhat at a loss to explain why it is not fully embraced to the exclusion of the numerous purportedly less reasonable alternatives. The analysis then ends with the hope that somehow uniformity might be imposed upon anyone who would mistakenly want to follow one of the other theories. This pattern is most clear in Chemerinsky's suggestion that the Court and each justice should adopt the practice of following a type of mission statement repeating, of course, his conclusion as to its purpose. In a later section of this chapter I explain why this pattern constantly reoccurs in legal theory and judicial reasoning. But first an outline of some opposing ideas as to constitutional function and democratic purpose is in order.

Popular Constitutionalism

Contrary to Chemerinsky's belief in the central importance of the Court's constitutional supremacy for the protection of otherwise vulnerable minorities are positions held by a series of legal scholars who argue for a more democratic conception and application of the United States Constitution and a lesser place for the Supreme Court in American Government. This is important. If theories of judicial supremacy like Chemerinsky's are not to be given a free ride, other options and the evidence available for them must be faced. This is even more clearly demanded in the face of such strong evidence as offered above that it is close to useless for the minorities it is supposed to protect under the "save the people from themselves protection from the tyranny of majority" theory of Court-driven constitutional law.

As it turns out, there are pretty good reasons why that theory is worthy of doubt. For example, Ran Hirschl, in *Towards Juristocracy*, offers an important and empirically informed investigation of legal systems in other countries that have adopted United States–style judicial review. He argues that the evidence makes it highly improbable that judicial review by a supreme court will be protective of minority rights.[16] Indeed, he finds the constitutionalization of rights and the move toward what he calls "juristocracy" is not only generally counterproductive for vulnerable minorities, but actually more often than not results in the entrenchment and protection of elites and their privileges. This protection of elites is, of course, the protection of a minority, but of a powerful and aristocratic minority. Indeed, he concludes that "the global trend toward judicial empowerment through constitutionalization should be understood as part and parcel of a large-scale process whereby policy-making authority is increasingly transferred by hegemonic elites from majoritarian policy-making arenas to semiautonomous professional policy-making bodies primarily in order to insulate their policy preferences from the vicissitudes of democratic politics."[17] Of course this would explain Chemerinsky's "failures" as really successes for the elites. Therefore, from the results of judicial empowerment and elite entrenchment Hirschl derives, and thinks the evidence ultimately proves, a "hegemonic preservation thesis."[18] This thesis holds that United States–style constitutional judicial review generally serves to insulate elite power from democratic process. Most dangerously, even the belief in the Court's position as protector of vulnerable minorities can help the deeper entrenchment of elites and their power and privilege against democratic challenge.

Richard D. Parker, in *"Here, the People Rule": A Constitutional Populist Manifesto*, offers a different reason to be suspicious of the tyranny of the majority story. He argues against the idea of constitutional law as higher and prior to democracy, and rather claims that rightly understood it should promote democracy rather than limit it. His main critique of the protect minorities from democratic tyranny thesis is that is constructs its defense upon a very questionable picture of "the people" as a mob. He claims that "Anti-Populist" sensibility is constructed on a narrative that sees political energy of the people as that of a mob, crowd, threat, irrational, etc.[19] He diagnoses this description of the people as generally attached to an analysis that demands against this threat a safe location of transcendence outside of political processes that is founded upon a hierarchy of quality.

Parker points out that if you combine the mob image with the assumption of a transcendent area of law that is based upon qualitative superior reasoning, the antimajoritarian concept of Constitution follows quite naturally. He, though, questions the accuracy of the picture of the people as a mob. Further, he also questions the belief in any superior quality of judicial decision making. Indeed, he identifies what he believes is a high rate of inflation in the characterization of judicial abilities. This exaggeration of judicial ability is then often combined with fetishism of the Constitution. Even further, the exaggeration of ability and fetishism of the Constitution will sometimes be combined with a further rhetoric of vulnerability where the Constitution is described as vulnerable (or delicate or fragile) and therefore in need of vigorous protection by the Court.[20] Given this image, in come the justices as transcendent, indeed almost heavenly saviors of the law, the Constitution, the people, justice, minorities, etc. Instead of this disdainful sensibility toward the people and such an inflated picture of judicial ability and the Court's position in protecting the Constitution, Parker argues that it would be better to rather try to create populist energies and see the central mission of Constitution as promoting majority rule.[21] Constitutional law as a separate legal domain should be deflated in importance and process-oriented. This would follow, be believes, once the fantasy that there are any "supra-political *guarantees* of anything" is given up.[22]

There is also historical evidence that the general understanding of United States Constitution's place in American government was not always dominated by ideals of judicial supremacy. In *The People Themselves: Popular Constitutionalism and Judicial Review*, Larry D. Kramer argues that the founding generation—the founders of the first country to be explicitly centered on the consent of the people—were more pro-democracy than current readings generally admit. Readings such as Chemerinsky's, that is, give way too much weight to purported fears of democracy than the founders actually had. Kramer argues that when read in the context of the governments of their time, the founders can be seen to be radically gambling on popular rule. Because of this, the Constitution was an act of popular will and therefore seeing judges as its supreme and final interpreter goes against the founding generation's central ideals.

So why the current emphasis upon the tyranny of the majority? For Kramer, echoing Hirschl and Parker, it has only evolved that way through interpreting the Constitution more like a normal professional-based piece of legislation than was originally intended. That is, through various causes a document of the people to be enforced and interpreted by the people and for the people has been handed off to legal elites who with a small set of professionalized tools are willing to propound their own central importance and therefore gain power, privilege and status in the process. This is, in another way of describing it, a move from the Constitution thought of as a public-based project of continuous reinterpretation within a broader political and social context to a set of game rules external to "the people" interpreted and enforced by legal experts. Once again, it is the quest to transcend through a qualitatively and authoritatively superior hierarchy. Of course such a story is very comforting to the professional elites that get put into the places of power.

For Kramer on the other hand, "eighteenth-century Americans had a less cramped image of popular constitutionalism. They took for granted the people's responsibility not only for making, but also for interpreting and enforcing their constitution—a background norm so widely shared and deeply ingrained that specific expression in the constitution was unnecessary."[23] Beyond the democratic foundation, he also notes that the evidence at the time of the making of constitution shows no clear consensus for or against judicial review."[24] But even with some support for judicial review, he argues that there was virtually no support for judicial supremacy as is practiced currently. Kramer therefore concludes "that the Founders expected constitutional limits to be enforced through politics and by the people rather than the courts is hardly surprising. Their history, their political theory, and their actual experience all taught that popular pressure was the only sure way to bring an unruly authority to heel."[25]

Instead of following this spirit we are now confronted with judicial supremacy constructed through the legal profession—an elite professional aristocracy. And this is a story written by a minority elite in pursuit, consciously or not, of a power grab from more democratic possibilities of governance. Indeed it is a type of Court activism that has brought with it such formalist legalist tools such as "a sharp distinction between public and private sphere" as well as "a pronounced tendency to emphasize broad, abstract legal categories, and a greater emphasis on deductive reasoning and bright-line classifications."[26] Rather than the (in Roosevelt's words) "layman's document" the Constitution should be, it has become a "lawyer's document."[27] This is, therefore, an unfortunate story of "judicial triumphalism" and "judicial monopoly" complete with a professional elite's self-aggrandizing tendencies trumping democratic possibilities.[28] This story, in turn, infects the public's picture of democracy with passivity wherein difficult issues are expected to be solved through legalist tools. Kramer's ultimate conclusion? "Simply put, supporters of judicial supremacy are today's aristocrats."[29]

Finally, Mark Tushnet, in *Taking the Constitution away from the Courts*, argues along the same lines, ultimately advocating for taking away interpretation from the courts and bringing it into the realm of the public's own deliberations.[30] But, as contrary to the story of professional capture offered by Kramer, he sees the move toward judicial supremacy as at least partially motivated by liberals scared of losing at the polls and therefore turning to "procedural subterfuges."[31] Instead of this subterfuge he argues that a properly populist constitutional law "treats constitutional law not as something in the hands of lawyers and judges but in the hands of the people themselves. Constitutional law creates the people of the United States *as a people* by providing a narrative that connects us to everyone who preceded us."[32] This is a project of the people that can only be done democratically. And rather than an appeal to higher law it is a politics of the Constitution that is constitutive because the Constitution sets the general story and aims for the ensuing and continuing democratic discussion (especially when combined with the Declaration of Independence). This, in turn, animates a continuing democratic project of "reconstruction" that results in the continuing construction of a political community.[33]

So, with all this evidence of consistent failures, institutional limits, plural possible purposes and explanations, an ambiguous history and democratic questions, why does judicial supremacy continue to be thought of as a necessary protector of the vulnerable? More importantly, why, given all these problems, does the "rule of law" and the countermajoritarian, transcendent, and hierarchical hope for easy "rule of constitutional law" solutions to difficult problems seem so convincing? Finally, if a more democratic conception of constitutional law is desirable, what would it look like in comparison?

Pragmatism and Democracy

The project of this book is to construct a pragmatist critique and solution to the problems identified above. Other pragmatists have attempted basic solutions to the problem of an aggrandizing Court. Sidney Hook, for instance, advocated for a legislative override to the Supreme Court or the requirement of a supermajority vote by the justices for their opinion to trump legislative acts.[34] These ideas seem quite helpful but still leave the antimajoritarian role of the Court largely unquestioned. The aim here will be much more ambitious. It will be to live up to, as far as possible, John Dewey's stringent demand that only democratic means be used for democratic ends. Democracy, that is, must be democratic "all the way down." More specifically, for Dewey law must be democratic in order to be justified democratically. This, of course, rules out seeing the constitution as an antimajoritarian source of a-priori game rules that, for instance, in systems like that of John Rawls's *Theory of Justice*, relegate democracy to a secondary place, only allowed to function after the system of constitutive rights or "side constraints" are in place.

To start the construction of "law as a democratic means" and critique the opposing save the people from themselves conception of constitutional law it is helpful to return to one of the earliest writings of the pragmatist canon. In "The Fixation of Belief," Charles Sanders Peirce, the founder of pragmatism and fellow member of the Cambridge Metaphysical Club with Oliver Wendell Holmes, Jr ., offers one of the most memorable explications of pragmatist methodology and how it contrasts with other available and standardly applied options for the settlement of doubt. As Peirce characterizes it, the pragmatist methodology of "inquiry" is useful for clarifying the meaning of terms or what beliefs should be held. That is, it is an interpretive method useful when the meaning of a term or statement is in question.

Peirce starts his article with a discussion of the relationship of belief to inquiry. Most basically, "the irritation of doubt causes a struggle to attain a state of belief. I shall term this struggle *inquiry*."[35] Further, "the sole object of inquiry is the settlement of opinion"—that is, the elimination of doubt.[36] Pragmatic inquiry as Peirce characterizes it is just one strategy among four that can be adopted for this aim. He labels the three other possible methods, those of "tenacity," "authority" and the "a priori."

According to Peirce, the first method, that of "tenacity," aims at fixing belief "by taking any answer to a question which we may fancy, and constantly reiterating it to ourselves, dwelling on all which may conduce to that belief, and learning to turn with contempt and hatred from anything which might disturb it."[37] Peirce admits that this method is for many individuals simple, direct, and often very effective for avoiding the pain of doubt. Further, it has a tendency to embody in an individual the seemingly admirable virtues of strength, simplicity, and decisiveness of character. But the method does have significant problems that ultimately counterbalance these virtues. First, it is not fact-driven but rather will-driven and dogmatic. It relies, therefore, upon an environment that is not too inharmonious to it or in need of flexible reactions. More important for Peirce is that, as tenacity, it is a form of inflexible individual activity, and because of this, "the social impulse is against it." Indeed, the method of tenacity is antisocial and treats other humans as impediments, not fellow citizens. Therefore, "unless we make ourselves hermits, we shall necessarily influence each other's opinion, so that the problem becomes how to fix belief, not in the individual merely, but in the community."[38]

So the need to live together limits the method of tenacity's usefulness. There is a need to form a community and, therefore, the method of tenacity becomes insufficient. In this case a group can adopt a second method of fixing belief, its own shared method of tenacity, that of "authority." Peirce states that this has all the tenacity and all the hostility to fact as the method of tenacity has above, yet requires the stubborn single-mindedness to be held in common by all members of the group. And because it is not driven by evidence or open conversation but rather is as will-driven and dogmatic as the method of tenacity, commonality to be created and continued under the method of authority must be externally induced. In short, authority as a form of social tenacity to be effective must be institutionalized and uniformly enforced.

Peirce believes that this method is ubiquitous and indeed is probably necessary to govern the "mass of mankind" who are and will remain, according to him, "intellectual slaves."[39] But Peirce also sees the method as much worse than the method of tenacity because the method of authority, requiring social uniformity, becomes fiercely and mercilessly enforced. And here is the major problem the method of authority brings on top of those also associated with tenacity: "Cruelties always accompany this system . . . for the officer of society does not feel justified in surrendering the interests of society for the sake of mercy, as he might his own private interests. It is natural, therefore, that sympathy and fellowship should thus produce a most ruthless power."[40] From a social spirit comes, counterintuitively but very plausibly, a belief in a purportedly justified demand for blind obedience and concomitant ruthless policing and coercion.

Ultimately, though, because others might have broader social feelings as well as doubts about the method and the need to ruthlessly enforce conformity, Peirce believes some will inevitably look for a more inclusive and less arbitrary, capricious and cruel method for fixing common beliefs. There is, therefore, a turn to open conversation, in current vocabulary "deliberation," and arrival at "natural preferences" which are "agreeable to reason."[41] That is, as opposed to tenacity and authority, there is open and reasoned discussion of various possibilities. But without further criteria external to natural preferences, Peirce claims that this method of "reason" is really only permission to believe what one or one's community already has inclination to believe, and because of this is really just an appeal to personal or social intuitions. This "a priori method," as he calls it, makes inquiry into something similar to taste, fashion, or feel. Using the a priori method does lead to conclusions comfortable to its practitioners. So far so good. But because it appeals to no real evidence beyond intuition and taste, Peirce believes that it encourages a type of individual vanity whereby personal or group inclinations get intuitively "verified" as universal and indisputable truths.

Once again, for Peirce the a priori method is a method much superior to the first two because it encourages discussion. But it ultimately fails and leads to conflicts because intuitions are not necessarily based upon evidence or guaranteed to harmonize between people. Further, the method offers no way to mediate between conflicting intuitions when they arise. That is, one person's "reason" is another person's absurdity. Peirce's example of the problem with a priori reasoning is the notorious combination of internal consistency with the external intractability of conflicting metaphysical systems in philosophy. For him each system is indeed a manifestation of "reason" as it appears to the specific philosopher, but ultimately there is no method and no shared evidence that can be appealed to between the systems for consensus. This problem, he claims, is also true of the intuitions of groups.

Therefore, Peirce turns to the last remaining method—the experimental or scientific method of inquiry, an emphatically empirical and experimental approach. He claims that this method not only brings all who follow it toward the same conclusions with the same evidence, but also that it is the only option in which method and results are in harmony. This is because "the test of whether I am truly following the method is not an immediate appeal to my feelings and purposes, but, on the contrary, itself involves the application of the method."[42] This method is, further, not only experimental but also social in that verification of results is a replicable social practice. Therefore, the method rests less upon internal will or comfortable intuitions and more upon reference to what Peirce described as results of beliefs methodologically facing the evidence of an experimental "outward clash" with the world. Indeed, he claims the method is solely determined by the world because beliefs can only be tested and fixed by the results they bring about in it.

Given this method of inquiry, the type of evidence appealed to necessarily changes as does the type of argument constructed. Peirce demands that inquiry "proceed only from tangible premises which can be subjected to careful scrutiny." And instead of an emphasis upon deduction or formal styles of reasoning, evidence in experimental inquiry needs to be empirical and broadly marshalled so we "trust rather to the multitude and variety of its arguments than to the conclusiveness of any one. Its reasoning should not form a chain which is no stronger than its weakest link, but a cable whose fibres may be ever so slender, provided they are sufficiently numerous and intimately connected."[43]

All this follows from the fact that Peirce thought inquiry a social and experimental process. Intuition is discounted in favor of replicable experiments tested by the outward clash of the world. In service of this he offers what has been termed the "pragmatic maxim." This method of clarifying a concept obeys the following rule: "Consider what effects, which might conceivably have practical bearings, we conceive the object of our conception to have. Then, our conception of these effects is the whole of our conception of the object."[44] Elsewhere he explained that for any assertion either there is a way to test through an experiment or else there is no sense in the statement. Once again, experiment is central to the method. As Cheryl Misak nicely puts this, the pragmatic maxim doesn't raise the question of the source or origin of a belief, but rather offers a test through which belief must pass.[45] It is a test the results of which will be determined by the world, not human intuition. In addition, it is thought by Peirce to be an experimental methodology that actually points toward the necessity of democratic practices for knowledge. This is because of the centrality of a community of inquirers, replicable experiments, and mutually identifiable results to the method.[46] The meaning of concepts is therefore intersubjective in that it relies on repeatable experimental results and not any individual thoughts, feelings, or intuitions.[47]

Building upon Peirce's analysis, John Dewey makes these requirements central to his philosophy of democracy. As Hilary Putnam explains, "For Dewey, the scientific method is simply the method of experimental inquiry combined with free and full discussion—which means, in the case of social problems, the maximum use of the capabilities of citizens for proposing courses of action, for testing them, and for evaluating the results."[48] Putnam calls this the "epistemological justification of democracy." As Misak describes it, this means that "inquiry, of any kind, must operate on democratic principles: it must provide opportunity and incentive to challenge accepted hypotheses, to criticize evidence and accepted norms, and to offer rival hypothesis."[49] Michael Sullivan gives a slightly different description: "Dewey's democratic theory is in large part merely a broader application of his pragmatism. The traits of Deweyan democracy—openness, participatory, transformative, future-directed, experimental, radical—are all part of the pragmatic method of inquiry."[50] As Putnam, Misak, and Sullivan note, for Dewey democracy and scientific inquiry are essentially intertwined.

This is because for Dewey the scientific "attitude" is most basically "freedom from control by routine, prejudice, dogma, unexamined tradition, sheer self-interest" as well as "the will to inquire, to examine, to discriminate, to draw conclusions only on the basis of evidence after taking pains to gather all available evidence." Further, and most importantly, it is "the experimental attitude which recognizes that while ideas are necessary to deal with facts, yet they are working hypotheses to be tested by the consequences they produce."[51] This, of course, is a loose paraphrase of Peirce's pragmatic maxim.

The same requirements are true of democracy. Dewey noted that while "democratic ends demand democratic methods for their realization," there was a tendency to wrongly accept authoritarian methods as necessary tools to protect democracy.[52] Indeed, he thought overly mechanical references to the Constitution to be a prime example of authoritarian methods pretending to be in service of democratic aims. Instead, he demanded that democracy be practiced in "in every phase of our common life" and claimed that "recourse to monistic, wholesale, absolutist procedures is a betrayal of human freedom no matter in which guise it presents itself."[53] For Dewey democracy is emphatically not a matter of "established mechanisms," "numerical contrivance," or other processes disciplined by unchangeable once-and-for-all side constraints or game rules, but rather a way of life.[54] Therefore, democracy requires a "primary emphasis upon the *means* by which these ends are to be fulfilled." And this is because "*the fundamental principle of democracy is that the ends of freedom and individuality for all can be attained only by means which accord with those ends.*"[55]

In short, for Dewey,

democracy as compared with other ways of life is the sole way of living which believes wholeheartedly in the process of experience as end and as means; as that which is capable of generating science which is the sole dependable authority for the direction of further experience and which releases emotions, needs and desires so as to call into being things that have not existed in the past. For every way of life that fails in its democracy limits the contacts, the exchanges, the communications, the interactions by which experience is steadied while it is also enlarged and enriched. The task of this release is steadied while it is also enlarged and enriched. The task of this release and enrichment is one that has to be carried on day by day. Since it is one that can have no end till experience itself comes to an end, the task of democracy is forever that of creation of a freer and more humane experience in which all share and to which all contribute.[56]

Dewey's further demands of democracy will be emphasized in the next chapter when his conception of democracy is more fully worked out in relationship to law. Here what should be emphasized is the essential link between democratic and experimental habits and the characterization of both as incompatible with authoritarian methods.

Dewey's Challenge: Law as a Democratic Means

One aspect of the argument I offer in this book is that almost all legal reasoning and theory exemplify the first three methods of thought outlined by Peirce. That is, legal reasoning as currently and historically practiced in the United States is accurately characterized as almost solely comprised of a mix of the methods of tenacity, authority, and a priori reasoning. Because of this, claims such as the purpose of law, the Constitution, and the Supreme Court as well as claims to correct and incorrect reasoning are held by legal scholars and Supreme Court justices even in the face of overwhelming evidence of their empirical inaccuracy, in the face of better explanations, and in the face of other equally plausible possibilities just as the reliance upon the methods of tenacity, authority, and the a priori would predictably entail.

In the chapters that follow cases and influential legal theories will be analyzed as to their reasoning and conclusions. The methods of tenacity, authority, and the a priori will be seen everywhere. Individual theorists and judges will create systems that are then expected to rule all other options out of the realm of possibility. Groups of professionals, alternatively, will find a theory so convincing that alternate view will be shouted out of the room or greeted with professional silence, and all will be claimed to be founded upon reason. Though, predictably following from Peirce's characterization of reason under the a priori method, one person's or group's reason is another person's or group's irrationality.

The other part of the argument offered herein is that a Deweyan conception of law, founded upon Peirce's method of science and using some-

thing like the pragmatic maxim and democratic experimentalism as developed by Dewey and further informed by the work of Charles Sabel,
Michael Dorf and others, can show a possible way to better satisfy Dewey's
demand that law be practiced as a democratic means. To satisfy this demand, law must be a democratic process itself and not just a transcendent
set of rules within which democracy can be practiced or, it goes without
saying, an expressly antimajoritarian tool to protect minorities from the
tyranny of the majority.[57] This, of course, would be recourse to authoritarian means no matter what the end. Therefore, the following chapters offer
a democratic understanding of constitutional law based upon pragmatic
inquiry. It will be argued throughout that a Deweyan conception of law
offers a greatly superior hope for constitutional law than that as currently
practiced. In this work the aim of greater and more effective democracy is
taken as a given. Indeed, this book accepts Jane Addams's claim that "the
cure for the ills of Democracy is more Democracy."[58] Therefore, constructing a more democratic conception of constitutional law along experimentalist lines is the project's goal.

CHAPTER TWO

Democratic Aims and Experimentalist Procedure

In the first chapter the question of law's proper place within democracy was accepted as important. This challenge, once again, comes in the form of a demand Dewey made of democracy—that democracy cannot legitimately use non-democratic means in furtherance of democratic aims. Given this demand, constitutional law as traditionally characterized is a problematic social institution. Law as traditionally characterized, that is, seems essentially attached to a top-down authority and command based model. The solution usually offered to this problem is not to try to reengineer law and legal practice as more democratic in its procedures, but rather to see constitutional law as a foundational command-based tool used for setting the constitutive rules of government within which democratic processes function.[1] Within this picture of law, democratic procedures are relegated to a lesser "moves within the game" role. The Constitution, under this conception, is democratic, if at all, only in its original pedigree. That is, it was ratified by the people in order to create nonnegotiable rules in order protect themselves from their own excesses. As the first chapter showed, this model can be clearly seen in Chemerinsky's analysis of the Court, and it is found in John Rawls's highly influential political philosophy as well. It is also shared by such disparate legal theories as those of Richard Epstein and Ronald Dworkin. If this picture is accepted then Dewey's demand for a democratic law process must be thought undesirable, avoidable, impracticable, or even impossible. Must Dewey's demand be rejected?

In this chapter I accept that the "democracy all the way down" demand is legitimate and important. Indeed, this chapter takes up Dewey's challenge by offering a plausible picture of law that functions as a democratic means within a larger democratic social and political framework. The claim is that the institution of law can itself embody a democratic procedure in service of democracy. To show how this is possible I start with a more detailed outline of the demands that Dewey makes of democracy than that offered in the last chapter. Then, in order to offer a more democratic conception of law, an initial theory of law is constructed out of Dewey's writings. Next, Dewey's analysis of law is supplemented by contemporary work in democratic experimentalism. Here I also combine Dewey's theories of democracy and law with a full outline, critique, and investigation of conceptions of democratic experimentalism offered in contemporary scholarship.

Dewey's Demanding Democracy

To understand what is demanded of constitutional law in order for it to be truly democratic, it is important to get a good idea of what Dewey's philosophy of democracy entails. While it might be difficult to offer a full picture of Deweyan democracy, indeed it cannot be offered because for Dewey democracy as an idea—as a social manner of existing and as a political organization—is always under construction; there are some core ideas within his writings that can be noted without much controversy.[2] In this sense an idea of democracy is best constructed through an awareness of the many strands or factors involved in the project.

First, democracy in its most central meaning is, for Dewey, a way of life that is broadly social before it is seen more narrowly as a political concept. Indeed, for him democratic habits "must affect all modes of human association."[3] Most important here is the claim that democratic political institutions are secondary to, and are the effects of, the underlying culture. That is, for there to be a working political democracy there is the antecedent need for various aspects of a democratic culture. Not only is it the case that a solely political democracy will not suffice, but we must "realize that democracy can be served only by the slow day to day adoption and contagious diffusion in every phase of our common life of methods that are identical with the ends to be reached and that recourse to monistic, wholesale, absolutist procedures is a betrayal of human freedom no matter in what guise it presents itself."[4] Dewey's colleague and sometimes co-author James H. Tufts not only required democracy to combine the two factors of equality and self-government, but also claimed that "the finest and largest meaning of democracy is that all people should share as largely as possible in the best life" and that "this is a view not so much about government itself as about what government is for."[5] Strikingly, this means that political majoritarianism through elections is itself only a possible tool of, and not (as it is often treated) a definitional aspect of, democracy. Ultimately, therefore, the claim is that democracy "must go all the way down."[6] This is, of course, in direct opposition to the claim that in the application of constitutional law the authoritarian ends justify the means. For Dewey, once again, democracy as an end can only be constructed from democratic means.

Second, for Dewey democracy entails pluralistic values and a decentered picture of social institutions. One reason this is important is that by having plural and decentered institutions as well as a form of life that practices democratic social habits there are created multiple avenues that allow for information to be communicated and solutions to be proposed. Another reason is that this pluralism allows for more inclusive dialogue. This, in turn, relates to Dewey's specific acceptance of the great complexity of causal forces in human society. For him, a "monistic view" just cannot handle the multiple forces, democratic or otherwise, that operate in human society. Indeed, one of the great challenges for human society is being able to coordinate, communicate, and understand such multiple and diffuse forces. Gregory Pappas argues that this means that for Dewey not only must democracy go "all the way down" but so must pluralism (and all the way up as well).[7]

As Dewey describes the process, social groups feel consequences before being able to label them. Noting and finding ways to control and solve unfortunate consequences of social life demands the construction of symbols. Common or "mutually understood" meanings are created through the construction of symbols and therefore animate a public discussion. This places primary responsibility for change on those who face a problem and therefore seems to burden the already suffering. But, John Shook rightly notes, any other possibility places the location of action in those who are not directly privy to the problem. This is even less ideal, and offers no guarantee of accuracy or responsiveness. Therefore, democratic change needs to be driven by those who directly feel the "shoe's pinch."[8] This whole process is optimized by the proliferation, interconnection, and overlapping of pluralistic and decentered associations.[9] Furthermore, coordination is not predicated on the arrival of a univocal stance, but also is protective of pluralist voices and values if at all possible.

Third, Dewey defines the public in functional terms. Here is where a distinctly political democracy comes into being. A public is created when social consequences that affect people beyond the immediate group are noted and found to be in need of social control.[10] Political democracy, therefore, comes into being where there is a recognized need to control consequences of social activity. Because problems are in constant change, states need to be continuously "re-made."[11] Indeed, the state is seen as a secondary type of association formed because of perceived externalities of individual or group activities on others and based upon the given fact of social and intersubjective life. Once it is accepted that the democratic state is defined by the consequences it is constructed in response to "the only statement which can be made is a purely formal one: the state is the organization of the public effected through officials for the protection of the interests shared by its members."[12] For Dewey, this eliminates the possibility that there is an a priori rule or procedure identifiable as sufficient to define democratic government. As a prime example of the naive and mistaken hope for an a priori solution to democracy, Dewey cites the imposition of constitutions "ready-made" upon governments.[13] In a properly democratic state, instead of a top-down constitutional structure determining the parameters of governmental rule, the state reacts to multiple groupings formed upon the basis of interests and acts in order to encourage more socially desirable activities. Dewey is particularly scornful of viewing democracy as only a numerical contrivance of vote aggregation— seeing this as a misunderstanding and simplification of the much greater multi-dimensional demands of a democratic culture.

Fourth, going back to democracy as a social way of life prior to the political and to the functional idea of the public as formed in relationship to specific and immediate social issues, Dewey claims that a living democratic society rests upon experimental intelligence. For Dewey, though, this is only taking a type of intelligence that has proven useful across various human societies and that every human being habitually enacts in everyday life and using it more consistently for the problems of governance.[14] This, of course, encompasses the experimental or scientific method in Peirce's terms, with its required democratic aspects of open communication, repeatability and social verification, etc. This is why Putnam notes that for Dewey, democracy is a precondition of full application of intelligence.[15]

But though this type of reasoning is proven effective it isn't always fully tasked in political activity. This is largely because fear of change and the psychological need for certainty have kept society from embracing this greater use of experimental intelligence in social life. Instead, "we have set undue store by established mechanisms." A blatant example of this, for Dewey, once again, is "idolatry of the Constitution."[16] As problems change the state must adapt and change as well. The idea of a static once-and-for-all solution is, just like the attempt to force any type of monoculture, a type of abdication of reason. Furthermore, by not focusing on the details of the problem at hand ideological frameworks can create problems by offering simplistic a priori frameworks that can create conceptual blinders that ignore or discount significant aspects of the problems.[17]

Fifth, the public and its government are institutions based upon real conflict. Democracy is based upon specific problems as problems. It is important to emphasize this because often Dewey has been accused of not understanding the tragic nature of human life and underestimating the extent of conflict. This critique is absurd. The whole reason for political democracy is the awareness of conflict in social activities. It bears no argument to acknowledge that here are real conflicts.[18] The only question worth answering is how to settle them. And Dewey does not expect utopian harmony—problems change and yet are continually arising. All he claims is that, given conflict, his version of democratic government built upon a wider democratic society is best at finding and creating the conditions for positive solutions—if they are at all possible.

Finally, as seen in the factors above, for Dewey democracy employs both scientific knowledge and creativity for communication and solution. Indeed, he believes it is the only form of social organization that can fully use these forces. But, importantly, social problems cannot be solved through the ultimate allocation of investigation, creativity, or decision making to technocrats. There are unavoidable problems in the appeal to expertise and "elite" democracy and where voting is relegated to the function of safety valve. For example, Dewey argues that if this theory of "elite" representative democracy is accepted it cannot account for democracy's usefulness because the populace's purported inability to understand, deliberate, and vote upon the complex and technical issues of the day is not remedied by representation of an elite due to the fact that the same problems are just replicated one step later. That is, the general claim is that governmental problems are too complex for the voters to understand, but why at one step removed and at the level of voting for representatives the issues would be better understood by the voters is unclear.[19] Not only that, but policies and values must be framed before technical expertise can be put to task and technocrats are not any better or more informed at foundational policy or value choice and quite possibly worse at such choices than the general populace. Just as important, the "elite" easily become isolated from the social world (or other publics) and therefore cannot represent the citizen's needs due to ignorance of them.[20] Therefore, the sixth factor is that there is no option but to locate the power to govern in the people. There is no other source of knowledge for what needs attention and whether programs are working.

To summarize, Dewey's theory of democracy demands that, first, democracy is to be a way of life that is broadly social before it is seen more narrowly as a political concept. Democratic habits "must affect all modes of human association." Second, democracy entails not only acknowledgment but also the respect of pluralistic values and a decentered picture of social institutions. Third, Dewey defines a public in functional terms. A public is created when social consequences that affect people beyond the immediate group are noted and found to be in need of social control. Political democracy, therefore, comes into being where there is a recognized need to regulate the consequences of social activity. And because problems constantly change, states need to be continuously "re-made." Fourth, Dewey claims that a living democratic society rests upon experimental intelligence. That is, intelligence is proven in its empirical results. Fifth, democracy is based upon specific problems as problems. In other words, it is constructed according to changing demands and is not to be defined in abstraction from these demands. And sixth, while democracy employs both scientific knowledge and creativity for communication and solution, social problems cannot be solved through allocation of decision making to technocrats. The appeal to expertise and "elite" democracy cannot avoid creating an undesirable distance from the knowledge of the concrete issues demanding solution. Therefore, ultimate power must always stay with the general public. As Robert Westbrook describing Dewey's theory puts it, "For him, it was always liberalism that that had to meet the demands of democracy, not democracy that had to answer to liberalism."[21] Importantly, if democracy is the aim, then law must answer to the same demands as well.

Dewey on Law

Though Dewey never wrote a book specifically on law, his various statements on law as found scattered throughout his voluminous writings neatly dovetail with his overall philosophy of democracy. Just as overly standardized or a priori theories of democracy were viewed as suspect by him, he was highly suspicious of legal pieties and dogmas. Indeed, Dewey was especially suspicious of legal institutions because, as Michael Sullivan puts it, "In his view, legal institutions were especially conservative and generally lagged behind other institutions in their responsiveness to the changing facts of our social lives."[22] Ultimately Dewey give law no unique status; rather, law is seen as just one of multiple social institutions that might, when used properly, further the social goal of a truly democratic society. It also, importantly, must satisfy the same set of democratic requirements expected of any other social organization.

To understand how it might be possible for a legal system to satisfy these requirements it is informative to start with a couple general statements Dewey makes about legal reasoning. For example, Dewey notes that properly understood, Oliver Wendell Holmes Jr's famous line claiming that "the life of law has been experience and not logic" is not really attacking logic in general but rather attacking a narrow picture of logic based solely upon "formal consistency." Actually, "the undoubted facts which Justice Holmes has in mind do not concern logic, but rather certain tendencies of the human creatures who use logic, tendencies which a sound logic will guard against."[23]

For Dewey real logic, or inquiry, "is ultimately an empirical and concrete discipline."[24] According to him, the opposing non-experimental formalist picture of logic is dangerous because attachment to it gets in the way of understanding the actual reasoning process used in law. In Holmes's terms it wrongly takes experience out of the realm of logic. This distortion, in turn, gives rise to an unrealistic expectation of certainty within the realm of legal reasoning. For instance, in the actual activity of legal practice, Dewey claims that premises are not just found readymade and already free-standing as standardly thought, but "only gradually emerge from analysis of the total situation."[25] Further, the lawyer usually begins with the conclusion that is hoped for, and then analyzes the facts so as to "form" premises. Both of these practices go against the idea of formally determined results deduced from previously existing legal rules. So, formalist hopes lead to distorted conceptions of legal inquiry.

But this is only part of the real story. Courts are also expected to justify their decisions in written opinions. This is, for Dewey, a quite different type of logic. The judge's exposition of a decision often aims at making the logic seem clearer, less provisional, vague and situational than it actually is or can be given the complexity of the legal issue. Dewey argues that this is where formalist legal reasoning comes most clearly into play—and most clearly distorts what is actually the case. Courts are tempted to substitute for the "vital logic" which had necessarily been used in the process in order to reach the conclusion, "forms of speech which are rigorous in appearance and which give an illusion of certitude."[26] But this tendency to pretend certainty is contradicted by the controversial and intractable nature of the controversies.

Such exposition may have the salutary effect (at best) of strengthening legal stability and regularity, but the artificial packaging also risks confusing a false form of apparent logical rigor with actual processes of legal reasoning and results in the world. The implication for Dewey is that legal reasoning should focus much more upon a "logic *relative to consequences rather than to antecedents.*"[27] Given this change logic is not useless, and it is not claimed that there is only the illusion of logical reasoning in law. Rather, what is argued is that there are various types of argumentation in law—various types of logic—and that a conflation of the various tasks and tools used creates mistaken expectations and distorts our understanding of actual legal process.

Not only can various types of logic be conflated, but "logic" is a term that can be used to cover up evasive forms of argumentation if attention to consequences is not kept centrally in focus. This, of course, parallels Peirce's claim about appeals to "reason." So, for example, Dewey's article, "Psychology and Justice," offers a critique of "legalistic" logic from an analysis of the Fuller Advisory Committee's report on the Sacco and Vanzetti case. Dewey contends that the final conclusions of the investigation rested upon the use of "strictly legalistic methods of reasoning" in a manner that enabled the committee to avoid the main issue at question by frittering the issue away into various legal subcategories.

According to his analysis the committee did this by, first, segregating the question of fair trial procedure from that of newly discovered evidence and, second, by splitting the issue of whether the speed to execution had constituted a miscarriage of justice into six separate and isolated questions.[28] Dewey claims that the important question was whether the cumulative impact of various irregularities gave reasonable ground for the possibility of a miscarriage of justice. But by investigating the six issues in isolation, and not keeping ultimate results firmly in mind, the commission moved from the conclusion that each issue by itself was inconclusive to the very different conclusion that all together must be inconclusive as well. This type of argument allowed the committee to wrongly "whittle down the significance of the admitted facts."[29] Further, as Dewey describes the process, this approach was used in combination with the further ability of the commission to shift the standards of evaluation throughout, therefore allowing them to conclude whatever they wanted. A concrete example of the shifting was the inconsistency in levels of credibility afforded the various participants. The jury was portrayed as accurate and unbiased. On the other hand, every statement made by the defendants was treated as highly suspicious. Here Dewey shows sensitivity to the way alternate legal procedures, different agenda setting strategies, and various levels of evidentiary scrutiny, can profoundly change the outcome. Once again, Dewey's analysis points to a claim made by Peirce. Instead of the separation of factors and isolation of issues resulting in a chain just as strong as its weakest link, Peirce offered the picture of best arguments being characterized as the braiding of multiple bits of evidence into one strong cable.

Dewey shows the same type of awareness in his article "Social Realities *versus* Police Court Fictions." Therein, he analyzes the case of *Kay v. Board of Higher Education of the City of New York (1940)*,[30] where Bertrand Russell was found morally unfit to teach at The College of the City of New York. The evidence the court used was Russell's own writings on ethics, marriage, and sex. In his analysis Dewey first admits that the passages cited by the court as evidence of moral turpitude are really contained in Russell's writings. "And yet," he explains, by adopting the same editing method employed by the court he could show that Russell's opinions were "in substantial harmony" with traditional views on the topics involved.[31] Dewey further notes that the Court's legal opinion is largely an attack upon Russell's views, which, "by the justice's own admission," were outside of his professional jurisdiction.[32]

Here Dewey highlights the virtues of legal process and properly constructed evidence laws, and therefore argues that it is important to encourage limits to judicial reach. What this shows is that Dewey is not properly read as a full "anti-formalist," or as against procedure or professionalism in law. He is not a legal skeptic. He clearly accepts the necessity and virtues of institutional rules. What is not accepted by him, on the other hand, are self-justifying institutional rules untested by empirical and scientific methods.

Dewey on Law and Democracy

For Dewey, once again, law is one of a number of institutions that, at best, helps further democratic society. As such, law is evaluated as a system in terms of its effectiveness toward this goal. He is critical of many of the methods of legal practice and uses, as seen above, the term "legalistic" pejoratively. On the other hand, he does not argue for a complete rejection of legal practice, and his writings show various hints at how law could be reengineered to more be a more effective social institution within a democracy. This can be seen more clearly by examining some further statements he makes on law structured around the factors required of democratic society identified earlier.

First, democracy is a way of life that is broadly social before it is seen more narrowly as a political concept. Democratic habits "must affect all modes of human association. This is, of course the demand that democratic society use democratic means as well as aim at democratic ends. It has already been noted that most contemporary theories of law do not accept this factor as legitimate and would fail it as a test. In this chapter, of course, it sets out the main challenge and goal. In this book it is accepted that this requirement would be fulfilled if the further five factors are satisfied.

The second requirement is the presence within legal practice of pluralistic values and a decentered picture of social institutions. These factors are clearly present in Dewey's theory of law. For instance, when Dewey examines the philosophical claims of legal positivism in "Austin's Theory of Sovereignty"[33] his criticism almost completely rests upon Austin's inability to accommodate a pluralist and decentered picture of law. On Dewey's view, Austin confuses sovereignty with a specific source of command. Further, Austin's search for the location of sovereignty is doomed from the start due to his unexamined assumption that sovereignty must be numerically determinate. Dewey tests the theory against what he sees as the actual practice of sovereignty in the United States. In this context Austin's theory is described as resting sovereignty on the electorate as an aggregate body. But Dewey counters that this raises innumerable problems for the concept of the numerically determinate sovereign. For instance, is this electorate a class or a set of particular members? And what happens to each individual when they vote with the minority or majority? These problems show that in this case "sovereignty is not determinate until after it is exercised," and this means that it fails to satisfy Austin's conceptual need for it to be always discretely or numerically identifiable.[34] Of course if publics are constructed as Dewey claims, then none of these issues create a conceptual problem—in fact they are quite easily explained.

What Dewey finds most problematic in Austin's positivism, though, is the identification of government with sovereignty. Dewey argues that law is only explainable on the theory that government is an organ of sovereignty, not sovereignty itself. First, in the United States constitutional law determines the type and limits of government, therefore there is some other force behind the government that determines its character. In order to avoid this problem, Austin famously denies that constitutional law is law at all, but calls it rather "positive morality," a type of pseudo-law. This claim Dewey believes is plainly unacceptable in relation to a document that is universally described as the law of the land. Further, for Dewey it appears that any change, from constitutional to the most minor modifications of daily government, is left conceptually unexplainable in Austin's theory. This problem is seen, for example, in the relationship of custom and development of law within the state. Austin's theory forces the claim that custom is not law until expressly declared by the judiciary. Dewey argues that the conception of sovereignty offered by the positivists leads to an overly intellectualized and narrow picture of the sources of law. That is, in the quest of a hope for crystalline conceptual clarity, the practices of actual law are ignored and distorted.

Dewey's legal theory, to the contrary, rules out any search for a unifying rule of recognition for sovereignty, government or law. Most importantly for this chapter, rejection of the hope for a determinate and unified single source of authority is not a negative result but rather allows for plural sources of law. Instead of Austin's answer to the sources of law, Dewey therefore can develop an empirically interesting description of law as often emanating from "the minor laws of subordinate institutions— institutions like the family, the school, the business partnership, the trade- union or fraternal organization."[35] This allows for a pluralistic and "bottom- up" conception of the sources of law, one that maps nicely on to the case- based and analogical reasoning central to the common-law tradition. Indeed, Dewey often highlights this part of the legal tradition as arising from everyday transaction and then in turn becoming "formative" of further activity.[36] Law under this description arises out of other habits, traditions and customs within society.

Importantly though, when law recognizes a custom, it also "represents the beginning of a *new* custom."[37] Further, Dewey observes "while there would not be laws unless there were social customs, yet neither would there be laws if all customs were mutually consistent and were universally adhered to."[38] Of course law itself is a type of custom itself, and Dewey notes that much of law is made up of the concepts it inherits from earlier decisions. So, in "Anthropology and Law," Dewey develops a historicized picture of law that, for example, explores the survival in modern maritime law of the concept of a ship as both a person and a responsible being.[39] For Dewey, this illustrates that in law, "the old is never annihilated at a stroke, the new never a creation ab initio. It is simply a question of morphology. But what controls the modification in the historic continuity is the practical usefulness of the institution or organ in question."[40]

Dewey's theory of law, therefore, is decentralized and flexible and so can allow for multiple sources for law and, he hopes, "the development of quite new organs of law-making."[41] This also makes it compatible with the third factor required of democracy—the definition of a public in functional terms. As noted above, a public is created when social consequences that affect people beyond the immediate group are noted and found to be in need of social control. Political democracy, therefore, comes into being where there is a recognized need to control consequences of social activity. And because problems constantly change, states need to be continuously "re-made." Dewey echoes this analysis in the realm of law in his article, "My Philosophy of Law."[42] Ultimately, for him, legal practices are products of their time and place and the issues relevant to that specific context. Legal standards cannot be judged outside of the acknowledgement of context. It follows that law "can be discussed only in terms of the social conditions in which it arises and of what it concretely does there."[43] This specificity of context and use "renders the use of the word 'law' as a single general term rather dangerous."[44] Just as in the case of the democratic state, reification of past or contemporary ideas of law without keeping an eye on its current and future effects can get in the way of creating effective institutional tools. Dewey writes, "A given legal arrangement *is* what it *does*, and what it does lies in the field of modifying and/or maintaining human activities as going concerns."[45]

Fourth, Dewey claims that a living democratic society rests upon experimental intelligence. Because of this, he is quite suspicious of appeals to natural law. It is not that the central importance of natural law in jurisprudential history is to be ignored. In fact, Dewey finds that in the past appeals to natural law have often served to promote legitimate and progressive human aims. Dewey, though, notes that "nature" is generally taken as an appeal to something given, something prior to inquiry. Therefore, appeal to natural law may be used to fossilize given values or rules.[46] Further, it is difficult to understand what type of knowledge claim an appeal to natural law makes. For Dewey, "the effect of any theory that identifies intelligence with the given, instead of with the foresight of better and worse, is denial of the function of intelligence."[47] And intelligence is shown in action through empirical results. Ultimately, therefore, appeals to natural law get in the way of the empirical testing of the results of legal decisions. Not only that, but appeals to an antecedently given standard can also frustrate creative problem-solving.

For Dewey, law, when properly used, can be thought of "as describing a method for employing force economically, efficiently, so as to get results with the least waste."[48] Law is not a substitute for force—but institutionalized force. Law should be justified, therefore, not by its harmony with an antecedently accepted picture of "lawfulness"—whether based upon natural law or some other purported "rule of law" foundation—but by whether or not it is "an effective and economical means of securing specific results." Indeed, if it is not effective and economical, then "we are using violence to relieve our immediate impulses and to save ourselves the labor of thought and construction."[49]

For instance, according to Dewey, Spencer's laissez-faire theory of human reason is a form of natural law theory and appeals to the "natural" aspect of markets simply to avoid acknowledgement of alternative possibilities. Dewey further outlines the implications of this recurring appeal to the "natural" idea in a series of legal decisions pertaining to ideas of *due diligence* and *undue negligence*. The analysis offered by courts within the highlighted cases use "reason" as a given or "natural" standard, and personal liability rests upon whether the question of whether or not the care and prudence exercised in each situation was "reasonable." Courts, Dewey notes, often equate the word "reasonable" with "the amount and kind of foresight that, as a matter of fact, are customary among men in like pursuits."[50] Further, this use of reasonable is then applied even though the results are undesirable. This, of course, is the a priori methodology analyzed by Peirce—and exhibits all the vices of the a priori method. Dewey would redefine reasonable functionally as the "kind foresight that would, in similar circumstances, conduce to desirable consequences."[51] This is proposing to use a forward-looking and empirically testable theory of reason to construct a workable standard of care instead of a customary and traditional conception of the reasonable.[52]

Dewey uses the same type of analysis to explore the concept of corporate personality used in law and considers the practical function it serves. He finds that the content of "person" as traditionally construed in law is attached to a "mass of non-legal considerations," among which are "considerations popular, historical, political, moral, philosophical, metaphysical and, in connection with the latter, theological."[53] Dewey argues that instead of following the various meanings resulting from the concept's historical attachments, the legal content of "person" should be centered upon the practical results created by adopting any specific construction of the doctrine. According to him any appeal to a "metaphysical" nature of person is misguided and results in legal confusion of earlier sources with contemporary needs and results. Instead he offers a decidedly pragmatic option—define a corporation, and more broadly a legal person, by the specific consequences that they bring about, not by any inner or intrinsic essence. The problem is that metaphysical conceptions of personhood, just as metaphysical notions of natural law, function as "rationalizations" to support specific parties in legal struggles. Dewey thus calls for the elimination of "*any* concept of personality which is other than a restatement that such and such rights and duties, benefits and burdens, accrue and are to be maintained and distributed in such and such ways, and in such and such situations."[54] Legal concepts are to be applied and understood in terms of consequences, and not intrinsic essences.

Fifth, democracy is based upon specific problems as real felt problems. Democracy is constructed according to changing demands and is not to be defined in abstraction from these demands. Law is thought of in exactly the same way and not of as a purportedly timeless institutional "rule of law" way to decide any type of issue that arises. Ultimately Dewey explicitly argues that law like all other social institutions is "social in origin, in purpose or end, and in application."[55] It is historically based and yet contextually varied. Indeed, law as an institution and as a concept "cannot be set up as if it were a separate entity, but can be discussed only in terms of the social conditions in which it arises and of what it concretely does there."[56]

Sixth, while democracy employs both scientific knowledge and creativity for communication and solution of social problems, these problems cannot be solved through allocation of decision making to technocrats—no matter how valuable their knowledge is to the process. This is because appeal to expertise and "elite" democracy as final decision makers cannot avoid an undesirable distance from essential knowledge of the concrete issues demanding solution. Experts will not feel where the shoes pinch and therefore will not be located in the primary and most privileged position of knowledge. This, of course, rests where there is an incipient public, where social activities are felt in need of governance. As much of "law" as possible should be bottom-up, contextual and constructed in response to specific issues. Professional legal tools are to be thought secondary to the specific public's framing of the issue.

As can be seen from above, Dewey effectively critiques positivist and natural law ideas. In addition, he is quite critical of many standard rule-of-law ideas, showing effectively how they are evasive or distorting of actual practice. Further, Dewey's writings on law show that he expected the same bottom-up pluralistic forward-looking democratic experimentalism that he demanded other areas of society and, more narrowly, political institutions to instantiate. But, as has been claimed even by theorists that find Dewey's critique important, such as Richard Posner, his philosophy of law does, admittedly, lack much in the way of concrete suggestions as to how to reengineer real-world legal institutions in order to maximize the possible democratic aspects of legal practice. His critique is much better at showing the limits of traditional legal practice than constructing the more democratic option. This is also true of some of the democratically inclined theories I analyzed in the last chapter. Fortunately, there were some early attempts at filling in the details and, more relevant to this chapter, are some contemporary theorists trying to construct concrete conceptions of just what such real-world democratic and experimental legal institutions could look like.

The Jurisprudence of Democratic Experimentalism

Early notable attempts at filling in Dewey's theory of democratic law where offered by various theorists often now classified as "legal realists"—a term that is so amorphous as to be virtually useless. Specifically, the work of Thurman W. Arnold emphasized the need for experimentalism as opposed to various attempts at other forms of "revealed" reasoning.[57] And Edward Steven Robinson argued against what he described as an internal priestly nature of the legal discipline and opposed to this a conception of responsibility to fact that William James and Dewey demanded (which he thought was exemplified in the jurisprudence of Holmes and Brandeis).[58]

More importantly, there are actually quite a number of contemporary theorists that are helping to construct a more systematic picture of what a workable jurisprudence of democratic experimentalism entails. But as will become quite apparent, most of these theories fail at least some of the requirements that Dewey sets out for democratic governance. For instance, one very influential variety of legal experimentalism within the academy seeks to use experimental results from fields such as behavioral economics in order to reengineer basic but ultimately local aspects of democratic procedure and debate. Perhaps most exemplary of this version are the works of Cass Sunstein.[59] In *Designing Democracy*, for instance, Sunstein uses the results of behavioral economics to investigate what conditions are helpful or harmful for democratic decision making. After finding problems such as "enclave deliberation" and "social cascades" that often lead to the holding of extreme conceptual positions, he tries to offer ways to engineer social space so as to encourage heterogeneity in deliberated opinions.[60] This result is all quite positive and certainly valuable for contemporary legal practice.

In this variety of democratic experimentalism, though, the basic assumptions and descriptions of governmental branches and their essential functions in government are largely taken for granted. The location of the experimentation, therefore, is within processes or branches of government taken as functionally and conceptually stable, and the experiments are restricted to making given systems more democratically responsive and informed. Most importantly, as Sunstein practices it, his analysis largely accepts the non-democratic legal means in service of democratic ends version of law. The implications of his analysis for law "proper," accordingly, are quite minimal. Indeed, Sunstein's legal scholarship steers clear of any great systemic experimental changes for legal practice and generally offers a quite traditional and non-experimental conception of law. So, for example, he is known for advocating judicial minimalism and "incompletely theorized agreements," a judicial stance that would intentionally relegate any policy experimentalism to decisions of other branches of government which he finds have better democratic pedigree.

Differing from Sunstein's local and largely conservative use of experimental results to inform democratic procedures, where a standard conception of law is taken as largely given and judges should take a deferential stance toward decisions of other governmental branches, a revolutionary in tone approach can be seen in Roberto Unger's work.[61] He aims to describe an experimentally based democratic society that through the ability to collectively learn enhances both "practical progress" and "the requirements of individual emancipation."[62]

According to Unger we are currently institutionally and democratically crippled from achieving this type of society because hampered by multiple (false) "necessitarian assumptions." Three of these assumptions are the idea that there is a closed and small list of possible institutional systems, that each of these institutions is indivisible—an essential type such as "law" with specific traits such as the necessary aspects of "the rule of law"—and that each of these systems are governed by lawlike and determinist forces.[63] He argues that we should instead accept the divisibility, indeterminacy, and contingency of institutional forms. Indeed, for him democratic experimentalism "requires freedom to recombine people, practices, and resources, unfettered by the prescriptions of rigid systems of social roles and entrenched social divisions and hierarchies."[64] It is important, that is, to develop alternative pluralisms. His plans range from progressive schooling and directed tax regimes to the creation of social institutions that exist in between those of purely private and purely public forms to an ultimate reconstruction of basic social concepts such as property (a social form he sees as particularly prone to fundamentalist and fetishistic constructions).

These ideas offer the outlines of a potential experimentalist and democratic regime. But while his work is a call to experimentation aimed at enhancing democracy, his proposals are highly abstract and largely programmatic. At least Sunstein's project, while institutionally conservative, relies on experimental results. Unger's work, to the contrary, is a top-down and god's eye "view from nowhere" philosophical treatise on the a priori foundational framework for a specific conception of experimental democracy with his main hopes resting on a core of revolutionary judges commanding experimentation from the bench. Experimental results or experimental institutional forms are not thought to originate from the bottom up. In other words, here the only experimentalism in relation to law is in Unger's hope that the judge as a democratic experimentalist prophet will use his or her position to further the experimentalist cause through commanding experimentation from the top down. Like Sunstein, Unger is, for all his experimentalist vocabulary, at heart a legal conservative or traditionalist and law as a formal process is seen as a practice largely outside of the realm of experimentation, let alone democratic decision making. And at least in Sunstein's case there is the use of empirical science—this is nowhere to be found in Unger's work (nor is there an obvious location where it would be used).

Another variety of democratic experimentalism that shows legal conservatism is offered in Knight and Johnson's *The Priority of Democracy: The Political Consequences of Pragmatism*. Therein they argue that given our political situation, characterized as unavoidably diverse, heterogeneous and yet wherein we are inevitably stuck together, the big issue is not to find a neutral starting point—there is none—but to find a best-possible manner with which to choose social institutions out of the plurality of feasible institutional forms.[65] A useful manner of institutional choice should, they claim, be able to: (1) coordinate "effective institutional experimentation"; (2) monitor specific institutional performance and; (3) monitor its own performance.[66] Knight and Johnson ultimately argue that "democracy as a political institution is due second-order priority because it embodies a reflexivity that renders it uniquely adept at the experimental task of determining which institutional arrangements to rely on across different domains."[67] In other words, while there are many different types and combinations of social institutions that might be best for first-order tasks, for the second-order task of choosing among institutions, monitoring them, and then reflexively evaluating whether the choice system was effective, democracy is superior.

But when it comes to law, Knight and Johnson explicitly accept and rely upon a standard "legal positivist" conception of law offered by H. L. A. Hart wherein "courts are primarily responsible for adjudicating controversies over how law is to be applied in particular cases."[68] In other words, courts are good at the first-order project of rule application but not the second-order project of the democratic choice of institutions and policy.[69] Further, they argue that because agenda-setting for courts is largely exogenous and standing requirements limit participation, there are further reasons, one being the problem of an under-inclusion of legitimate stakeholders, as to why courts are less than ideal institutions to choose first-order institutions.[70] Most importantly, they identify the "real weakness" of the court system as its inability to assess institutional outcomes.[71] This is because such assessment requires ongoing evaluation of experiments tried, as well as interests and social commitments, and courts, because they are restricted to a specific case or controversy, cannot handle these issues.

In this variety of democratic experimentalism, democracy is largely accepted in its standard already familiar forms and the institutional forms themselves are portrayed as representing ideal and essential types. The essential aspects of law are accepted as contrary to democracy. As one of the institutions accepted in essentialized, albeit "Hartrian" legal positivism form, law is once again described as outside of the experimental arena, indeed as being merely a rule-applying forum characterized by all the traditional "rule of law" characteristics. Just as with Sunstein and Unger's work, it seems that in Knight and Johnson's work pragmatist experimental methodology, and democracy, stops at the entrance to the legal realm. All three clearly fail Dewey's requirement that democratic ends entail the use democratic means through and through.

Law as a Democratic Means

There are, though, scholars developing a more "all the way down" picture of experimentalist democracy and law. For instance, Christopher Ansell, in *Pragmatist Democracy: Evolutionary Learning as Public Philosophy*, goes much further toward constructing a through-going democratic experimentalism where law is, itself, necessarily more democratic and experimental. His theory starts by locating democratic hope in mid-level institutions such as administrative agencies that are traditionally thought embarrassing to democracy. Ansell contrasts his democratic agency conception of democracy with what he describes as a "traditional model" where public agencies are conceived of "as the final link in a chain of representation that begins with the electorate, moves on to the legislature, then to appointed agency officials, and finally reaches the street-level bureaucrat."[72] The problem with this model, according to him, is that it is characterized by a number of principal/agent "pathologies." For instance, such a model rests upon a clear distinction between politics and administration that breaks down under the complexity of contemporary issues. Further, Ansell argues that such an organizational form typically seeks control through the use of rules, but "the vacuous nature of the rules often leads to a vicious cycle, where the failure of existing rules is met with new systems of rule-oriented control," but "new rules only add to the complexity of the formal environment and create new opportunities to 'game' the system."[73]

Ansell's alternative, like Dewey's, starts with the concrete and local problems of affected stakeholders and then creates the grounds of public action through collaborative governance. Ansell offers a general conception of an agency that embodies evolutionary learning. This is the main component of his "problem-solving democracy," that builds consent through a focus smaller "publics" focused on specific problems that is characterized by "three generative conditions for evolutionary learning." These are: (1) a problem-driven perspective; (2) reflexivity; and (3) deliberation.[74] Evolutionary learning, though it is characterized as situationally focused upon the specific, is also attached to an ecological perspective that values holism, because public issues are both spatially and temporally "multidimensional and complexly linked."[75] And, importantly, the identities of both the problem and the relevant problem-solvers and stakeholders are often constructed and altered in the process of solving a problem. That is, problem solving entails the communication of both the problem and the values that should be served, and because these are related to the specific problem at hand, therefore helps confer identity on the problem itself.

But how exactly does this fit in with the idea of administrative agencies as democracy enhancing public institutions? Most succinctly put, "*institutions are relationships between the symbolic artifacts that mediate social life and people's experience of those artifacts.*"[76] Ansell next proposes (following Dewey) that we "call an audience that has become collectively self-reflective a *public*" and, finally, that "a *community* is a public that can act collectively to arbitrate the interpretation of concepts and control their meaning."[77] Once institutions are acknowledged to be conceptual ecologies, "symbolic politics" becomes necessary and a primary source of institutional action.

In the relational pragmatic institution, organizational levels are loosely coupled and often act quite autonomously. The top level sets the overall policy direction of the organization as well as defines the central purposes of the organization. The other semiautonomous subunits, because infused with the meta-norms and meta-concepts and of clear capacity and competence, can be allowed latitude in decision making. Of course in light of this change in structure, democratic consent changes in characterization. Instead of the principal-agent problems attached to a picture of "monistic sovereignty," which creates the traditional desire to keep agencies separate from their regulated environment, pragmatist institutions emphasize relational authority, and the authority of joint inquiry. And because of this, agencies cannot only more effectively gather information, but they also can more directly engage interested publics.

This starts to fill in aspects of what a legal system aimed at being democratic in Dewey's form might look like. A discussion specific to "law" proper is notably missing from Ansell's analysis, though. Is law, as a specific branch of democracy, to be reconceived in the "quasi-law" forms that contemporary administrative agencies are often described as exemplifying? Is law to be reconceived more radically as an experimental evolutionary system itself? I take it that the latter option is more true to Ansell's version of pragmatic democratic experimentalism. But this conclusion is never explicitly stated. This is where the work of William Simon can help. His characterization of "Toyota Democracy" also emphasizes the instantiation of pragmatist learning in specific democratic institutions and specifically notes the way in which experimentalism in firms can be translated into a more dynamic form of democratic governance within law.[78]

Simon argues that contemporary commercial institutions have developed practices that can be used to translate Dewey's democratic and experimental vision of pragmatism into concrete operating strategies. These institutions have the ability to provide stability at the same time that they enable continuous revision, learning, and adaptation—especially through the use of rolling rule regimes where institutions learn from other institutional experiments and constantly raise the baseline expectations. Further, he claims that these same institutions can empower local democratic decision making and coordinate multiple and often distant activities, all the while allowing for a diversity of interests through adoption of the Deweyan starting points of instrumentalism, contextualism, and the centrality of incremental experimentation.

Simon notes three operational strategies in particular that have been used in modern institutions that could be employed to further the Deweyan project. These three strategies are "lean production," "standardization," and "team-based decision making." Briefly, lean production is exemplified by the Toyota Production System where, as opposed to the practices of end-of-the-pipe correction or ad hoc adjustment, the aim is to catch problems as they arise and use them as sources of learning opportunities. For instance, rather than building up excess parts or shunting off problems through relaxing the demands of precision, problems are faced immediately, used as information, and solutions are searched for in ways that resonate throughout the process, creating an institution engineered for constant improvement. Standardization, somewhat counterintuitively, by creating uniformity in testing and results, makes practices more transparent and, in the process, easier to compare and coordinate with other institution's practices. Of course any specific standardization can be challenged and treated as a problem to be solved as well. Finally, nested team-based decision making both encourages group learning and helps create cooperative norms.

As opposed to the work of Sunstein, Unger and Knight, and Johnson, the work of Ansell and Simon does not accept as given non-democratic and non-experimental conceptions of legal process. On the other hand, both remain largely in the abstract and do not give concrete examples of how a specific legal system could satisfy the six aspects of democracy demanded by Dewey. It is a real virtue of the work of Michael Dorf and Charles Sabel that it starts to do just that. That is, the work of Dorf and Sabel actually fleshes out a more specific and concrete proposal for what a specifically experimental practice of law might look like in a fully experimental democratic regime.

Their article, "A Constitution of Democratic Experimentalism," offers what they describe as a "Madisonian" conception of constitutionally systematized "Democratic Experimentalism" that while compatible with traditional United States governmental organization would dramatically change the understanding of how government, and therefore the court system, ought to function.[79] Furthermore, their conception of legal process is explicitly pragmatic. The authors first note that the pragmatist's acceptance of the "reciprocal determination of means and ends" is an important realization because inevitable due to the "pervasiveness of unintended consequences" that, in turn, makes it impossible to come up with "first principles that survive the effort to realize them."[80] Second, they note the Peircean thought that doubt properly understood and utilized is a spur toward creative solution. Third, Dorf and Sabel also accept that the inquiry following from doubt is "irreducibly social," indeed our understanding of our individual projects "depends on how others interpret and react to them."[81] Fourth, they adopt ideals from classical pragmatism because "as a theory of thought and action through problem solving by collaborative, continuous reelaboration of means and ends, pragmatism suggests that advances in accommodating change in one area often have extensive implications for problem solving in others."[82] All of this relates clearly to Peirce's idea of inquiry and Dewey's elaboration of the relationship between inquiry and democracy.

One of the most important implications of pragmatism is, for them as well, that it questions a clear-cut distinctions and essentialist understandings of political branch functions and fixed conceptions of the line between public and private. Dorf and Sabel, as did Simon, note that once essentialist notions of institutional purity are questioned, democratic experimentalism as a program can look to private firms, indeed all available examples of successful social institutions, for possible solutions to problems of democratic governance. They argue that because markets have become "so differentiated and fast changing that prices can serve as only a general framework and limit on decisionmaking," innovative private firms have had to "resort to a collaborative exploration of disruptive possibilities that has more in common with pragmatist ideas of social inquiry than familiar ideas of market exchange."[83] Specifically, these firms have adopted "federated" and open strategies of benchmarking, simultaneous engineering, and learning by monitoring. Benchmarking entails "an exacting survey of current or promising products and processes which identifies those products and processes superior to those the company presently uses, yet are within its capacity to emulate and eventually surpass."[84] Simultaneous engineering on its part entails "continuous adjustment of means and ends and vice versa, as in pragmatism, the means and end of collaboration among the producers." Further, because "the exchanges of information required to engage in benchmarking, simultaneous engineering, and error correction also allow the independent collaborators to monitor one another's activities closely enough to detect performance failures and deception before these latter have disastrous consequences," this type of collaboration encourages "learning by monitoring."[85] Indeed, in these firms, group discussion becomes central in pooling plans, problems, and perspectives. This type of organization yields flexibility in purpose and output as well as creates self-reinforcing habits of inquiry and transparency.

Once institutional fundamentalism is questioned, it is not as startling to think that business conditions might require democratic types of information gathering and institutional monitoring. From this, Dorf and Sabel argue that a political system built along the same lines could actually be democracy-enhancing. In this specifically political system of democratic experimentalism the roles of various branches remain somewhat distinct, but their functions are partially reconceived. As Dewey requires, governmental activity would be presumptively local. Congress would encourage and allow subunits to experiment as to means and, to a lesser extent to ends, "on condition that those who engage in the experiment publicly declare their goals and propose measures of their progress, periodically refining those measures through exchanges among themselves and with the help of correspondingly reorganized administrative agencies." Congress would also ensure that information, such as the results of various experiments in governance, would be made generally available, therefore creating an information pooling resource of successful and unsuccessful regulatory choices. Administrative agencies would be chiefly charged with assisting subunits in experimentation as well. More specifically, with congressional authorization they could set regulatory standards, most often following "rolling best-practice rules," thereby encouraging effective benchmarking.[86]

Citizens continue to evaluate their representatives through voting in general elections, but elections would be informed through the use of the pooled benchmarking information. That is, the same governmental process that encourages the development of benchmark information in furtherance of solutions to current political issues creates a record that can help inform votes. Further, citizens serve a more active stakeholder role (possibly as constructed publics?) on various governance councils in more directly democratic venues focused on bringing together members centered upon pressing current governance issues. Dorf and Sabel describe this form of democratic process happening in multiple places through multiple publics as a "polyarchy" This decentered picture of democracy is, of course, very reminiscent of Dewey's characterization of sovereignty as plural and decentered. Therefore, "experimentalism links benchmarking, rulemaking, and revision so closely with operating experience that rulemakers and operating-world actors work literally side by side—but, to repeat, in plain view of the public-and thus, largely overcome the distinction between the detached staff of honest but imperfectly informed experts and the knowledgeable but devious insiders they regulate."[87]

Most important for this chapter, the conceptualization of the role of the courts, and law in general, changes. Courts function to make sure that the local government experiments fall within the broad aims authorized in Congress's legislation, respect the rights of citizens, and are performed in a properly systematic and transparent manner. Communities would get freedom and support for their experiments, but in return for this liberty they must develop a record of options and choices considered (which would be virtually automatic given the requirements of benchmarking, simultaneous engineering, and learning by monitoring). A court would look at the possibilities revealed by the process in order to decide whether or not any rights or policies are unlawfully thwarted. An interested party challenges governmental choices in court by pointing out better choices revealed in other experiments in governance.

This picture of the legal system does not eliminate the use of traditional rule of law virtues; it just limits their import. What it does do, though, is change the dominant role of the system, and the judge in particular, from ultimate rule-giver to active collaborator in a broadly democratic and bottom up experimentalist system. It also changes the manner of inquiry expected of the courts. The aim is much less to police decisions for their proper correspondence to a priori rules than it is to encourage transparent, informed, and democratically responsive collective responses to social issues.[88]

As Dorf and Sabel put it, "In this way the vindication of individual rights encourages mutual learning and vice versa, and judges' discretion in applying broad principles is schooled and disciplined by actual experimentation with possibilities they could have never imagined."[89] Once again, courts would not eliminate traditional doctrines but would have to embrace two ideals in order to function properly within democratic experimentalism. First, courts would have to combine a sense of "fundamental legal norms" with an understanding that these norms can properly be exposed to experimental elaboration. Second, "experimentalist courts defer to the political actors' exploration of means and ends only on the condition that the actors have in fact created the kind of record that makes possible an assessment of their linking of principle and practice."[90]

Because of this, "judicial review by experimentalist courts accordingly becomes a review of the admissibility of the reasons private and political actors themselves give for their decisions, and the respect they actually accord those reasons: a review, that is, of whether the protagonists have themselves been sufficiently attentive to the legal factors that constrain the framing of alternatives and the process of choosing among them."[91] And, of course these reasons would have to be tested through use of the pragmatic maxim. The virtue of this is that the process creates data so, as opposed to courts currently that have to act as if empirical questions are questions of pure reasoning, the court within democratic experimentalism will have an experimentally informed record to work from. Further, under a statute authorizing experimentalist administration, the courts do not conceptualize themselves as needed to supply any final authoritative meaning. Instead, agencies and other actors jointly provide the aims and baselines required for judging proposed solutions through identification of rolling best-practice standards.[92] Judges therefore function less as a referee and more as part of an active problem-solving process.[93] But the activity does not, tellingly, fit the accusation made against judges in tradition roles, as "activist" because the judge does not aim to make determinant once-and-for-all rules. Rather, the collaboration is based upon the information developed and documented in the record and an understanding that social needs and institutional solutions are both constantly changing. Any legal determination must be potentially revisable in the light of further social experimentation and the evidence this provides.

Dorf and Sabel develop the most through-going pragmatic version of democratic experimentalism in specific relationship to law "proper" of all of the systems analyzed in this chapter. Their conception of democratic experimentalism actually entails that the legal system itself is an experimental and democratic system. While the Court and the judges still have a role to play, that role is decentered and better thought of as a democratic facilitation than rule making. If, indeed, democracy (and therefore law within a democratic regime) is taken as an experimental project of construction (as they do and Dewey did before them) and not an already identified system of foundational rules and essential procedure, then this entails that understanding democracy and law is also a creative, comparative, and forward-looking project. That is, we only understand democracy and law by experimentally constructing it democratically—as can be seen by the characterization of law that Dorf and Sable law can be reconceptualized to emphasize both democratic and experimental features.

And democratic experimentalism, as they construct it, does an excellent job of satisfying the demands that Dewey makes of democracy. First, law as a mode of human association is broadly democratic—especially when contrasted with the top-down command form it is traditionally found to manifest. Where traditional pictures of the "rule of law" fixate on command and control structures, in the jurisprudence of democratic experimentalism the presumption is in favor of the choices made by various citizen publics. Second, pluralistic values and a decentered picture of social institutions is built into the system. The system pools information and encourages experimentation through its decentered and federated structure. The system is predicated upon evolutionary learning with local venues rather than hopes for unmoving foundations or top-down decision making. Third, publics are functional in that they are organized to solve specific problems and are continuously "re-made" in relationship to the social issues needing attention. Fourth, experimental intelligence is centrally encouraged. Fifth, democratic procedure is constructed according to changing demands and is not to be defined in abstraction from these demands. And sixth, while a legal system organized along the lines of democratic experimentalism expressly uses experimental and scientific knowledge and also encourages creative solutions to social problems, the appeal to expertise is disciplined by both the practice of benchmarking and the constant creation of and monitoring by (the participation of) citizen-stakeholder publics. Ultimate power always stays with the general public. Further, this power is not just exercised through voting, but through a much more pluralistic set of social institutions.

In many ways Dorf and Sabel's democratic experimentalism seems to be a very successful imaging of how Dewey's stringent democratic demands could be experimentally institutionalized through benchmarking, learning by monitoring, etc. And democratic habits can be even further encouraged through the Court deferring to localized and pluralistic interpretive possibilities also generated through democratic processes as Kramer and

Tushnet envision. That is, not only should democratic experimentalism encourage local experimentation as to legislative and means, but also as to constitutional interpretation. This would democratize the constitution rather than allowing the opposite tendency of constitutionalizing political issues therefore encouraging pluralism and incrementalism as against legal formalism and anti-democratic foundationalist rule-making.

So, the conclusion to be had from this chapter is that it is possible to conceive of a legal system of democratic experimentalism that is both empirically plausible and that satisfies Dewey's demand that democracy only utilize democratic means. This is a startling result and should at the very least raise questions about the amazing lack of constructive imagination in contemporary legal thought and practice. This raises the question—Why exactly are the traditional rule of law "virtues" thought to be virtues? Indeed, this critique invites the possibility that many of the ideas of contemporary jurisprudence are actually specific to certain quite possibly narrowly parochial practices. Further, the repetitive discourse and standardized moves (indeed the fetishized quest for essential standardized moves) might be limiting our search for more democratic possibilities. Might these comfortable conceptions of law have been invented in times where an experimental outlook was frowned upon and democratic rule seen as threatening to an entrenched elite? That is, might it be the case that many of the cliché "rule of law" virtues often glorified in legal theory actually made virtues out of earlier institutional limitations—limitations that now can properly be seen as vices to be experimentally overcome?

This conclusion seems quite plausible. In this spirit, in the next chapter I investigate in greater detail one aspect of the model of democratic experimentalist law outlined above—its aim of information production. This systemic goal of producing and making the greatest possible pool of information available for a legal decision will be contrasted with influential contemporary theories of law—most centrally the "public meaning originalism" theory of Antonin Scalia—that explicitly attempt to exclude information in order to limit decisions to "properly legal" reasons because of an appeal to rule of law virtues. This investigation will be made concrete through and investigation of Scalia's *Heller* opinion and Richard Posner's Seventh Circuit opinion on much the same issue in *Moore v. Madigan*.

CHAPTER THREE

Information-Rich Jurisprudence

In August of 2014, *Slate* published an article entitled "Listen to a Conservative Judge Brutally Destroy Arguments against Gay Marriage."[1] The case was *Baskin v. Bogan*. The judge was Richard Posner, whose information-rich theory of judging informs much of this chapter and whose judicial decision making will help show a few strands of what the jurisprudence of democratic experimentalism looks like in practice. The article excerpted recorded sections of Posner's cross-examination of attorneys for Indiana and Wisconsin that were charged with trying to justify state bans on same-sex marriage. The exchanges are notable because the lawyers continuously tried to rest their reasoning on legal doctrine, abstract hypotheticals, and various other legalist strategies. Posner, on the other hand, confounded them by repeatedly asking for empirical facts. Ultimately realizing the states could offer no real facts as to the purported harms that legalizing same-sex marriage would cause, he became exasperated.

Posner's opinion for a unanimous Seventh Circuit finding the bans unconstitutional, *Baskin v. Bogan*, decided the next month, September 4, 2014, shows an equal attention to empirical facts and brevity with legal formalities.[2] Posner's opinion uses as little legal jargon as possible. And where he felt it necessary to use legal terminology he explained it as clearly and with as few citations as possible. As in oral arguments, the whole analysis ends on the fact that state lawyers offered no empirical evidence for their claims that same-sex marriage had undesirable results and therefore was justifiably banned. The opinion is forty pages long and gives the startling impression (at least startling in the context of legal argumentation and judicial decision making) that scientific literature and proven empirical harms are more important than standard legal form. The author of the first *Slate* article on the oral arguments, Mark Joseph Stern, followed the decision up with a new article titled "Judge Posner's Gay Marriage Opinion

Is a Witty, Deeply Moral Masterpiece,"[3] wherein he notes, favorably and insightfully, that Posner was "fixated on the facts on hand."

Later on, Posner's opinion on same-sex marriage will further analyzed and contrasted with the Supreme Court decision on the same subject, *Obergefell*. But even the brief description offered above of Posner's *Baskin v. Bogan* decision helps highlight one intriguing aspect of the conception of democratic experimentalism offered in the previous chapter. This is the characterization of the legal system as a tool to produce and pool factual information for judicial decision making. This contrasts with influential conceptions of law that are aptly described as purposefully "information excluding." That is, traditional conceptions of law are often centered upon the project of excluding from legal reasoning what are thought of as illegitimate and non-legal reasons. This exclusionary tendency brings together seemingly quite opposite theories of proper constitutional interpretation. For example, both Ronald Dworkin and Antonin Scalia police the borders of law to eliminate what they consider improper non-legal reasons from being used (though they disagree on what is to be included as well as what reasons are properly legal ones).

I argue in this chapter that a conception of the legal process, and the judge's position within it, as an information-production system is possible that is greatly superior to the traditional information excluding type of legal decision making. To do this I have supplemented the jurisprudence of democratic experimentalism offered in the last chapter with an analysis of Richard Posner's recent pragmatist jurisprudence. To show the import of this stance, it will be contrasted with Antonin Scalia's jurisprudential theory, "public meaning originalism," an explicitly information excluding conception of law. The analysis will use as its focal point a defining opinion for Scalia's legal philosophy, *Heller*, a United States Supreme Court opinion that interprets the Second Amendment's "right to bear arms" clause. I then conclude with an investigation of a Posner opinion—*Moore v. Madigan*—that arguably exemplifies the jurisprudence of democratic experimentalism on the very same legal issue. I will show that the conception of law offered by democratic experimentalism as information-producing would result in a much more desirable legal methodology.

District of Columbia v. Heller

Heller is arguably the defining opinion for Scalia's jurisprudential philosophy.[4] The facts were close to perfect for implementation of his theory.

There was a clear constitutional text; the "bear arms" clause of the Second Amendment—"A well regulated Militia, being necessary to the security of a free State, the right of the people to keep and bear Arms shall not be infringed"—and very few precedents to worry about. Further, the facts were simple and undisputed. The District of Columbia had a set of legal codes that made it extremely difficult to legally possess a handgun. A one-year license was possible but rare and only allowed via being issued by the chief of police. Heller, a D.C. special police officer applied for a permit and was refused. He filed suit under the Second Amendment. The District Court dismissed, the Court of Appeals for the D.C. Circuit reversed and the Supreme Court granted certiorari.

The majority opinion, written by Scalia, reads as if the Court had officially adopted his originalist methodology. As it stated, "In interpreting this text, we are guided by the principle that '[t]he Constitution was written to be understood by the voters; its words and phrases were used in their normal and ordinary as distinguished from technical meaning." Of course for him this is the meaning of the founding generation. Purportedly using this methodology, that is, through investigation of the textual structure of the amendment as well as the normal public meaning of the text at the time of the founding, the *Heller* Court ultimately found that the Second Amendment "protects an individual right to possess a firearm unconnected with service in a militia, and to use that arm for traditionally lawful purposes, such as self-defense within the home."[5]

The Court did this by offering a reading of the text based upon the following analysis. First, the Court divided the text into a "prefatory clause" and an "operative clause." Then it explained that, "apart from the clarifying function, a prefatory clause does not limit or expand the scope of the operative clause."[6] Therefore, it seems, if the original meaning of the operative clause is reasonably and fairly clear, reference to the prefatory clause becomes unnecessary. But in this case this leaves very little explicit content left to go by. Even so, the Court's analysis of the "operative clause" has every appearance of a tortured formalist wonder. "First, the "right of the people" was found to be unambiguously a right of individuals, not of a collective "people" or any type of corporate rights. Therefore, the Court found a strong presumption that the Second Amendment Right is exercised individually and belongs to all Americans. Then, in "to keep and bear Arms" it was found that the contemporary meaning of "arms" is no different than that of the eighteenth century. In addition, "to bear" was found by the Court's majority to mean to "carry" for the purpose of "confrontation."[7] From this it was concluded that "bear arms" was unambiguously used to refer to the carrying of weapons outside of an organized militia.

To bolster such an analysis public meaning originalism uses public historical sources. Scalia in *Heller* claimed that these sources show that the Second Amendment codified a preexisting right that had "nothing whatever to do with service in a militia."[8] Further, the Court found that in the phrase "security of a free state," the word "state" means "the people composing a particular nation or community." To support this reading the opinion switched away from constitutional text and surveyed postratification summaries and treatises, pre–Civil War case law, post–Civil War legislation, constitutional commentators, and earlier Supreme Court precedents. From this Scalia concluded, "Nothing in our precedents forecloses our adoption of the original understanding of the Second Amendment."[9] Therefore, the Court held "the inherent right of self-defense has been central to the Second Amendment right. The handgun ban amounts to a prohibition of an entire class of 'arms' that is overwhelmingly chosen by American society for that lawful purpose. The prohibition extends, moreover, to the home, where the need for defense of self, family, and property is most acute. Under any of the standards of scrutiny that we have applied to enumerated constitutional rights, banning from the home 'the most preferred firearm in the nation to 'keep' and use for protection of one's home and family' would fail constitutional muster."[10] The Court then affirmed the judgment of the Court of Appeals and the D.C. handgun "ban" was found unconstitutional.

Importantly, the opinion also noted that "nothing in our opinion should be taken to cast doubt on longstanding prohibitions on the possession of firearms by felons and the mentally ill, or laws forbidding the carrying of firearms in sensitive places such as schools and government buildings, or laws imposing conditions and qualifications on the commercial sale of arms." Not only this, but the Court also accepted that the holding should be limited to the types of weapons in common use at the time of enactment.

Both Stevens and Breyer wrote dissents. Stevens started his by defining the issue as whether the Second Amendment protects any gun rights for nonmilitary purposes. He also stated that "the Second Amendment was adopted to protect the right of the people of each of the several States to maintain a well-regulated militia. It was a response to concerns raised during the ratification of the Constitution that the power of Congress to disarm the state militias and create a standing army posed an intolerable threat to the sovereignty of the several States."[11]

Further, Stevens argued that *Miller*, the Court's only relevant precedent, also situated the right to bear arms in the context of a "reasonable relationship" to militia activity. As to the first part of the constitutional text in question, instead of "prefatory clause," he labeled it a "preamble" and found that it shows the purpose of the Amendment was the preservation of militias, that such militias were thought necessary to the security of a free state, and that these militias must be well-regulated.[12] Stevens noted that the majority opinion ignores the preamble so it can pretend to "find" its preferred reading but that only through ignoring the preamble's content can the majority make such a reading compatible with the text. Stevens further noted that even this truncated compatibility is questionable given the majority's inconsistent reading of such terms as "the people."[13]

Breyer started his own dissent by agreeing with Stevens that the majority's opinion is incorrect on originalist grounds and then added the claim that it was also incorrect because it ignored constitutionally legitimate limitations to Second Amendment rights. Breyer ultimately advocated an explicit "interest balancing inquiry."[14] Given this interpretive methodology, a methodology that encourages the use of social data, he then offered a detailed statistical survey of gun-related social issues and argued that because of the importance of the issues, and the amount of uncertainty in the results of various legislative policies, judges should defer to legislators. Breyer noted that deference to legislative judgment is appropriate where the judgment has been made by a local legislature with particular knowledge of local problems and workable solutions. Further, he argued that room should be made for local experiments when solutions are not clearly apparent.

Analytical reaction to the majority opinion in *Heller* was overwhelmingly negative. Some found that its version of "law office history" smelled of partialist advocacy.[15] Others noted how naive the picture of history and meaning must be for an originalist to come up with a determinate meaning, with Mark Tushnet describing such history as based on a "simulacrum of historical inquiry" that results in "history-in-law" that necessarily ignores contested truths. Tushnet noted that because Scalia has to ignore these contested truths and come up with a single determinant meaning he has to dismiss much actual historical evidence that would make his purportedly objective and certain conclusions more tentative.[16] This claim is especially true if Samuel Issacharaoff was correct in stating that "there is every reason to believe that constitutional terms were deliberately vague so as to garner agreement when the specifics could not be worked out." This was a situation where "the Framers were embarking on a bold venture into representative democracy, with few historical milestones to guide how the various pieces would hold together." Therefore, "they were specific when they could be and aspirational when they reached the limits of their understandings or their ability to agree."[17]

Another damning claim, this one made by Reva Siegal, was that, though the rhetoric was of judicial humility in the face of a clear textual mandate, the actuality of the matter was that originalism actually functioned in *Heller* "as conservatives' living constitution" because it "gave jurisprudential expression to the coalition politics of the New Right."[18] That is, originalism acted as a jurisprudential theory that could justify (and disguise) the activism of the current conservative members of the Court. Finally, multiple commentators noted that the real "operative" aspects of the majority's opinion, the disclaimer of what the case does not rule out, offers virtually no guidance for lower courts in figuring out what they should do.[19]

As it stands, the case represents a bright-line and universal rule purportedly based upon original public meaning that stands for the minimal content that virtual "bans" of handguns in the home are unconstitutional and then a laundry list of exceptions with no explanation as to why they pass constitutional muster. That is, there is no guidance as to how to move from this minimal baseline to the exceptions in a reasoned, principled or empirically helpful or predictable manner.

Of great interest is Posner's *New Republic* critique.[20] He finds *Heller* "questionable in both method and result." He sees the decoupling strategy between the "prefatory" and "operative" clauses used by the majority as textual evasion, argues that the context of the Second Amendment's ratification gives strong support to the accuracy of Stevens's dissent, and notes that at the time of the constitution's ratification the reigning conception of textual construction was that of Blackstone's which was "loose," "flexible," and "nonliteral." Therefore, an originalist true to his or her theory should be a loose constructionist. To support this claim he points out the fact that the Constitution's great expositor, John Marshall, was also a "loose constructionist." Posner also notes that at the time of ratification "arms" meant "muskets" but the Court properly ignored this detail because "using that detail in a modern interpretation would be 'preposterous.'"

Ultimately Posner is at a loss to explain *Heller* as anything but a version of "payback" or "turnabout is fair play" in response to earlier liberal courts using loose interpretation. But Posner offers other reasons to worry about the *Heller* opinion rather than just its historical inaccuracy, political motivation, and unexplained looseness. First, Posner allows that it might be important to use a loose construction of the Constitution when the group seeking the enlargement of protection "does not have good access to the political process to protect its interests." But, he observes, gun advocates are not without such access; indeed they are a strongly organized and well-funded group. Second, "*Heller* gives short shrift to the values of federalism, and to the related values of cultural diversity, local preference, and social experimentation."

One would think that in the light of this criticism, indeed criticism coming from figures even to the right of the Court's political preferences such as Richard Epstein, that the Court would back off of its conclusions.[21] That was not the case. Two years later in *McDonald v. City of Chicago* the Court extended the *Heller* holding to states under the Due Process Clause (thereby further supporting Posner's "turnabout" analysis).[22] Scalia's concurrence reiterated his originalist interpretation in *Heller* and, though noting the imperfection of originalist methodology, argued that it was still the "best means available" to constrain judicial excess.[23]

Stevens, in dissent, noted the irony that the Second Amendment was "directed at preserving the autonomy of the sovereign States and its logic therefore 'resists' incorporation by a federal court *against* the States." Further, he critiqued Scalia's purportedly "objective" and "neutral" method as one that just ignores all the questions that need to be answered in order to start a proper inquiry, including, for instance, what level of generality the analysis should be framed and what "vision of democracy" Scalia holds.[24]

Excluding Information in Order to Constrain

In order to see why Scalia thought Stevens, Breyer, and Posner are wrong-headed in their critiques it is important to understand that Scalia's legal formalism rests upon an ideology that might be summed up as "exclude in order to bind." Indeed, the chief virtue claimed of Scalia's own interpretive scheme is that it excludes so many factors from what the judge can legitimately notice when interpreting a statute or constitutional text. In contrast to his theory's virtuous exclusion, Scalia argues that the legal profession has an unfortunate idea of the "great judge" that encourages a picture of the judge as "the man (or woman) who has the intelligence to discern the best rule of law for the case at hand and then the skill to perform the broken-field running through earlier cases that leaves him free to impose the rule."[25] This ideal exacerbates what he sees as a grave danger in constitutional interpretation, which is that a judge will mistake his or her own preferences for official constitutional doctrine. Scalia thinks the ultimate problem with this ideal is in relationship to democratic governance. This is because the common-law judge's "attitude" is wrong for an "age of legislation" where "most new law is statutory law."[26] Indeed, he claims that when it comes to statutory interpretation "attacking the enterprise with the Mr. Fix-it mentality of the common-law judge is a sure recipe for incompetence and usurpation."[27] And this is because in a government of laws, not of men, "it is the *law* that governs, not the intent of the lawgiver."[28] As Scalia explains, "It is simply not compatible with democratic theory that laws mean whatever they ought to mean, and that unelected judges decide what that is."[29]

This is an admittedly formalist doctrine—and Scalia proudly accepts that description for his theory of interpretation because in his opinion, "the rule of law is *about* form."[30] Once this simple theory is accepted, Scalia thinks that some of the great tricks of the legal trade can be eliminated. Most importantly, there is legislative history. Scalia is adamant that legislative history should not be used as dispositive in statutory interpretation because legislative history is easily manipulated and therefore a likely source of false information.

Scalia thinks the same originalist interpretive doctrine is even more appropriate for constitutional issues. Scalia notes that in a standard constitutional law class the text of the actual Constitution will take a back seat to Supreme Court cases, and that "the new issue will presumptively be decided according to the logic that those cases expressed, with no regard for how far that logic, thus extended, has distanced us from the original text and understanding. Worse still, however, it is known and understood that if that logic fails to produce what in the view of the current Supreme Court is the *desirable* result for the case at hand, then like good common-law judges, the Court will distinguish its precedents, or narrow them, or if all else fails overrule them, in order that the Constitution might mean what it *ought* to mean."[31] And this is wrong because it is "not the way of construing a democratically adopted text."[32]

One of the most egregious types of such a stance, he writes, is that of "the living constitution" where it is held that the Constitution needs to be interpreted in a flexible and evolutionary manner so it can "provide the 'flexibility' that a changing society requires."[33] Ironically, Scalia sees the result of such a stance toward the Constitution as resulting in the creation of less flexibility through a promulgation of multiple Court-created

restrictions upon democratic government. For example, there is the exclusion of prayer at public school graduations.[34] Or, more importantly for
Scalia, there are various Court-created (in his view) erosions on property
rights or the fact that gun laws are limiting our right to bear arms in con-
tradistinction to the Founders' expressed wishes.[35]

Ultimately, the great virtue of original meaning textualism for Scalia
is that "the originalist at least knows what he is looking for: the original
meaning of the text."[36] Of course Scalia also acknowledges that there are
problems with originalism. But he thinks that even when meaning might
be somewhat difficult to discern, "the difficulties and uncertainties of determining original meaning and applying it to modern circumstances are
negligible compared with the difficulties and uncertainties of the philosophy which says that the Constitution *changes*; that the very act which it
once prohibited it now permits, and which it once permitted it now forbids;
and that the key to the change is unknown and unknowable. The originalist,
if he does not have all the answers, has many of them."[37]

But Scalia's textualist originalism does not exhaust his jurisprudential
philosophy. It is supplemented with a conception of "the rule of law as a
law of rules." According to him, "rightly constituted laws should be the
final sovereign; and personal rule, whether it be exercised by a single person or a body of persons, should be sovereign only in those matters on
which law is unable, owing to the difficulty of framing general rules for all
contingencies, to make an exact pronouncement."[38] As in the originalist
stance that Scalia adopts, this conception of law of rules is also justified
by its link to democratic values: "In a democratic system, of course, the
general rule of law has a special claim to preference, since it is the normal
product of that branch of government most responsive to the people."[39]

Best, according to him, is to follow the law as written. But, as Scalia
noted above, originalist meanings can often be quite difficult or impossible to determine. This is not fatal to Scalia's originalism, though, because,
"the value of perfection in judicial decisions should not be overrated,"
indeed, "it is just one of a number of competing values. One of the most
substantial of those competing values, which often contradicts the search
for perfection, is the appearance of equal treatment."[40] So, in cases where
original meaning is indeterminate or contested, the judge should work
toward an *appearance* of equal protection, because "the Equal Protection
Clause epitomizes justice more than any other provision of the Constitution. And the trouble with the discretion-conferring approach to judicial
law making is that it does not satisfy this sense of justice very well."[41]

Therefore, it is "much better, even at the expense of the mild substantive distortion that any generalization introduces, to have a clear, previously enunciated rule that one can point to in explanation of the decision."[42]

Further, rules have according to him another great virtue: predictability. Indeed, for Scalia, because having rules that have the appearance of equal protection is so central a value to the rule of law, "there are times when even a bad rule is better than no rule at all."[43] This is, once again, attached to his picture of judicial humility: "Only by announcing rules do we hedge ourselves in."[44]

But, somewhat paradoxically, "While announcing a firm rule of decision can thus inhibit courts, strangely enough it can embolden them as well. Judges are sometimes called upon to be courageous, because they must sometimes stand up to what is generally supreme in a democracy: the popular will. Their most significant roles, in our system, are to protect the individual criminal defendant against the occasional excesses of that popular will, and to preserve the checks and balances within our constitutional system that are precisely designed to inhibit swift and complete accomplishment of that popular will."[45] Indeed, for Scalia the conception of the "rule of law as the law of rules" is so central to a properly functioning legal system that "we should recognize that, at the point where an appellate judge says that the remaining issue must be decided on the basis of the totality of the circumstances, or by a balancing of all the factors involved, he begins to resemble a finder of fact more than a determiner of law" and "to reach such a stage is, in a way, a regrettable concession of defeat." He continues, "The unfortunate practical consequences" is that "equality of treatment is difficult to demonstrate and, in a multi-tiered judicial system, impossible to achieve; predictability is destroyed; judicial arbitrariness is facilitated; judicial courage is impaired."[46] But this parade of horribles is not arrived at very often, because "it is rare, however, that even the most vague and general text cannot be given some precise, principled content—and that is indeed the essence of the judicial craft."[47]

 Importantly, Scalia allows for a little post-originalist contamination in his methodology in the use of *stare* decisis, but, as he puts it, "*stare decisis* is not *part* of my originalist philosophy; it is a pragmatic *exception* to it."[48] This is because a purer use of textual originalism is too strong a medicine to swallow, and therefore he admits when it comes to originalism he is often "faint-hearted." But, to return to his textual originalism, Scalia notes that, "of course, the extent to which one can elaborate general rules from a statutory or constitutional command depends considerably upon how clear and categorical one understands the command to be, which in turn depends considerably upon one's method of textual exegesis. For example, it is perhaps easier for me than it is for some judges to develop general rules, because I am more inclined to adhere closely to the plain meaning of a text."[49]

In a nutshell, this can be thought of as the "Scalia two-step." First, use the original text and common understandings of the time in which statute or constitution was ratified to determine the meaning of the language in question. Second, if the meaning cannot be made determinate, create a clear rule of law in order to facilitate both predictability and clarity, therefore limiting the possibility of future judicial interference with democratic governance. If this rule is problematic, expect that the legislative branch will fashion a proper, democratic, remedy. His interpretive method is ultimately, therefore, justified by an appeal to its democratic virtues. This is because Scalia thinks that a democratic society does not need constitutional guarantees to insure that its laws will reflect popular values. Elections are where these get represented. The purpose of constitutional guarantees is to prevent the electorate from enacting certain changes in original values that the Constitution protects as fundamental. This, of course, is a variation on the themes of protection from the tyranny of the majority and the enforcement of foundational ground rules picture of judicial supremacy. This, Scalia thinks, determines the result in *Heller.*

Including Information in Interpretation

If, for Scalia, the whole point of an interpretive legal philosophy is to constrain the judge through a drastic limitation of the legally cognizable facts and policy choices, for Posner such a theory is descriptively inaccurate and functionally unworkable. He advocates for more information-rich judicial decision making both because he thinks it more descriptively accurate and because it would, if pursued consciously, he claims, bring about more predictable, informed, and desirable judicial decisions.[50]

Posner offers a sustained argument for the conclusion that American judges, especially federal judges, necessarily are "*constrained* pragmatists" who utilize broad types of information in order to arrive at their legal decisions. This conflicts with what he sees as the official party line of the legal profession that he labels "legalism." Posner argues that given the personal, professional, and institutional constraints that American judges face, legalism is unworkable and a type of "professional mystification" adopted in a way that exaggerates the disinterested and professional aspects of legal practice.[51] Reminiscent of Dewey's analysis in the last chapter, Posner claims that as "the judiciary's 'official' theory of judicial behavior" legalism, though false as a description of what judges actually do, determines much in the way of judicial opinion writing, legal education and appellate advocacy.

Posner gives multiple conceptions of "legalism." One instantiation of the legalist idea that Posner highlights is Scalia's originalism. Another comes from the confirmation hearings for Chief Justice John Roberts where Roberts described the judge's role, even the Supreme Court justice's, as that of "merely an umpire calling balls and strikes."[52] Legalism starts with such a picture of judicial neutrality but also includes slogans such as "a government of laws not men" and "the rule of law," which Posner derides as standard "Law Day" rhetoric. Legalists further claim that judicial decisions "are determined by 'the law' conceived of as a body of preexisting rules found stated in canonical legal materials" or, if not preexisting, then, "derivable from those materials by logical operations."[53] Such a decision-making process does not rely on any traits personal to the judge or extrinsic to the legal materials and therefore treats law as an "autonomous discipline" running on rules specific to its own internal legal logic.[54] Because of this doctrine, and "since the rules are given and have only to be applied, requiring only (besides fact-finding) reading legal materials and performing logical operations, the legalist judge is uninterested professionally in the social sciences, philosophy, or any other possible sources of guidance for making policy judgments."[55] For the legalist, the orthodox tools such as reasoning from precedent, adopting deterministic rules, including canons of construction of such rules (such as originalism), and argument from analogy are enough to decide, that is fully determine, even the most difficult case. Further, explicitly using any other facts or tools to help decide is to allow extra-legal issues to improperly intrude. At its most extreme, Posner thinks that legalism encourages a position where lawyers "are like mathematicians in wanting to manipulate symbols" and attempt to "think words not things."[56]

Posner admits that legalism does do a lot of the mundane work of the courts, but notes that as one reaches the appellate level legalist tools become less and less useful, because "there are too many vague statutes and even vaguer constitutional provisions, statutory gaps and inconsistencies, professedly discretionary domains, obsolete and conflicting precedents, and factual aporias."[57] In such cases the orthodox legalist tools are inadequate to properly "determine" an outcome. And because the cases that reach appellate levels are more often the cases that legalist tools cannot decide, and are also the cases that are most determinative of the further development of the law, legalist tools give out right where the most difficult and important cases begin. There is an "open area" of what Posner describes as "*involuntary* freedom" where judges have "decisional discretion."[58]

Returning to Roberts's claim to be merely calling balls and strikes, Posner writes, "Roberts knows that when legalist methods of judicial decision making fall short, judges draw on beliefs and intuitions that may have a political hue" and this is because "the judicial imperative is to decide cases, with reasonable dispatch, as best one can. The judge cannot throw up his hands, or stew indefinitely, just because he is confronted with a case in which the orthodox materials of judicial decision making, honestly deployed, will not produce an acceptable result."[59] For Posner this conclusion shows that judges cannot, because of their professional role and responsibilities, rest in legalist materials. Further, by following legalist ideology and focusing exclusively on orthodox legalist materials, the legal profession is left with a situation where "nothing in their training equips them to deal with the nonroutine case."[60]

Once again, the argument is that legalist tools cannot handle the toughest cases and therefore the orthodox tools are too limited to do all of the work that they are expected to do. This is not to argue that they should be ignored or rejected, just that these tools have severe limitations that, when ignored, get in the way of the development of better and more effective legal decision making right where it is most desperately needed. This limitation has been noted by other legal theorists, one being Scalia, and various tools of a legalist quality have been offered as filling in the vacuum. The most notable are those Posner describes as "comprehensive judicial philosophies," such as Scalia's "originalism." Such philosophies are meant to patch up the open areas of involuntary judicial freedom through a sort of meta-rule that constrains the judge and, once again, determines a correct decision based upon purely orthodox legal materials. Posner sees such stances as being in all actuality either rationalizations or rhetorical weapons.[61]

As rationalizations, such philosophies allow the judge greater ability to "fig-leaf" decisions that match personal preferences. Thereby actually enhancing the ability of the judge to perform broken-field running rather than constraining it as Scalia claims. This is seen, for example, in how the search for a constraining authentic and foundational "Ur text" meaning for a statute of constitutional clause actually allows for greater "manipulation of meaning in the name of historical reconstruction or intellectual

archeology."[62] As rhetorical weapons, such comprehensive theories help
bolster the legalist ideals behind the "Law Day" banner so as to help judges
avoid scrutiny for their uninformed policy choices. More directly, Posner
notes that there are various competitors for such a meta-rule, for instance,
his own "law and economics" option (which he properly notes is controversial as a normative stance), Scalia's originalism, Dworkin's "law as integrity,"
or Stephen Breyer's "active liberty,"[63] and that all of these are unable to
command the substantive agreement necessary (short of the use of coercive
force as necessary under Peirce's description of the method of authority)
for the legalist's required systemic closure.

Posner finds originalism, as a variant of the "strict construction school"
of constitutional and statutory interpretation, an especially absurd version
of legalist ideology. First, he sees it as an ideology purportedly based upon
democratic ideals but in reality based upon hostility to big government,
indeed a non-democratic hostility at that.[64] Originalism as a form of strict
construction, that is, because its cramps the manner of judicial interpretation, creates both overbroad and overnarrow results, ignores changes in
context and blinkers the judge from the realities of the legislative process
or any other helpful facts outside of its quite narrow allowed data-set,
generates often insurmountable roadblocks for government by placing
"an unbearable information load on our legislatures."[65] Such an interpretive strategy would, because of its severely constricting the information a
judge can legitimately use, seem to impose a requirement of virtual omniscience on the legislative branch requiring the anticipation of all ambiguities and future changes in society. If such omniscience is lacking (as
it clearly is) adoption of this type of interpretive strategy would require
constant legislative and constitutional amendment. But, of course, "The
legislative process is inertial, legislative capacity limited, the legislative
agenda crowded, and as a result amending legislation is difficult and time-
consuming."[66] These problems are further compounded when strict constructionist methodologies such as originalism are used to interpret the
"220-year-old Constitution" where legislative correction would have to
proceed through the elaborate process of constitutional amendment.

To make his point Posner lists a parade of absurdities that seem likely
to be required by such a method:

> A strict construction of the equal protection clause of the Fourteenth Amend-
> ment is that it forbids affirmative action (unequal benefits) but not the racial
> segregation of public schools (mere separation); of the Sixth Amendment that

it requires jury trials in courts-martial; of the First Amendment that it abolishes the tort of defamation and forbids the criminalizing of criminal solicitations, the legal protection of trade secrets, and the censorship of military secrets; of the Second Amendment that it entitles Americans to carry any weapon that one person can operate, including shoulder-launched surface-to-air missiles; of the Fifth Amendment that it permits evidence obtained by torture to be introduced in federal criminal trials provided the torture was not conducted in the courtroom itself; of the Eleventh Amendment that it permits a person to sue in the federal court of the state of which he is a citizen though no other state; and of Article I, section 8, that Congress cannot establish the Air Force as a separate branch of the armed forces or regulate military aviation at all.[67]

Cases deciding along these lines would, indeed, create a lot of extra work for a legislative branch that seems less than omniscient and quite overburdened as it is.

Because of the limits of legalism and the absurd consequences and implausibility of the adoption of any of the possible comprehensive judicial philosophies, Posner argues that American judges are necessarily pragmatists. That is, the American judge, because he or she is confronted with a demanding caseload that must be decided and a set of legalist tools that are incomplete at best and obstructionist at worst, must have recourse to purpose and consequences, to tools outside of the orthodox legalist toolkit, in order to decide cases in a reasonable and effective manner. Of course the legalist regards this as allowing extra-legal materials into the mix, materials that should be excluded, therefore diluting the purity of the law and allowing "politics" and "policy" to taint the legal process. Posner, in response, first notes that multiple descriptive theories of law (he references nine) in contemporary academia find that politics, as well as many other factors, influence legal decisions.[68] This is a scandalous finding for the legalist.

This is not a problem for the pragmatist judge, though, because Posner rejects the law versus politics dualism. Indeed, Posner embraces the fact that law, especially appellate and constitutional law, is inextricably political. But the accusation of "political" must be analyzed. As he puts it, "partisan politics is not the only politics."[69] Judges, that is, may use political ideas to help decide tough cases but not be following some local or partisan political agenda. For instance, a judge might believe that American law rests upon Lockean property rights, and therefore have a strong "political" interpretation of the Constitution that does indeed influence his or her vote, without being a devoted and party-following Republican.

Further, as Posner notes, it is highly unlikely that any judge makes a decision by thinking "what would George Bush (or Ronald Reagan, Barack Obama, etc.) want me to decide?" Indeed, it seems correct to say, as Posner does, that "virtually all judges would be distressed to be regarded as politicians in robes, because if they thought of themselves in that light they could not regard themselves as being good judges."[70] The pejorative accusation of political judging rests upon the legalist belief that the autonomous and unique tools of law are sufficient to decide the tough cases—and this is now taken as patently absurd and resting upon a mistaken picture of law and the judge's role. Indeed, the main problem with the accusation of political judging once legalism is rejected is not that political factors should be excluded, or that it is descriptively inaccurate, but that it ignores all the other supposedly non-legal factors that also are involved in determining a judges' decision.

For Posner, "'law' in a judicial setting is simply the material, in the broadest sense, out of which judges fashion their decisions."[71] This material includes legalist tools, but also must include vast materials foreign to the legalist view. For instance, there are market incentives and institutional norms. Some of these norms are professional. Judges are socialized through their law school training and their membership in the legal profession and therefore have institutionalized norms and limits attached to the role of judge that they inhabit—a judge cannot take bribes decide cases by flipping a coin, appeal to partisan political affiliation, etc.—that create powerful constrains upon what is allowable.[72] Therefore, the desire to have the reputation of being a "good judge" is a powerful limit on reasons that a judge will think acceptable to offer.[73] Many limits also come from broader social norms; indeed, Posner argues that the pragmatist judge's chosen consequences are determined by "the prevailing norms of particular societies.[74]

This suffices to overcome the legalist claim that if the limits of legalism are relaxed and consequentialist reasons are allowed into judicial decision making, "everything is permitted."[75] For Posner, therefore, American judges are not properly seen as willful legislators, they are in fact *involuntary* and occasional legislators, reluctantly legislating in the open area where and when legalist tools give out. The pragmatist judge is not engaged in an ad hoc anything goes process of willfully imposing unconstrained and possibly idiosyncratic consequentialist ideals on otherwise clear areas (where the legal equivalent of balls and strikes are defined in advance). The pragmatist judge is rather reluctantly but necessarily a pragmatist because the other options are false and result in absurd and costly decisions that ultimately force the legislative branch into a position that requires virtual omniscience to function. In contrast to this, the pragmatist judge, by looking to context, purpose, and consequences, "shares out the information burden between legislators and judges."[76]

Ultimately, for Posner the pragmatist judge is not lawless, but the conception of a legally correct decision under legal pragmatism is indeed more flexible, less determinate, and attached to the idea of a "zone of reasonableness" within which decision making is constrained.[77] This is best seen in the following passage where Posner describes what might be thought of as a pragmatist, non-correspondence theory of legal decision making; "when we say that a judge's decisions are in conformity with 'the law,' we do not mean that we can put his decision next to something called 'law' and see whether they are the same. We mean that the determinants of the decisions were things that it is lawful for judges to take into account consciously and unconsciously."[78] Therefore, American judges are "*constrained* pragmatists" because they are "boxed in . . . by norms that require of judges impartiality, awareness of the importance of the law's being predictable enough to guide behavior of those subject to it (including judges!), and a due regard for the integrity of the written word in contracts and statutes."[79] They are also boxed in by systemic functions and limits, as well as professional, institutional, and social norms.

Law as an Information-Producing Machine

Posner's argument that American judges are necessarily constrained pragmatists is founded upon the judge's need for more information than that allowed for within a legalist framework such as Scalia's. In this sense, if Scalia's system is premised upon the idea of "exclude information in order to bind," then Posner's pragmatism slogan might be thought of as "include information for the sake of effectivity and efficiency." This is a huge distinction. But what if a court system could be part of a system that aims for information production? That is, of course, what the jurisprudence of democratic experimentalism aims at doing. As seen in the last chapter, the aim is to use ideas found in Deweyan pragmatism to dramatically change the understanding of how government, and therefore the court system, ought to function.[80]

Earlier it was argued that democratic experimentalism offers a picture of law that functions as a democratic, experimental, and information-producing system. Once again, this picture of democratic governance starts with governmental activity being presumptively local. Congress, administrative agencies and the like do less rule making than they are expected to do presently and are, rather, more aimed at assisting local units with information (by expressly aiming at the function of information pooling) and resources to support experimentation. They also, along with the courts, set basic standards and ensure transparency through investigation of the decision making process utilized in political choices. This is rendered less invasive and top down because the basic standards are created by and through the process required of local government. Through strategies such as benchmarking, simultaneous engineering, and learning by monitoring, local government would be required, in return for the freedom to experiment, to create an informed record as to the content and manner of decision making.

What courts do in particular is to make sure the broad aims set out in legislative rules are followed and decision making at every level is sufficiently informed and transparent. This is done largely through evaluation of the record created during decision making of benchmarks and alternatives considered, etc. A challenger to a governmental decision offers the claim that the process disclosed or should have disclosed better options than those chosen by the governmental unit in question. An experimentalist court, in turn, defers to the judgments of local governmental unit only if the unit developed a record that makes the choices made and the reasons for the choices properly transparent. Review is deferential, but only if the record shows a certain level of diligence. The judge's reasoning, that is, turns to the reasons given and that of evaluating the sufficiency and transparency of the process rather than to the finality of a rule. In this way, judges function less as referees calling balls and strikes and more as pragmatic collaborators in an active problem-solving process. This, in turn, if practiced effectively, creates a process that encourages mutual learning. Of course basic legalist tools are used, but when their usefulness runs out, instead of the judge turning to his or her own favorite information excluding theory and then crafting a somewhat arbitrary rule, the judge learns from the record placed before the court. First, if the record is insufficient, the judge learns that that the decision making process of the governmental unit in question was not properly informed. Second, if the record is sufficient, and shows proper benchmarking, deliberation, monitoring, etc., then the judge is offered an informed and information-rich record from which to evaluate the ultimate legislative decision.

This type of review would, therefore, function at a "metalevel."[81] The virtue of this is that the process creates data so, as opposed to courts currently that have to act as if empirical questions are questions of pure legal reasoning, the court within democratic experimentalism will have real empirical information to work from. So, for example, under a statute authorizing experimentalist administration, the courts do not themselves supply authoritative meaning; the agencies and other actors jointly provide the baseline through rolling best-practice standards."[82] Judges therefore function less as a rule-making referee and more as part of an active problem-solving process.[83] The judge becomes more like a partner and less like an external rule finder. Indeed, the ideal is that the empirical evidence, the rules and the interpretive strategies are democratically created elsewhere in the process and are always open to change in the face of new data.

From Information Exclusion to Information Production

Heller as actually decided starkly shows the result of Scalia's information exclusion-based jurisprudence. First, it excludes the prefatory clause, then any broader context, then any legislative record to find intent, and then it finally rests upon the ability to identify an independently existing identifiable discrete and coherent meaning supposedly locatable in historical records. This meaning is then used to derive a decision without any recourse to social facts, changing circumstances, or social consequences in general. As he notes, this first part of the two-step is often difficult so he follows this with a strong presumption in favor of bright-line rules even if the rule chosen is not fully attached to an original meaning and therefore potentially causes substantive distortion on the theory's own terms. This is because Scalia believes rules hedge judicial discretion in and therefore keep the judge in role—that is, applying democratically produced rules in neutral fashion to specific cases. It is interesting to note in this regard the information excluding aspects of this stance not only allow the judge to not notice the actual effects of a decision (good or bad), but also explains Scalia's blinkered analysis of what he means by "democracy." As a judge, and given his conception of his role, that is none of his business. It also, of course, means that even if Stevens's claim that the historical record was ambiguous, Scalia believes he was still justified in making a bright-line rule because judges need to be hemmed in and the rule of law requires rules.

It must be admitted that this conception of the law and the judge's role within it might be seen as attractive. First, if accurate, it can explain and justify the save the people from themselves/tyranny of the majority picture of American law, and give a real, clear meaning to such slogans as "the rule of law as the law of rules" and to the often-heard critique of decisions not so justified as evidence of judicial activism. Second, given the institutional position of a judge, and the purported institutional limits of the court system, it explains how justified decisions can be made without the societal information that other branches of government can more easily make effective use of.

Unfortunately for Scalia's picture, though, the identification of original meaning is a naive pipe dream. First, in the case of the United States Constitution, the context would rather point to a document incompletely theorized, meant to be loosely understood, and full of aspirational, vague, and even some evasive terminology that would have to be filled in later with meaning. Given the nature of the document it would be fully reasonable to expect that the founder's expected future generations to fill in the general words with content that functioned best for the later times. Of course, the historical data available is radically incomplete. Finally, from a pragmatist point of view, Scalia's originalism rests upon a sort of "myth of the given" in the sense that he appears to believe that a specific univocal original meaning can often be identified outside of the specific inquiry, the specific controversy, in question.

Beyond the problems with originalism there is also the assumption that rules are better at constraining a judge and that this is better for democratic government. As Posner notes, this seems to be an empirical claim, but claims like this are almost always offered in the constitutional and legal context without any empirical support, and are therefore really unsupported legalist dogma resting upon judicial intuition. Indeed, and again from a pragmatist point of view, this fixation upon rules looks a lot like the misguided and pathological quest for certainty that Dewey so effectively critiqued. Finally, when the two-step originalism and rule picture Scalia offered got its seemingly perfect moment in *Heller*, the actual legal traction of the decision rested largely upon the exceptions to the legally determined rule. In other words, for all the purported virtues of the information excluding picture of law he offers, it seems that more information than legally proper under his own jurisprudential philosophy was necessary even in the ideal case.

Of course this is all as Posner would predict. He sees legal ideals such as Scalia's to be too trapped in legalist ideology and full of rhetorical,

"Law Day" flourishes that are better explained as professional mystification than—even in best-case scenarios such as *Heller*—descriptive accuracy. Posner offers instead a conception of the judge as constrained pragmatist forced into an open area of involuntary freedom due to the fact
that legalist materials and legalist comprehensive judicial philosophies
such as Scalia's are inherently unable to function as demanded. Instead
of the willful discretion of the common-law Mr. Fix-It judge that Scalia
fears, Posner highlights the inherent insufficiency of the materials that
Scalia claims are determinative. A judge has to "affix" a decision in the
sense that controversies must be settled and therefore if legalist materials
are insufficient then other materials, and other information, must do the
job. Further, of course, Posner highlights the absurdly naive picture of
legislative process that Scalia's jurisprudence requires. The constrained
pragmatist judge, to the contrary, is expected to use as accurate a conception of legislative ability as possible.

Posner argues that the legally necessary materials are multiple and
diverse, but that this isn't really the problem that Scalia and legalists in
general think it is once a more descriptively accurate picture of judicial
decision making is accepted. Here is where another aspect of Scalia's philosophy appears to a pragmatist to be fatal in fact. Through developing a
"non-correspondence" conception of law where multiple factors are combined in order to determine a legal decision and the decision is not imagined as being determined through the process of holding a decision up
against something called "law" in order to test the accuracy of the correspondence, Posner highlights how often much of the legalist system relies
upon an intuitive acceptance of something very close to a correspondence
theory of legal decision making with all the ensuing difficulties.

Ultimately, Posner's constrained pragmatist is constrained not only by
the need to decide a heavy caseload in a timely fashion without any guarantees of certainty, but the judge is also hemmed in by professional norms
and general social values and beliefs. Therefore, even in an "information
including" system of law only a small set of reasons and decisions will be
actually possible. These decisions fall within a "zone of reasonableness."
Posner thinks it actually a virtue that a judge has to admit that the zone
of reasonableness does not determine a specific result but only a family
of acceptable possibilities. In this case the judge cannot fully hide behind
a rhetorical appeal to "the law" and therefore must admit to personal responsibility for the actual decision. This would, he thinks, properly give
the judge a feeling of skating on thin ice and, therefore, tend to move

judges in general toward a more modest position.[84] It would also, it seems, encourage the judge to want to know more about facts and specific policy options. So, instead of beating judges over the head with legalist materials, lawyers would be moved toward emphasizing the consequentialist stakes (both short- and long-term) of possible decisions.

As to how this relates to *Heller*, certainly Breyer's dissent has more in common with Posner's constrained pragmatist judge than either the majority opinion or the Stevens dissent (which serves largely as a *reductio ad absurdum* to Scalia's claims to certainty in historical meaning, truth, knowledge, certainty, constraint, etc). Breyer emphasizes social statistics relating to gun use, the difficulty of knowing what policies are more effective in specific situations, and the need to allow for as large an area of social experimentation as possible so as to let local governments try various options in the face of serious social problems. This seems fully compatible with Posner's constrained pragmatist judge. Further, Breyer argues that there are conflicting aims in the Constitution and that, therefore, the Court's opinion is overly absolutist in its picture of just one of the enumerated rights, and maybe not even the most important of the rights—especially given the changed circumstances from the royal tyranny of revolutionary times to the crimes of the modern inner city—aspects Scalia's system cannot notice. This, of course, is an argument for looking to purpose over a more literalist reading (a strategy which is plainly true of the Court's jurisprudence in relationship to other rights such as, for example, free speech and equal protection). On the other hand, it is not so clear that Posner's judge would immediately turn to balancing tests to decide as Breyer does. All-in-all, though, Breyer's dissent would almost assuredly fit within the constrained pragmatist judge's zone of reasonableness.

Would the same be true of the majority's decision? Certainly the methodology would be seen as a sham—as it should be from a pragmatist's point of view. What about the result? In all actuality the result was not much of note. First a relatively miniscule bright-line rule is announced to the effect that a virtual ban of handguns for personal protection is unconstitutional. Beyond that, the Court offers a set of exceptions that seem completely ad hoc and founded upon nothing but previous general legislative enactment or judicial decision. Posner's constrained pragmatist would want a more developed argument at this point. But, of course, the Court's legalist tools have no argument to offer here, and so the Court goes silent right where the real need for even the most basic legal guidance begins. Therefore, the constrained pragmatist would have a difficult time seeing any virtue to the *Heller* decision, and would wonder how the Court thought that this offered any but the most minimal constraint to lower court judges based upon a sham simulacrum of historical analysis. The most predictable result seems to be more litigation in the lower courts with less guidance as to what short of an absolute ban is allowed.

But the constrained pragmatist judge would be constrained in another way less than ideal—that is, constrained in the type of information offered the court even if the attorneys on either side decided to use facts instead of more legalist arguments in their cases. This is because, just as the originalist judge ends up with a result prepackaged on both sides, and therefore a type of "history in law," the constrained pragmatist would get a type of "nothing but the facts of the case" in that each side would be willing to only offer those options that clearly favored their side. The virtue of democratic experimentalism is that it would, if effective, solve this problem and actually enlist the court system in the production of a more thorough set of information in regards to the policies and rights at issue.

In the case of *Heller*, it is difficult to know from the Court's opinion what options were considered. Under the governance scheme offered in democratic experimentalism an empirically informed record of options considered and why specific policies were chosen would be most likely the largest part of the Court's data. Upon a challenging of the law, the lower court would often use normal legalist tools to decide an easy case. But given a more uncertain, difficult, or strongly contested case, the record developed by the local government through the use of benchmarking, data collection, and policy options generated, as well as results from the locality and others dealing with the same issues, would be available in order to ensure that principle and practice were sufficiently linked.

The role of the judge here is not to solve controversial problems through the somewhat arbitrary settling via a clear rule, or identification of some original meaning, but rather to encourage democratically transparent and accountable constitutional analysis and problem solving where the rules of law come from democratic processes and not a judicial oligarchy. This offers a democratic and experiment-encouraging rule of law that discounts judicial rules in favor of greater information production and policy testing. There isn't the certainty purportedly offered by Scalia's jurisprudential theory, but this is a virtue given the dogmatic hubris so apparent in Scalia's purported modesty. Of course one might see exclusion of information (judicial ignorance?) to be a doubtful virtue to begin with. As to how a judge under the democratic experimentalist methodology would decide *Heller*, we have only hints. But Posner has recently given us a start at what it might look like.

Posner's *Moore v. Madigan* and the Information-Producing Judicial Opinion

As Posner's fact-based adjudication started this chapter, it will end it as well. This time, though, instead of same-sex marriage the case was gun rights and the issues were almost identical to those in *Heller*. But, as will be seen, the methodology is quite different. Posner's *Moore v. Madigan* exemplifies many of the factors central to democratic experimentalist jurisprudence, such as placing a heavy emphasis upon empirical evidence, treating judicial decision making as centered upon systemic collaboration, and a preference for informed democratic processes over legalistic boundary setting.

Moore v. Madigan was argued in front of the Seventh Circuit June 8, 2012, and decided December 11 of the same year. Posner wrote the court's twenty-one-page opinion. Williams wrote a twenty-five-page dissent. Posner began his opinion with a description of the challenged law. The Illinois law in question forbade a person, with narrow exceptions, to carry a gun ready to use other than in his or her home, his or her fixed place of business or on another's property with permission of the property owner. Appellants claimed that this restriction was unconstitutionally narrow under *Heller* as applied to the states via *McDonald*. As seen above, *Heller* held that the Second Amendment protected a core right to self-defense in the home. The question before the court in *Moore v. Madigan* was whether the interpretation of the Second Amendment offered in those two Supreme Court cases also required a right to carry a gun for self-defense outside of the home.

To answer this question Posner started his opinion with a description of the record before the court as "hundreds of pages of argument" largely focusing on the historical understanding of the constitutional clause at the time of its enactment and before.[85] He noted that the historical analysis offered in the voluminous record goes back to fourteenth-century statutes, cases in the 1600s and a reading of Blackstone. He then wrote of the various conclusions as to this historical analysis: "All this is debatable of course, but we are bound by the Supreme Court's historical analysis because it was central to the Court's holding in *Heller*."[86] Posner, therefore, quickly deflected this issue by refusing to revisit the history as constructed by the Supreme Court majority and used to decide the issue in *Heller*.

Instead he rested his first move on an expressly functionalist premise. He argued that if the Second Amendment protects a right to self-defense, then "one doesn't have to be a historian to realize that a right to keep and bear arms for personal self-defense in the eighteenth century could not rationally have been limited to the home."[87] Further, he argued that there is a significant historical continuity in that, as in earlier times, people are more likely in the present day to be attacked outside of the home than in it. Therefore, functionally a self-defense justification for the right to bear arms must encompass more than just the home. That is, if self-defense is the point of the Second Amendment, then the project must be taken as more than that of just protecting the castle (one of the purported historical understandings found in Blackstone). Posner rejected this by arguing that this narrow view would conflate a self-defense right with a defense of property rights. His argument here is colorful enough to quote in full: "To confine the right to be armed to the home is to divorce the Second Amendment from the right of self-defense described in *Heller* and *McDonald*. It is not a property right—a right to kill a houseguest who in a fit of aesthetic fury tries to slash your copy of Norman Rockwell's painting *Santa with Elves*. That is not self-defense, and this case, like *Heller* and *McDonald* is just about self-defense."[88]

At this point, from pages eight to fifteen, the opinion changed from a functional analysis of the meaning of self-defense to a wide-ranging investigation of empirical literature on the effect of public bearing of guns. He cited a substantial set of studies investigating the evidence available for the claim that guns are effective for self-defense as well those investigating the effects of gun legislation. Ultimately, though, he found that the empirical evidence is ambiguous and when read carefully "fails to establish a pragmatic defense of the Illinois law."[89] He noted further that more is required than merely the judicial finding that the law is "not irrational." Such a "blanket prohibition" in the core of the Second Amendment rather requires more justification than a ban on guns in specific places such as public schools because in this case, "a person can preserve an undiminished right of self-defense by not entering those places; since that's a lesser burden, the state doesn't need to prove so strong a need."[90] Therefore the court can expect to see at least some positive empirical evidence in favor of the legislature's chosen law.

Having surveyed the data and distinguished the standard of review, Posner turned to the matter of options. As he put it, "Illinois has lots of options for protecting its people from being shot without having to eliminate all possibility of armed self-defense in public."[91] In this section of the opinion, therefore, benchmarking anchors the analysis. He continued, "Remarkably, Illinois is the *only* state that maintains a flat ban on carrying ready-to-use guns outside the home."[92] Part of the benchmarking he offered entails a survey of the laws of other states that enables him, in turn, to describe the Illinois law the most restrictive among all of the states. He concluded, "If the Illinois approach were demonstrably superior, one would expect at least one or two other states to have emulated it."[93] But because of the benchmarking process the opinion doesn't just end on a negative holding but includes a discussion of alternatives. Alternative possibilities offered as tentatively acceptable include competency tests, training, bans from specific premises such as churches, and demonstration of "proper cause" in order to be allowed to get a license.[94]

So, the *Moore v. Madigan* opinion requires evidence for the specific regulatory regime chosen, and expects the evidence to be more than just an argument that the connection between the aim and the means is not irrational. But ultimately he explained that "our analysis is not based on degrees of scrutiny, but on Illinois's failure to justify the most restrictive gun law of any of the 50 states."[95] That is, the analysis rests largely upon the combination of lack of empirical justification with other less restrictive means available learned of through an investigation of other state strategies in the same legal realm. Indeed, he continued, "the key legislative facts in this case are the effects of the Illinois law; the state has failed to show that those effects are positive."[96] Therefore the court found the law unconstitutional and reversed and remanded. Yet here Posner avoided setting down a bright-line rule but rather handed that task off to the state legislature—"we order our mandate stayed for 180 days to allow the Illinois legislature to craft a new gun law that will impose reasonable limitations, consistent with the public safety and the Second Amendment, as interpreted in this opinion, on the carrying of guns in public."[97]

Posner's opinion shows many of the most important aspects of an information-producing court design as demanded by democratic experimentalism. The opinion treats the project of gun regulation as a collaborative project and then analyzes the aim functionally. Further, he supplements the traditional venue-surveying benchmarking already practiced within the federalism of the United States system with a careful investigation of the scientific and academic evidence on the effectiveness of guns and gun-control legislation for the aim of self-defense. Finally, he refuses to lay down a bright-line prohibition but rather prods the legislature to find and offer empirical justification for a more effective and less restrictive strategy for the implementation of its aims. Instead of creating a determinant rule himself, he, if successful, forces the legislature to make transparent the information and reasoning behind the choice of regulation it ultimately makes.

Admittedly, reactions to the case have been mixed. For instance, after the decision the Defendants petitioned the Seventh Circuit for an en banc rehearing. Williams, in dissent, argued that the court should have been more deferential to legislative judgments. On the other hand, Posner's benchmarking analysis outlines the multiple other options available and was supported by an extensive investigation into the information available on the matter. It is important here to emphasize that in an experimentalist court individual intuitions—the traditionally dominant (and determinant) tool of legal analysis—are discounted in favor of empirical investigation and decisions based upon a factual record. In this sense, the whole point of an information-producing court is to discipline intuitions through empirical fact, rather than be controlled by them. Of course this is in harmony with Pierce's claim that intuitions, even if offered under the terminology of "reason" are really just matters of a priori taste if not disciplined by experimental methodology.

In any case, *Moore v. Madigan's* requirement of a higher standard of empirical evidence is information-forcing and, ideally, information-producing rather than information eliminating if the legislature follows its requirements. Further, the case is also more democratic than the standard case that hands down a bright-line judicially created rule in order to police boundaries. By remanding to the legislature with a requirement of supporting evidence, Posner avoided the legalist tendency exemplified in Scalia's jurisprudence to see the courts as final rule givers trumping other sources of law while also forcing the more democratic branches to offer up tangible evidence for their ultimate decisions. Of course, as in this case, the empirical evidence might be ambiguous as well. But here the ambiguity can, at times, at least discipline judicial intuitions by keeping the judge from deciding the absolute limits of an area too soon. And, if the system works as imagined, the iterative process will produce an expanding pool of information with which to inform further decision making. It is worthy of note that by remanding the choice from remaining options back to the Illinois legislature rather than creating any bright-line statement of law, Posner showed a different type of judicial deference by declining to determine one option just for the sake of having a determinant judicially created (or in Scalia's case purportedly "found") outcome.

From this chapter's analysis it seems that the jurisprudential theories that included or actually aimed at producing information could create more justifiable and desirable outcomes. They are also more democratic. Furthermore, as Posner's opinion shows, they may even be more constrained than those offered by proponents of theories expressly aimed at constraining judges. How can this be? This second version of judicial constraint can be summed up in a slogan such as "discipline by facts rather than dogma and intuition." Therefore, in just demanding constitutional law to be information-rich, democratic experimentalism not only offers a more disciplined interpretive strategy, but also one that is much more democratic in form and function.

CHAPTER FOUR

Epstein, Holmes, and Regulatory Takings Jurisprudence

The information-rich jurisprudence of democratic experimentalism and Richard Posner has an important precedent in the legal thought of Oliver Wendell Holmes, Jr. And this means that American jurisprudence has within its tradition a powerful strand of support for a more empirical, experimental, and democratic conception of constitutional law. With Justice Brandeis, Holmes helped forge a strong and broad tradition of free-speech protection that is taken for granted by all Americans. His dissent in *Lochner* (to be analyzed later) is often pointed to as a central constitutional moment, possibly the greatest dissent of all time.[1] Finally, there is at least one area of contemporary constitutional jurisprudence where a Holmes-written opinion is central and yet it is legitimate question as to whether this fact is something to celebrate or to condemn. The area is that of "regulatory takings." The case is *Pennsylvania Coal Co. v. Mahon*. The Court in *Mahon* found that a land use regulation went "too far" and therefore constituted a taking of property that required "just compensation." Holmes and an almost unanimous Court—save for a lone dissent penned by Brandeis—found a state land-use regulation passed under the aegis of Pennsylvania's police powers as going so far that it, in effect, created a "regulatory taking," analogous enough to the traditional takings criteria of expulsion or occupation to require compensation.

Holmes's holding in the case has been used ever since by the Court to explain why takings can be found beyond traditional exclusion or seizure of property by the government. Holmes's reasoning has also been strongly criticized by Richard Epstein, a leader in contemporary conservative foundationalist constitutional theory and the "takings revival" in

Supreme Court jurisprudence.[2] The contrast between Holmes's and Epstein's reasoning starkly highlights the difference between a formal deductivist "links in a chain" understanding of jurisprudence and one that finds this methodology too limited, distorting, and rather emphasizing empirical analysis and, most central to this chapter, the braiding of reasons à la Peirce, Dewey, and the jurisprudence of democratic experimentalism.

In addition to the theoretic import, the contrast in reasoning method is also important because *Mahon* "has become a virtual surrogate for the original understanding of the Takings Clause,"[3] and is considered "both the most important and most mysterious writing in takings law."[4] In relation to this, Mark Tushnet observes that "the modern Supreme Court has decided more cases involving takings and land use regulations than any other category of economic regulation."[5]

So, Holmes's opinion is a central one in American constitutional law and grounds the Court's most active area of economic decision making. And yet, surprisingly, it is also considered poorly or incompletely reasoned by some of the legal theorists and justices most influenced by it such as Epstein and Scalia. Furthermore, as Frederic R. Kellogg notes, *Mahon* shows that despite standard contemporary readings, Holmes was not against all use of the Fourteenth Amendment to overrule state legislation.[6] Therefore it is an important decision to face in order to understand Holmes's own jurisprudence. Somewhat ironically, then, Holmes is notable for writing the most famous dissent in Supreme Court history, a dissent noted for its strong advocacy of judicial deference to legislation and rejection of the Supreme Court's striking down of democratically passed economic regulation in *Lochner*, as well as *Mahon*, the foundational case in the contemporary area most active in striking down regulations and legislation affecting economic issues.

But, once again, for all the citation of *Mahon* as the founding legal precedent for the Court's great takings revival the academy's great prophet of the movement, and the broader contemporary movement in "conservative foundationalist constitutional theory," Richard Epstein thinks that the in- fluence of Holmes and the reasoning in *Mahon* has ultimately led the law of regulatory takings "into intellectual incoherence" because "Holmes's 'too far' question turns a bright-line question into a matter of degree for no good reason."[7]

This chapter will first outline *Mahon* and some of the most important regulatory takings cases following from it. Then it will turn to Epstein's critique and, after outlining it, compare the demands of his theory with that of Holmes's. The ultimate conclusion will be that Epstein's theory is, indeed, a conceptually coherent system, but one that must dogmatically ignore any disagreement with a significant number of controversial assumptions it rests upon to be accepted. Indeed, Epstein offers a striking example of legal analysis utilizing the methods of tenacity, authority, and a priori reasoning as outlined by Peirce. Furthermore, from the pragmatic perspective Epstein's reasoning, rather than principled, is better seen as a "flight from the complexity of the world."[8]

In contrast, for all the difficulties it presents, Holmes's reasoning in *Mahon* properly resists reduction to such simplistic formulas and exemplifies a democratically inclined and multi-fibred method of analysis that allows room for experimentalist methodology. Therefore, Holmes's opinion and his jurisprudence offer an influential precedent that points toward the possibility of a jurisprudence of democratic experimentalism and law as a democratic means. The aim will be to show that Holmes's fact-based and democratically minded jurisprudence offers a coherent and more judicially constrained method of constitutional decision making than Epstein's dogmatic, aggressively formalist and democratically dismissive stance.

Mahon

The facts in *Mahon* were not in dispute.[9] After being given notice of Pennsylvania Coal's plans to mine coal under his residence in a manner that could cause surface subsidence, Mahon sued to prevent the company from acting on this intent. The deed executed in 1878, and that still governed the property, conveyed surface rights to the homeowner but expressly reserved to Pennsylvania Coal the right to mine all coal underneath. The deed also included an express waiver to all damages to the surface caused by mining the coal. This meant under Pennsylvania law that the company had contractually reserved an explicit ownership of a separate support estate.

Mahon argued that passage of Pennsylvania's Kohler Act in 1921, which forbid, among other things, the mining of coal in a manner that causes subsidence of land where there is a structure used for human habitation, unless the property is owned by the company doing the mining, had eliminated Pennsylvania Coal's right to mine. The Pennsylvania Court of Common Pleas found the statute unconstitutional. The Supreme Court of the State held the statute a legitimate exercise of the state's police power. Pennsylvania Coal appealed to the United States Supreme Court. Holmes wrote the majority opinion wherein the Court found the Kohler Act's regulation to be an unconstitutional taking of property without just compensation. Brandeis filed a lone dissent.

Holmes began the opinion with a description of the effect of the Act: "As applied to this case, the statute is admitted to destroy previously existing rights of property and contract. The question is whether the police power can be stretched so far."[10] He then summed up the interpretive framework that would be applied:

> Government hardly could go on if, to some extent, values incident to property could not be diminished without paying for every such change in the general law. As long recognized, some values are enjoyed under an implied limitation, and must yield to the police power. But obviously the implied limitation must have its limits, or the contract and due process clauses are gone. One fact for consideration in determining such limits is the extent of the diminution. When it reaches a certain magnitude, in most if not in all cases, there must be an exercise of imminent domain and compensation to sustain the act. So the question depends upon the particular facts. The greatest weight is given to the judgment of the legislature, but it is always open to interested parties to contend that the legislature has gone beyond its constitutional power.[11]

Holmes found that in this case the public interest was limited because it was litigation over the matter of a single private residence. He saw this as removing the case from the realm of public nuisance. Further, Holmes reasoned that because the act did not apply to land where the surface was owned by the company, this showed to him that the statute's aim was to help or constrain specific property owners, and not to serve a general public interest. The issue of safety could be handled, he reasoned, through notice (as it had been handled). On the other hand, he noted that "the extent of the taking is great" because it not only completely took what was under Pennsylvania law a full estate in land, it also abolished an explicit contractual agreement. Therefore, as applied to Mahon, the Court found that "we should think it clear that the statute does not disclose a public interest sufficient to warrant so extensive a destruction of the defendant's constitutionally protected rights."[12]

Holmes then proceeded to discuss the general validity of the Act. Other parts of the Act disallowed mining that causes subsidence under public lands including streets and utilities. The Court found, though, that the legal result was the same: "It is our opinion that the act cannot be sustained as an exercise of the police power, so far as it affects the mining of coal under streets or cities in places where the right to mine such coal has been reserved," because "to make it commercially impracticable to mine certain coal has very nearly the same effect for constitutional purposes as appropriating it or destroying it."[13] Holmes then distinguished this from other cases, including a case where a court upheld as valid under police power a legislative requirement to leave a pillar of coal along the edge of adjoining property, with a similar requirement for the company on the other side of the property line. This requirement he found justified be-cause it was for the safety of the mine's employees and also because it secured "an average reciprocity of advantage" between the parties regu-lated. He continued:

> The rights of the public in a street purchased or laid out by eminent domain are those that it has paid for. If in any case its representatives have been so short sighted as to acquire only surface rights without the right of support, we see no more authority for supplying the latter without compensation than there was for taking the right of way in the first place and refusing to pay for it because the public wanted it very much. The protection of private property in the Fifth Amendment presupposes that it is wanted for public use, but provides that it shall not be taken for such use without compensation. A similar assumption is made in the decisions upon the Fourteenth Amendment.[14]

Holmes went on to claim that when the "seemingly absolute protection" is noticed in practice to be qualified by the state's police power, "the natural tendency of human nature is to extend the qualification more and more, until at last private property disappears."[15] According to Holmes the Con-stitution does not allow this.

From this analysis he derived an underlying rule: "The general rule, at least, is that, while property may be regulated to a certain extent, if regula-tion goes too far, it will be recognized as a taking."[16] What is, for Holmes, questionable is the citizen's use of a statute in the face of "misfortunes" or "necessities" to shift the costs "to his neighbor's shoulders." What is un-questionable, on the other hand, is that "a strong public desire to improve the public condition is not enough to warrant achieving the desire by a shorter cut that the constitutional way of paying for the change."[17] Holmes noted that this is still a matter of degree, and therefore analysis requires, in order to arrive at a proper decision, not a general proposition but rather a fact-specific inquiry. He then concluded: "But the question at bottom is upon whom the loss of the changes desired should fall. So far as private persons or communities have seen fit to take the risk of acquiring only surface right, we cannot see that the fact that their risk has become a danger warrants the giving to them greater rights than they bought."[18]

The *Mahon* majority opinion is terse, commanding and Delphic in quality, as is somewhat to be expected from Holmes. Though lengthier and more detailed, Brandeis's dissent is easier to summarize. He started by describing the property at issue in a different manner. "Coal in place is land, and the right of the owner to use his land is not absolute. He may not so use it as to create a public nuisance, and uses, once harmless, may, owing to changed conditions, seriously threaten the public welfare. Whenever they do, the legislature has power to prohibit such uses without paying compensation, and the power to prohibit extends alike to the manner, the character, and the purpose of the use."[19] This is because a "restriction imposed to protect the public health, safety or morals from dangers is not a taking" and, according to Brandeis, the Kohler act merely prohibits a noxious use.[20] Therefore, the end of the statute is a proper public interest under the police power. Further, the means utilized is constitutionally acceptable as well because to keep the pillars of coal in place is appropriate to prevent subsidence. To support this, he cited multiple other cases that have held that regulatory restrictions under the police power do not necessarily become unconstitutional even if they deprive the owner of the only profitable use of the property.

Brandeis then returned to the issue of the property taken, this time in relationship to Holmes's reference to "diminution of value." This, he pointed out, depends how the property being evaluated is framed. If instead of considering the coal that the act requires to be left in place, the pillar, what is compared is the total value left in all of the land owned by the coal company, "the value of the coal kept in place may be negligible."[21] He also questioned whether the Court really did show proper deference to the Pennsylvania legislature or state courts in terms of the safety issues by raising doubts as to whether the Court had enough information to properly overturn the decision of institutions that have greater local knowledge. He then repeated his claim that the accepted law is that if public safety is truly in danger then the property or contract rights cannot win against the state's police power regulation.

Therefore, Brandeis concluded, the legal question is whether public safety is, indeed, in danger. He turned to an analysis of the Kohler Act and argued that though it covers private houses it also covered public structures, public passageways such as streets, roads, and bridges, as well as railway

tracks, rights of way, pipes, conduits and wires, all of which were threat-
ened by the mining regulated under the act. He also concluded that there
were clear public interests in these related to safety and health that cannot, as the majority opinion mistakenly claimed, be remedied sufficiently
through notice. Brandeis ultimately offered that the real principle underlying Holmes's decision must be that of not finding an "average reciprocity of
advantage" between the various parties. He agreed with Holmes that this
test might be useful in the case of legislation aimed at giving benefits to adjoining owners or a neighborhood, such as abutting mining areas, but saw
the Kohler Act as aiming at a more general harm. Therefore, for Brandeis,
"where the police power is exercised not to confer benefits upon property
owners but to protect the public from detriment and danger, there is, in my
opinion, no room for considering reciprocity of advantage" unless "it be
the advantage of living and doing business in a civilized community. That
advantage is given by the act to the coal operators."[22]

Later Supreme Court Regulatory Takings Jurisprudence

Mahon was more or less absent from Supreme Court jurisprudence for
over fifty years. But, in the late 1970s this changed when it was rediscov-
ered as the centerpiece of a "takings revival." For instance, *Penn Central*,
a case that is perhaps only second in importance to *Mahon* in regulatory
takings, repeatedly cited Holmes's *Mahon* opinion as its legal grounding.[23]

Penn Central involved a challenge to an attempt to use regulations to
preserve a historic New York building. A landmarks preservation act was
passed with the expressed aims of fostering civic pride in the beauty and
accomplishments of the city's past, enhancing tourist appeal, stimulating
business, and generally protecting the educative, pleasure, and welfare
benefits the landmarks provide. Though preservation was the central aim,
the law expressly focused on ways to ensure the owners a "reasonable return" on their investments and maximum flexibility to use their property
for purposes consistent with the preservation goals.

Final designation as landmark resulted in specific restrictions. There was
a duty placed upon the owner to keep the exterior of the building in good
repair and, second, a commission had to approve in advance any proposal
to alter the exterior features. If the owner wanted to alter a landmark desig-
nated under the act, three procedures were available. The owner could apply to the Commission for "certificate of no effect," a "certificate of 'appropriateness,'" or seek acceptance of the project on grounds of "insufficient

return" in order to avoid undue economic hardship. If any of these applications were denied the owner could have recourse to judicial review. Designation also had a positive aspect in that it provided "transfer development rights" whereby development rights the owner would have had but for the landmark designation could be used on nearby property.

Penn Central, owners of New York's Grand Central Terminal, an eight-story structure that was, "one of New York City's most famous buildings," and a "magnificent example of the French beaux-arts style," asked the Commission under the "no effect" and "appropriateness" certificates to allow a fifty-three- to fifty-five-story office building to be built above the terminal. Two plans designed by Marcel Breuer were denied certification. Breuer II was rejected because it directly tore down parts of the terminal's facade. Breuer I was rejected on non-structural reasons. Penn Central filed suit claiming property had been taken without just compensation.

The Court, through an opinion by Justice Brennan, started by explaining that the Fifth Amendment is at bottom "designed to bar Government from forcing some people alone to bear public burdens which, in all fairness and justice, should be borne by the public as a whole." The opinion continued on to explain that the Court had been unable to develop any set formula for determining when "justice and fairness" would require that injuries caused by public regulations be compensated by the government because determination depends on particular circumstances and an ad hoc factual analysis. Brennan then identified several factors as particularly significant: "The economic impact of the regulation on the claimant and, particularly, the extent to which the regulation has interfered with distinct investment-backed expectations are, of course relevant considerations. So, too, is the character of the governmental action."[24] This statement has become the *Penn Central* test. As explained, a "taking" may more readily be found when the interference with property can be characterized as a physical invasion by government, than when interference arises from some public program adjusting the benefits and burdens of economic life to promote the common good."[25] The Court continued, "More importantly for the present case, in instances in which a state tribunal reasonably concluded that 'the health, safety, morals, or general welfare' would be promoted by prohibiting particular contemplated uses of land, the Court has upheld land use regulations that destroyed or adversely affected recognized real property interests."[26]

To Penn Central's argument that the airspace above terminal is a discrete property interest that had been fully deprived them, the Court responded that " 'taking' jurisprudence does not divide a single parcel into discrete segments and attempt to determine whether rights in a particular segment have been entirely abrogated. In deciding whether a particular governmental action has effected a taking, this Court focuses rather both on the character of the action and on the nature and extent of the interference with rights in the parcel as a whole."[27] Penn Central also argued that because the regulation singled out specific property it represented discriminatory "reverse spot" zoning. The Court disagreed and rather emphasized that the plan was "comprehensive" and included four hundred landmarks and thirty-one districts. The Court then noted that the regulation in question left current use undiminished and allowed a "reasonable return" on property. Further, air rights were made transferrable so there was some mitigation of the regulation's impact. Given this, the Court concluded that New York City's Landmark Law had not brought about a taking of Penn Central's property.

Rehnquist wrote a dissent in *Penn Central* that started by arguing that "the question in this case is whether the cost associated with the city of New York's desire to preserve a limited number of 'landmarks' within its borders must be borne by all of its taxpayers, or whether it can, instead, be imposed entirely on the owners of the individual properties."[28] He then distinguished the Landmark Act from an acceptable zoning law: "Typical zoning restrictions may, it is true, so limit the prospective uses of a piece of property as to diminish the value of that property in the abstract because it may not be used for forbidden purposes. But any such abstract decrease in value will more than likely be at least partially offset by an increase in value which flows from similar restrictions as to use on neighboring properties."[29]

Rehnquist went on, "In the words of Mr. Justice Holmes, speaking for the Court in *Pennsylvania Coal Co. v. Mahon*, there is 'an average reciprocity of advantage.' Where a relatively few individual buildings, all separated from one another, are singled out and treated differently from surrounding buildings, no such reciprocity exists."[30] Here, he observed, the cost to each owner may be significant, without necessarily bringing reciprocal benefits, forcing some to bear public burdens which should "in all fairness and justice" be borne by all. Rehnquist continued; "As Mr. Justice Holmes pointed out in *Pennsylvania Coal Co. v. Mahon*, 'the question at bottom' in an eminent domain case 'is upon whom the loss of the changes desired should fall.' "[31] Here he found the benefits widely distributed but the burdens all too property specific. Finally, Rehnquist turned once again to *Mahon* with the following concluding section of his dissent:

Over 50 years ago, Mr. Justice Holmes, speaking for the Court, warned that the courts were "in danger of forgetting that a strong public desire to improve the public condition is not enough to warrant achieving the desire by a shorter cut than the constitutional way of paying for the change." The Court's opinion in this case demonstrates that the danger thus foreseen has not abated. The city of New York is in a precarious financial state, and some may believe that the costs of landmark preservation will be more easily borne by corporations such as Penn Central than the overburdened individual taxpayers of New York. But these concerns do not allow us to ignore past precedents construing the Eminent Domain Clause to the end that the desire to improve the public condition is, indeed, achieved by a shorter cut than the constitutional way of paying for the change.[32]

Two years after *Penn Central*, Rehnquist wrote the majority opinion in a case that implicated both the Takings Clause and the First Amendment, *Pruneyard Shopping Center v. Robins.*[33] Pruneyard was a privately owned shopping center open to the public. High school students sought to solicit support for their opposition to a United Nations resolution against Zionism. They set up a card table in a corner of Pruneyard's central courtyard to distribute pamphlets and ask shoppers to sign petitions. A security guard informed them that they would have to leave because the activity violated Pruneyard regulations. They left and filed a lawsuit to enjoin appellants from denying them access for the purpose of circulating their petitions. The question addressed by the Supreme Court was whether state constitutional provisions protecting free speech and petition rights on the private property of a shopping center open to the public violate the shopping center owner's rights under the First, Fifth, and Fourteenth Amendments.

The Court started its analysis by noting that "one of the essential sticks in the bundle of property rights is the right to exclude others" but also that not every destruction or injury to property by governmental action is a taking.[34] To determine whether a taking occurred "requires an examination of whether the restriction on private property forces some people alone to bear public burdens which, in all fairness and justice, should be borne by the public as a whole." And this entails a set of factors (the *Penn Central* test) such as, the character of the governmental action and the economic impact, as well as how much interference with reasonable investment-backed expectations there is. Quoting the *Mahon* principle that when "regulation goes too far, it will be recognized as a taking," Rehnquist found that the student activities would not unreasonably impair the value or use of Pruneyard's property and that Pruneyard had failed to demonstrate that the right to exclude others was so essential to the use or economic value of their property that the state's constitutional limitation of it amounted to a taking.

Marshall concurred and cited *Munn* as precedent for a broad right of the state to define property.[35] He claimed that rights of property created by the common law cannot be taken away without due process, but the law may be changed at the will of the legislature because the purpose of statutes is to remedy defects in the common law and to adapt to changing circumstances. He warned that any decision holding otherwise "would represent a return to the era of *Lochner*."[36]

Seven years later, in *Keystone,* a divided Court analyzed a 1966 Pennsylvania statute with great similarities to the Kohler Act. The Court's majority opinion, delivered by Stevens, started with the following:

> In *Pennsylvania Coal Co., v. Mahon,* 260 U.S. 393 (1922), the Court reviewed the constitutionality of a Pennsylvania statute that admittedly destroyed "previously existing rights of property and contract." Writing for the Court, Justice Holmes explained: "Government hardly could go on if, to some extent, values incident to property could not be diminished without paying for every such change in the general law. As long recognized, some values are enjoyed under an implied limitation and must yield to the police power. But obviously the implied limitation must have its limits, or the contract and due process clauses are gone. One fact for consideration in determining such limits is the extent of the diminution. When it reaches a certain magnitude, in most if not in all cases there must be an exercise of eminent domain, and compensation to sustain the act. So the question depends upon the particular facts." In that case, the "particular facts" led the Court to hold that the Pennsylvania Legislature had gone beyond its constitutional powers when it enacted a statute prohibiting the mining of anthracite coal in a manner that would cause the subsidence of land on which certain structures were located. Now, 65 years later, we address a different set of "particular facts," involving the Pennsylvania Legislature's 1966 conclusion that the Commonwealth's existing mine subsidence legislation had failed to protect the public interest in safety, land conservation, preservation of affected municipalities' tax bases, and land development in the Commonwealth.[37]

Invoking the later legislature's detailed findings of fact, the Court's opinion held that the situation was different enough to conclude that *Mahon* did not control and therefore the 1966 Act was not unconstitutional on its face.

Briefly put, the 1966 Subsidence Act authorized a state agency to im-
plement and enforce a "comprehensive program to prevent or minimize
subsidence and to regulate its consequences." The act covered mining that
causes subsidence damage to public buildings, noncommercial buildings
generally used by the public, dwellings used for human habitation and
cemeteries. The agency's formula for necessary support required in the
range of 50 percent of the coal beneath structures protected to be left
intact. In 1982, petitioners, an association of mine operators, filed action
alleging a taking. They alleged that the Act deprived them of the "support
estate," an estate recognized by Pennsylvania law as a valuable "strand"
in the bundle of rights defining ownership of property. The petitioners argued that the case was decided by a straightforward application of *Mahon*.

The majority opinion found that the similarities were less significant
than the differences. First, the Court noted that in *Mahon* the case was that
of a conflict between the owners of a single private house balanced against
a large loss to the coal company. Second, Stevens read the more general
part of *Mahon* as an "advisory opinion," and one that was uncharacter-
istic of Holmes's normally case-specific jurisprudence. This part of the
opinion, he found, forwarded "two propositions." First, that because the
Kohler act served only private interests it was not a proper exercise of
the state's police power. Second, the statute's effect was to make it "commercially impracticable" to mine "certain coal."[38]

Two factors, Stevens explained, have become "integral parts" of the
Court's taking analysis. First, that land use regulation can be a taking if it
does not "substantially advance" legitimate state interests. And, second, if
it denies an owner economically valuable use of his land. The Court then
found that the 1966 act was aimed at a "significant threat to the common
welfare" of a level "akin to a public nuisance" and cited Harlan's opinion
in *Mugler* where he wrote that a "prohibition simply upon the use of property for purposes that are declared, by valid legislation, to be injurious to
the health, morals, or safety of the community, cannot, in any just sense,
be deemed a taking or appropriation of property."[39] The Court then noted
that Holmes later joined the unanimous decision in *Miller v. Schoene* that
did not find a taking in the case of a total destruction of property.[40] This,
the Court explained, shows that a comparison of values before and after a
regulation is relevant but not conclusive. In fact, restraining uses of property that are "tantamount to public nuisances" satisfies the "reciprocity of
advantage" reasoning shown in *Pennsylvania Coal*.[41]

As to the second commercial value factor, the Court found that the petitioners had not shown that the Act made it impossible for them to earn a

profit or had interfered with their investment-backed expectations. First, in the situation of a facial challenge, the test is simply whether or not the regulation denied the owner "economically viable use of his land." In this case that had not been shown. According to the Court's analysis the Act would require less than 2 percent of the total amount of coal in the mines to stay in place and some of this 2 percent might have been necessary to leave in place regardless of the law. Petitioners argued that it was the specific 2 percent that was taken, or, alternatively, the whole "support estate" that had been appropriated. Here, the Court cited *Penn Central* statement that the proper focus was on the parcel as a whole and destruction of one "strand" of the full "bundle" of property rights is not necessarily a taking, "because the aggregate must be viewed in its entirety."[42] Furthermore, the Court explained in the case of the separate support estate that "our takings jurisprudence forecloses reliance on such legalistic distinctions within a bundle of property rights" and rather uses a functional test which showed that "the support estate has value only insofar as it protects or enhances the value of the estate with which it is associated. Its value is merely a part of the entire bundle of rights."[43]

Rehnquist's dissent reached a sharply different conclusion. In it, *Mahon* is both described as central to regulatory takings jurisprudence and as under attack by the majority. As he put it, the case is "the foundation" of the Court's regulatory takings jurisprudence, a foundation that the majority opinion "attempts to undermine" by treating most of it as advisory.[44] He claimed that the differences between the issues in *Keystone* and those in *Mahon* were insignificant. First, the same public interests were invoked in both cases, and because of this the same reasoning, in particular Holmes's statements that the "strong public interest" in preventing subsidence in Kohler was "insufficient" to overcome the takings requirement in the latter case, applied as well. Further, the "nuisance exception" was, according to the dissent, much narrower than the majority read it. This narrow reading was compelled by the policy aim of making sure that the public interests are not disproportionately loaded upon individual property owners. Therefore, nuisance regulations must be "discrete and narrow" and, more importantly, not applicable to cases that "allow complete extinction of the value of a parcel of property."[45] The Court's refusal to recognize this as a separate segment of property was wrong, because the coal left is "an identifiable and separable property interest." Rehnquist concluded, "This complete interference with a property right extinguishes its value, and must be accompanied by just compensation."[46]

Scalia wrote the Court's most notorious regulatory takings opinion (to date) five years later, wherein it was found that a statewide environmental regulation was a taking under the constitution. In 1986, Lucas bought two beachfront lots in South Carolina for $975,000. In 1988, the South Carolina Legislature passed the Beachfront Management Act and, in effect, at least as found by the trial court, rendered the lots valueless. Lucas did not question the validity of the Act, but just demanded compensation as a taking.

Scalia's opinion started the discussion of law as follows:

> Prior to Justice Holmes's exposition in *Pennsylvania Coal Co. v. Mahon*, it was generally thought that the Takings Clause reached only a "direct appropriation" of property, or the functional equivalent of a "practical ouster of [the owner's] possession." Justice Holmes recognized in *Mahon*, however, that if the protection against physical appropriations of private property was to be meaningfully enforced, the government's power to redefine the range of interests included in the ownership of property was necessarily constrained by constitutional limits. If, instead, the uses of private property were subject to unbridled, uncompensated qualification under the police power, "the natural tendency of human nature [would be] to extend the qualification more and more until at least property disappear[ed]." These considerations gave birth in that case to the oft-cited maxim that, "while property may be regulated to a certain extent, if regulation goes too far it will be recognized as a taking." Nevertheless, our decision in *Mahon* offered little insight into when, and under what circumstances, a given regulation would be seen as going "too far" for purposes of the Fifth Amendment.[47]

He then explained that the standard test is *Penn Central*'s ad hoc factual inquiry. There were, according to the Court's take on the law, though, two areas where this inquiry was not needed, where there is physical invasion (at least where permanent), and where all economic or productive value is denied.[48] The Court's opinion then claimed:

> Surely, at least, in the extraordinary circumstance when *no* productive or economically beneficial use of land is permitted, it is less realistic to indulge our usual assumption that the legislature is simply "adjusting the benefits and burdens of economic life," in a manner that secures an "average reciprocity of advantage" to everyone concerned. And the *functional* basis for permitting the government, by regulation, to affect property values without compensation—that "Government hardly could go on if to some extent values incident to

property could not be diminished without paying for every such change in general law,"—does not apply to the relatively rare situations where the government has deprived a landowner of all economically beneficial uses.[49]

Scalia continued, "On the other side of the balance" is the "fact" that a regulation that leaves land without economic options poses "a heightened risk that private property is being pressed into some form of public service under the guise of mitigating serious public harm."[50] Therefore, Scalia created a bright-line categorical rule that "when the owner of real property has been called upon to sacrifice *all* economically beneficial uses in the name of the common good, that is, to leave his property economically idle, he has suffered a taking."[51] He allowed that the purpose of government regulation can be broader than harmful or noxious use and just needs to be reasonably related to policy aimed at broad public benefit and general in effects on property. Further, the Court even allowed a narrow exception to the new categorical rule. Even such a total elimination of value will not be a taking if the owner's estate did not have the use in question in the title to begin with under the "restrictions that background principles of the State's law of property and nuisance already place upon land ownership."[52]

Blackmun's impassioned dissent started with the following line: "Today the Court launches a missile to kill a mouse." The Court's decision, he claimed, "ignores its jurisdictional limits, remakes its traditional rules of review, and creates simultaneously a new categorical rule and an exception (neither of which is rooted in our prior case law, common law, or common sense)." He therefore dissented, he stated, not because he thought he could intercept the missile or save the "targeted mouse," but rather to "limit the collateral damage."[53]

He then proceeded to offer much more information about the case than Scalia did in the majority opinion. Blackmun's descriptive facts about the property noted that about half of the last forty years the two Lucas plots were part of the beach or flooded twice daily. From 1957 to 1963 they were under water, and from 1963 to 1973 the shoreline was 100 to 150 feet into the land. Finally, from 1981 to 1983 the island they were on had experienced twelve emergency orders.

Further, he argued that the South Carolina Supreme Court had accepted two premises that were accepted by the U.S. Supreme Court until *Lucas*. First, each state "has the power to prevent any use of property it finds to be harmful to its citizens." And, second, that "a state statute is entitled to a presumption of constitutionality."[54] Here the legislature's findings were not challenged by petitioner yet the Court allocated to the state the burden of showing the regulation was not a taking. He went on: "The Court offers no justification for its sudden hostility toward state legislators, and I doubt that it could."[55] Then he questioned why the creation of a new categorical rule, especially when previous cases all reject the claim that even total diminution of value by itself is enough to decide: "Instead, the cases depended on whether the government interest was sufficient to prohibit the activity, given the significant private cost."[56]

Blackmun also pointed out, as Brandeis had in *Mahon*, that determining the "threshold" requirement—loss of all economic value—will depend on how the property is defined, but noted that there is no "objective" way to define this. Finally, he questioned the use of state's common law of nuisance, "If judges in the 18th and 19th centuries can distinguish a harm from a benefit, why not judges in the 20th century, and if judges can, why not legislatures?"[57]

Stevens also vigorously dissented. He started by stating:

> As the Court recognizes, *Pennsylvania Coal Co. v. Mahon*, provides no support for its—or, indeed, any—categorical rule. To the contrary, Justice Holmes recognized that such absolute rules ill fit the inquiry into "regulatory takings." Thus, in the paragraph that contains his famous observation that a regulation may go "too far" and thereby constitute a taking, the Justice wrote: "As we already have said, this is a question of degree—and therefore cannot be disposed of by general propositions."[58]

Stevens saw this as also showing that economic injury or "extent of the diminution" is merely one factor to be weighed. Indeed, there are cases that repeatedly acknowledge that complete destruction of a property's value might not be a taking because comparison of value before and after is just one relevant factor. Plus, he noted that the categorical rule was arbitrary because all depended on the definition of the property right in question. Indeed, a developer could sell very narrow rights, severing one small strand from the overall bundle, so that any regulation at all could be a "total" taking. Further, and very significantly, he claimed that the narrowness and inflexibility of the "nuisance exception" brought back the discredited heightened legal scrutiny of legislation characteristic of *Lochner*.[59] Finally, he thought that the Court's opinion set up a rule that ignores the important factor of the character of the regulatory action. One aspect of the character of legislation traditionally emphasized is its general and broad applicability. Stevens noted that the Beachfront Management Act is very general in that it covered the entire state. Therefore, he concluded, "in view of all of these factors, even assuming that petitioner's property was rendered valueless, the risk inherent in investments of the sort made by petitioner, the generality of the Act, and the compelling purpose motivating the South Carolina Legislature persuade me that the Act did not effect a taking of petitioner's property."[60]

Epstein on Takings

To understand the resistant undercurrent to *Mahon's* "matter of degree" and "too far" analysis of takings in *Lucas*, itself purportedly founded upon Holmes's opinion, it is useful to turn to Epstein's highly influential and much more categorical and deductive conception of takings. Before this, though, it is informative to briefly turn to his analysis of *Mahon*.

Epstein claims that Holmes's *Mahon* opinion "lurches unhappily between brilliant insight and utter nonsense," and this "because his instincts are not disciplined by any overriding theoretical approach."[61] He sees Holmes's real problem as that of lacking a coherent philosophy and, because of that, not having enough of a commitment to constitutional structure. Indeed, "at every critical juncture, Holmes shrugged off hard choices with the observation that 'every hard question is a matter of degree,' thus treating an intellectual evasion as a judicial insight."[62]

According to Epstein some of Holmes's flaws due to lack of proper theory include the following: failure to see that one can only apply the "average reciprocity of advantage" principle to general laws; a centering of the law of takings upon a vague "too far" diminution of value test instead of on all of the value taken; the neglect to specify what particular property right is being evaluated for loss; the tendency toward balancing without explaining how to balance or even what exactly is being balanced; and the inclination to let decision making rest upon mistaken judicial deference following from an ungrounded skepticism.

In effect, Epstein demands of Holmes's theory a fully formed legal test for takings with an acknowledged theory of government that gives a central place to the Takings Clause. Further, the test should rely upon determinant conceptual clarity and the use of clear "bright-line" rules. It should be highly protective of property and highly suspicious of legislative intervention in the market. Therefore, though Holmes, according to Epstein, rightly found the Kohler act to be a taking, his analysis was too under-theorized, undisciplined and unprincipled. Ultimately, Holmes's Supreme Court takings jurisprudence with his deferential and "matters of degree" stance is seen as incoherent because, in Epstein's words, "it takes judicial energy and moral conviction to intervene, and Holmes has neither."[63]

 Epstein's own takings theory is, admittedly, much more conceptually determinate than Holmes's. And, indeed, it rests upon an internally coherent and quite detailed theoretical foundation. Most important, to both fully understand his critique of *Mahon* and the foundation of his own takings jurisprudence is to understand what he takes to be the only proper aim of government. This he makes clear in the following statement:

> The entire program of state regulation becomes utterly incoherent in the absence of its proper end: <u>unrestrained competition</u>. Should regulators have any doubts about the primacy of competition, the entire system will necessarily fall of its own weight. There will be no prior established norm against which particular institutional arrangements can be checked; the choice of institutional arrangements and objectives thus becomes a pure political play.[64]

Proper market competition is the underlying value, and no other values are proper as ends of regulation.

From this foundation he argues through an appeal to the Coase theorem that a society founded upon markets with low transaction costs creates positive externalities wherein any negative externalities are offset by the overall gains. Basically, that is, if markets are functioning properly everybody is better off (or those that are not better off could be more than compensated from the gains to others).

Under Epstein's theory not only is the aim of government clear, but its basic means are settled as well. Because for him the substantive correctness of his ideas of liberty, social welfare, etc., are beyond doubt and "admit of permanent solutions," he claims that there is no need to waste time debating them.[65] Therefore, "we do not leave these issues for the legislature to sort out because we know that its interests, or those of its many members, often deviate from what a robust system requires."[66]

More specifically, in the regulation of private property Epstein demands a solution that takes it fully out of the political realm and avoids "needless debate" as well. Government is just created in order to protect the previously existing rights of individual liberty and property. It is not that property rules descended from heaven fully formed. Rather, Epstein claims that though "the creation of private property that binds all individuals is necessarily *social* at its core," it cannot continue to be socially "redetermined" after the initial creation because requiring group consent beyond the initial creation would entail prohibitive transaction costs. Therefore, any legislative changing of previously vested property rights, indeed all governmental action of any type, "should be examined under a presumption of error."[67]

The "correct" understanding of the Takings Clause starts with a "proper respect for the primacy of private property and liberty of action," which necessarily limits government regulation to only two specific areas; acts of aggression and monopoly power.[68] Aggression is wholly made up of various types of wrongful force and fraud. Regulation of these harms is just a prospective version of the remedial common law of tort and criminal sanctions. The problem here, according to Epstein, is that once government is allowed to prevent even such a narrow group of harms there will inevitably be legislative overreaching.

To ensure that legislative and administrative branches "behave well" they must be subjected to external control. Courts, therefore, are necessary watchdogs and should use "intermediate scrutiny" to ensure that proper limits are maintained. The process is simple: if the aims of legislation are within an area of aggression, a proper police power end, then the presumption is in favor of the regulation. And if the regulation is legitimate, then no compensation is required. This presumption or legitimacy can be overcome, though, through a showing that the regulation is selectively applied, has "disparate impact," or was passed for some "invidious motive." If the aim is regulation of monopoly, then various remedies and regulations can be applied. For collusion, for example, an injunction may be sufficient. For cases of natural monopoly regulation analogous to that of rate-setting of common carriers is allowed.

Epstein claims that this "correct" understanding of the takings test is central, indeed truly foundational, quite simple to outline, and mostly easy to apply. Epstein further simplifies the matter by claiming that the test applies equally to both state and federal government because, in his opinion, this is consistent with the U.S. government's "basic Lockean design."[69] The test in outline form goes as follows: first, is there a taking of private property? If not, then the inquiry stops. If so, is there any justification for taking the private property in question? If there is, within narrow boundaries,

then it is allowed without compensation. If it does not fit the allowed justifications, then is the taking for public use? If not, then it is disallowed. If
there is a legitimate public use, then there must be proper compensation.

First, it must be established whether or not property is taken. Epstein
offers a truly clear and bright-line rule to this problem. For him, private
property is simply "the sum of the goods that the individual gets to keep
outside of the control of the state."[70] Any and all property is covered under the Takings Clause. Epstein puts it this way: "The takings clause says,
'Nor shall private property be taken for public use, without just compensation,' it means, 'nor shall private property, in whole or in part, be taken for
public use, without just compensation.' "[71] For Epstein, therefore, strictly
speaking, there is no such thing as a partial or regulatory taking. Every
stick in the bundle is a full property right, therefore every stick of the bundle is individually protected. For instance, takings would cover business
goodwill, defamation by a state official, any tax or zoning law as well as
contract rights. Therefore, Epstein concludes, what constitutes a taking
"is a question that admits to a rigid logical answer," because "*all* regulations, *all* taxes, and *all* modifications of liability rules are takings of private
property prima facie compensable by the state."[72]

Once private property is taken, the next step is to see if it is justified under the police power. The police powers of the state are there only to protect against private violations of pre-political natural rights boundaries.
Just because the state needs resources for this necessary role of protection, it must be allowed to coerce its citizens. But to keep the government
from going beyond this function it must be strictly limited.

First, he outlines the acceptable ends. As stated above, Epstein analogizes the police power area to that of self-defense in private law, a situation where harm is caused by the wrongful conduct of the other: "Where
the harm threatens a large portion of the population, the state has the
sum of their individual rights. The police power as a ground for legitimate
public intervention is, then, exactly the same as when a private party acts
on its own behalf."[73] In such acts of aggression, "the wrong of the citizen
justifies conduct otherwise wrongful by the state as representative of and
in defense of its other citizens."[74] Indeed, all the state really is allowed to
do is protect the rights that each individual citizen has before entering the
political realm. Therefore, the state can only control public nuisances collectively within the same bounds as the individuals could have controlled
them on their own. The Court must throw out as unconstitutional any ends
outside of this narrowly justified area.

Second, the Court also must analyze the means. This, according to Epstein, requires an "intermediate standard of review" such as exemplified in *Lochner* instead of the modern practice of using the weak "rational relation" test.[75] Generally, "the court should defer where it believes that a legislative decision is likely to be more accurate than its own, or more precisely, where it believes that the additional costs of its own extended supervision . . . is not justified by an incremental improvement in fitting means to ends."[76] If both the means and ends are deemed legitimate by the court, then the regulation is allowed without compensation.

If it does not fit the narrow nuisance justification for police powers, then the question is whether or not the taking is for public use. If not, then it is disallowed. Once again, Epstein's take on what is legitimate public use is also very limited. For him public use most centrally includes "public goods"—that is, goods where exclusivity is unavailable and marginal costs for further units of the good are very low (his example is national defense). But limiting public use to public goods is too narrow even for Epstein. So, it also must include projects akin to that of roads, for example. These he analogizes to "common carriers" in private law. Here, general public access is sufficient to allow the regulation as long as just compensation is provided. Outside of these two areas there is a strong presumption against the aim. Most importantly, indirect public benefit is not enough.

Finally, if it is a genuine public good being aimed at then there must be compensation. First, explicit monetary compensation, when required, must be higher than market value. This is because market value does not take into consideration use values, or even such obvious factors such as relocation costs. But with general legislation there will often be implicit in-kind compensation. To evaluate this some of the "matters of degree" analysis creeps into Epstein's analysis. Ultimately, implicit in-kind compensation analysis uses factors such as "direct measurement of the consequences of regulation, theoretical predictions of economic loss, disproportionate impact tests, and examination of local motive."[77]

Epstein v. Holmes

Epstein's takings theory certainly seems internally coherent and is based upon a fully worked out theoretical foundation. And whether or not Holmes has "moral conviction" there is no doubt that Epstein does. Indeed, Epstein has remarkably few doubts at all. He determines the one

and only proper aim of government and the uniquely optimal and specific means to bring about that end. In the realm of takings, a realm only
slightly narrower than all of government activity for Epstein, the definition
of property is found housed in common law. Using the common law as a
foundation he then uses it to define property expansively and settle the
rules once and for all. He gives a determinant and expansive reading of the
Takings Clause, explaining that it means all parts of the property bundle
individually and collectively, and then offers bright-line rules for legal application. He eliminates any recourse to the extent of the diminution of
value because in his system any loss of value is enough to trigger the clause.
Even in the case of remedial measures for nuisances that happen through
factors such as changing conditions, Epstein defines the legislative powers

in an exceedingly narrow fashion. And he gives the Court the last word
on the whole system as the keeper of proper rights under rigorous judicial
oversight. Overall, legislative acts are to be judged by the Court under a
general suspicion of endemic overreaching. If a legislative act overcomes
this suspicion by fitting into one of the police power or public use exceptions then it is presumptively good, though challengeable under an intermediate standard of review. He even gives us a proper precedent for this
type of analysis, Justice Peckham's majority opinion in *Lochner*. Finally,
Epstein explains the intricacies of what just compensation means.

Epstein appears to believe the single-mindedness, internal coherence,
formalist reasoning and precise line-drawing that characterizes his system
are all legal virtues, and that the isolated plausibility of each individual
piece makes the overall system stronger, therefore forming an unimpeach-
able framework for the Takings Clause.

On the other hand, coherence and precise line drawing may create a
system that is so closely linked formally that it ceases to function at all
with the elimination of any one of the links. For example, it seems highly
questionable, to say the least, to think that there is any unanimity over
the one and only proper end of government. Even if economic prosperity is a major goal of government it is difficult to believe it is the only legitimate goal. The same critique can be used on the identification of only
one means—market competition. Even if one accepts that the market
is generally superior to other forms of social organization, thinking of it
as the only means beyond the narrow exceptions Epstein allows seems
extreme. If his whole system of takings necessarily rests upon this type of
foundation, it may be that theoretical subsidence is setting in already. It
seems an act of theoretical hubris or imperiousness, a blatant use of the

method of tenacity and authority, to justify top-down rules that define even the judicial discussion of other options off the table. Epstein exemplifies, therefore, a very extreme and aggressive version of the "exclude in order to bind" version of constitutional decision making.

But even assuming that economic prosperity, defined specifically as Epstein defines it, is accepted as the sole proper aim of government, it does not follow necessarily that the common law is the only and best way to bring this about. Epstein references Coase's theorem a lot for his claims. But Epstein underemphasizes what is a very important message of Coase's work—that there are always transaction costs and it is an empirical, not solely theoretical question, as to how to optimize social welfare even through markets. Yes, Coase's theorem can and has been used to critique uncritical government-centered solutions. But, and this is crucial, it can also be used to critique overly optimistic "frictionless" pictures of markets, an error that Epstein seems to find it difficult to avoid.[78] Coase explicitly warns of this problem, lamenting that "in modern economic theory the market itself has an even more shadowy role than the firm." Further, Epstein would be wise to contend with this statement of Coase, "for anything approaching perfect competition to exist, an intricate system of rules and regulations would normally be needed. Economists observing the regulations of the exchanges often assume that they represent an attempt to exercise monopoly power and aim to restrain competition. They ignore or, at any rate, fail to emphasize an alternative explanation for the regulations: that they exist in order to reduce transaction costs and therefore to increase the volume of trade."[79] So, if there is any dispute over proper means as to what will get us to the greatest amount of economic prosperity, once again the coherence of Epstein's system becomes less of a virtue in that it treats an empirical question as a matter of theoretic definition. Epstein may already have achieved certainty, but his certainty in both the realms of means and of ends is not universally shared. More worrisome, his certainty allows him to enthusiastically propound a constitutional theory that renders any opposing voice without either political or legal recourse.

Imagine in further detail what his Constitution would look like. It is Court-centered, with the legislature's role being severely limited and disciplined by the Takings Clause placed as the central foundational pillar for government. It takes as its positive precedent the reasoning exemplified in *Lochner*, one of the most infamous "antiprecedents" in U.S. Supreme Court history. Further, the Takings Clause is applied equally to both the federal government and the states therefore issues of federalism

are ignored. He claims this is warranted because of the Constitution's
Lockean roots. Of course, to think the Constitution instantiates Locke's
philosophy is plenty questionable. Then there is the reading of the property in question as any and every separate stick of the bundle—an extremely expansive definition of property covered.

Every step of this is questionable. First, as Jeremy Waldron has
shown, a Lockean constitution might not be as court-centered or as antidemocratic as Epstein imagines. Locke might even be characterized as a
"proto-theorist of deliberative democracy."[80] Furthermore, defining federalism out of the picture ignores the essential state-based location of property law.

Then there is his more general picture of property. First, common law
is less helpful to his theory than Epstein thinks it is. He likes to quote
Blackstone's definition of property to show how clear and strong common
law was with regards to property rights. But this is dubious support. For
instance, in Daniel J. Boorstin's investigation of Blackstone's *Commentaries* he finds the treatment of property as purposefully "obscure," "circu-
lar," and "mysterious," so as to keep it out of the gaze of the "vulgar" and
"ill-intentioned." Maybe more telling, it is described as Blackstone's tool
that "forced people to be free."[81]

On top of this there is plenty of scholarship, of which Carol M. Rose's
work can serve as an example, where different traditions of property rights
are identified and contrasted. Her example is a property tradition of repub-
licanism and "propertarianism" whereby property, in its proper forms and
not in excessive amounts, is thought to be useful in fostering civic virtue.[82]
This tradition conflicts with the one of defining property solely in terms of
wealth acquisition. Her claim, interestingly, is that Holmes's takings test allows for both types of property and so therefore "in takings doctrine, the
tradition of property's civic responsibility is embodied in a test that balances
public benefits against private losses from a particular measure."[83]

This analysis could help explain the result in *Pruneyard* that balanced
the property rights of the shopping center owners with the free speech
rights of the students whereas Epstein's theory cannot. The ironic limit
to this is Epstein's evasion of the work of theorists like Charles A. Reich,
whose classic article, "The New Property," challenges just about every
limit that Epstein would want to put on the concept of property.[84] Finally
even Scalia's *Lucas* opinion acknowledges that the expansive definition of
property advocated by Epstein is historically inaccurate as a description
of property covered under the Takings Clause (therefore not part of the
common law Epstein purportedly is relying upon).

Epstein's system offers the hope for a clear and uncomplicated test for whether or not a taking has occurred. But, if each of the links is a necessary component of the test, doubt as to the validity of any one of the links raises doubts as to the system itself. If the ideal is a formal deduction from the premises, then a missing necessary premise renders the conclusion unsupported. This may be enough to eliminate Epstein's theory as an option given how extreme some of his premises are.

More appropriately for the argument of this chapter, though, his theory can also be critiqued through a "matters of degree" analysis. That is, instead of accepting the idea that the coherence of his whole system makes each component more plausible or that there is a need to find any one link to be completely wrong, what if the system was evaluated by the plausibility of each part multiplied by all the others? In other words, if Epstein's theory rests upon ten discrete assumptions, each given the highly charitable 50 percent likely to be correct evaluation, the likelihood of the whole system being "robust" in its justification is the likelihood of $.5 * .5 * .5 * .5 * .5 * .5 * .5 * .5 * .5 * .5$. This means that as a complete and coherent system Epstein's takings jurisprudence would have a likelihood of .000976. This is not the type of theory a "bettabilitarian" as Holmes liked to characterize himself as would want to bet on.

That Epstein's theory seems plausible in the face of this possibility demands explanation. One explanation is that Epstein's theory falls prey to the same mistake in reasoning as exemplified in the hypothetical "Linda" example offered in Thaler and Sunstein's *Nudge*.[85] Therein Linda is described as "single, outspoken, and very bright" as well as having participated in antinuclear demonstrations and been a philosophy major interested in discrimination and social justice. When test subjects were asked to rank possibilities for Linda they ranked as more probable that she was a "bank teller active in the feminist movement" rather than just a bank teller. This is a mistake that finds the combination of two events (a * b) more likely that either one individually. Thaler and Sunstein describe this as a "representativeness" bias based upon stereotype. Of course that Epstein has a bias toward a priori definitions and formalistic reasoning might bias him toward overconfidence in both the individual assumptions of his theory as well as the probability of them all being true together.

Holmes's factor-based decision woven from multiple threads of inquiry starts to look quite intelligent in comparison. First, it acknowledges undisputed fact that property and contract rights were destroyed through legislation. Second, it doesn't treat this as dispositive because there are cases of nuisance, and other police power cases, that have acknowledged that

there are wrongful uses of "property" that government should not necessarily protect. And what is wrongful or a nuisance can change because
of context.

It is worth noting along these lines that Holmes, the Civil War veteran,
had perhaps the greatest "antiprecedent" for trying to solve political issues through Court authority, *Dred Scott,* in his recent memory. Therein,
Taney invalidated the Missouri Compromise and found slaves to be property protected by the Constitution. Indeed, an argument can be made that
Dred Scott was the first regulatory takings case.[86]

It could also arguably be a case that shows why a categorical rule like
that offered by Scalia in *Lucas* is not a very good idea. Holmes might, in
light of the events that followed this earlier more "bright-line" application
of property law, certainly be allowed a little skepticism toward the wisdom
of any belief in the Court being able to settle social controversies through
judicial fiat, let alone settling them correctly through a bright-line rule. So,
Holmes allows for play in the joints, and settles for the investigation of multiple factors to analyze the case at hand such as diminution of value, the
extent of the burden upon the regulated party, the obvious meaning of the
constitution's words, the property rights in question, the fact that they were
expressly contracted for and who is feeling the pinch of the regulation as
opposed to who is getting the benefit. He does not, though, expect to find
easy categorical lines between property and other legal concepts, or to be
able to solve this problem though facile definitions. And, of course, he does
not try to arrest the evolving path of law at a specific moment in time.

Further, he gives this factor-based analysis some additional predictability by practicing judicial deference to legislative activity given its greater
democratic pedigree. Because of this structuring appeal to deference, the
balance weights strongly in favor of the validity of government regulation, and the analysis becomes acceptably predictable. As an example of
deference there is *Tyson,* where Holmes wrote, "I think the proper course
is to recognize that a state legislature can do whatever it sees fit to do unless it is restrained by some express prohibition in the Constitution of the
United States or of the State, and that Courts should be careful not to
extend such prohibitions beyond their obvious meaning by reading into
them conceptions of public policy that the particular Court may happen
to entertain. . . . The truth seems to me that, subject to compensation
when compensation is due, the legislature may forbid or restrict any business when it has a sufficient force of public opinion behind it."[87] Here is
strong deference to democracy and legislative activity, but notice the one
requirement; that of "compensation when compensation is due."

As Kellogg notes (and *Mahon* shows), Holmes did not give a free ride to all police power regulation. So, for example, in *Missouri Pacific Railway,* Holmes held that a Nebraska statute that required the railway to build tracks to privately owned grain elevators was a taking because they were only private connections.[88] Therefore Holmes advocated judicial deference, not judicial abdication. And Holmes allowed that there could be broader public purposes than those commonly recited under traditional police power doctrine.[89]

Holmes's takings jurisprudence was structured upon a deference to majoritarian decision makers that was, in turn, founded upon the belief that "what prevents the friction between competing conceptions of the way of life should be from overheating and leading to violence is democracy."[90] As Jeremy Waldron would put it, the "circumstances of politics" demand that we show respect for persons through showing a proper "respect for the reality and implications of disagreement."[91] This is surely an intelligent response to the absolutism of *Dred Scott, Lochner* and, in our time, the type of reasoning that is exemplified in Epstein's conception of takings and to a lesser extent in Scalia's *Lucas* opinion.

Holmes famously wrote that "certitude is not the test of certainty." In the same place he continued, "property, friendship and truth have a common root in time. One cannot be wrenched from the rocky crevices into which one has grown for many years without feeling that one is attacked in one's life."[92] Having good reason to be wary of Court-created absolutes, Holmes could plausibly adopt a stance of judicial deference. Further, that combined with a "matters of degree" analysis could give legislatures great weight, but still find, at the extremes, moments where they wrongfully try to read sections of the Constitution out of the document.

In a letter to Franklin Ford on Supreme Court letterhead, December 29, 1908, Holmes wrote, "My own opinion often expressed through many years is that the only use of the phrase Police Power is to express the fact that you can't carry out constitutional provisions to their logical extremes." He then gave an example: "A law forbidding the building of houses more than 80 feet high I presume might be good under the police power, one forbidding you to build more than one foot would be a taking and would have to be paid for."[93] Such a matter of degree analysis maps on to the Court cases outlined above quite well, including such seemingly absolutist cases as *Lucas,* but without falling in to the vice of creating needless absolutes.

Mahon is a case that exemplifies a well thought-out, antifoundational, evolutionary, flexible, multi-factored, or braided analysis that largely rests upon the particular facts of the case at hand. It is not an overly frustrating case unless one is mesmerized by a conception of law as best exemplified by bright-line rules and simple deductive tests where defining terms and applying general principles in absolute fashion is a categorical require-ment. If rid of this dogmatic conception of what law is and must be, and its vestiges in the Court's takings jurisprudence, then the cases analyzed above can be seen as exemplifying vigorous debate over precisely the fac-tors that should be confronted every time in fact-patterns that are hon-estly difficult to legally decide. And, if one were to add an awareness of alternate conceptions of property and democracy-enhancing factor to *Ma-hon*'s reasoning, as *Pruneyard* could be read to do, then the democratic aspect of Holmes's reasoning becomes even clearer. Holmes's reasoning is therefore wrongly criticized by Richard Epstein. Indeed, Epstein's theory exemplified not only the vices of a formal deductivist understanding of jurisprudence in an extreme manner, but also helps show the virtues of a legal analysis such as Holmes's that finds the limits of this methodology too distorting and rather emphasizes empirical analysis and the braiding of reasons as advocated by Peirce, Dewey, and the jurisprudence of demo-cratic experimentalism.

CHAPTER FIVE

Lochnering

The last chapter contrasted Epstein's takings jurisprudence with Holmes's reasoning as exemplified in *Mahon*. What was noticeable was conflicting references to what is often thought of as one of the most controversial cases in United States Supreme Court history, *Lochner v. New York*.[1] In the case history on takings both conservative and liberal justices alike were ready to accuse their opposition of "Lochnering." Only one person referenced in the last chapter was willing to embrace *Lochner*, and that was Epstein. While the others seemed to disagree on who was falling into the jurisprudential traps of the case, all of them seemed to agree that it is a trap to avoid. *Lochner*, therefore, represents a central case in the constitutional law of the United States. Further, Lochner is usually criticized as an example of judicial overreaching thwarting democratic results. Indeed, in *Obergefell* (to be analyzed later) Roberts rested his very strongly worded dissent largely upon what he saw as the majority replicating *Lochner's* antidemocratic vices. Therefore, the issues and analysis involved in the decision directly highlight the question of the place of judicial review within democratic government.

I begin this chapter with an analysis of contemporary stances on *Lochner*. After that, Peckham's infamous majority opinion along with the famous dissents by Harlan and Holmes will be outlined. Then, *Lochner* will be evaluated through the theory of Epstein, the philosophy of Ronald Dworkin, and last from the perspective of Deweyan democratic experimentalism. My conclusion here is that *Lochner* indeed is rightfully seen as something of a litmus test for the relationship between law and democracy.

At least if democracy is the aim of constitutional culture, contra theorists like Epstein, *Lochner* is properly thought of as an "antiprecedent." This will be shown through a construction of what a properly democratic and experimental result in the case would have looked like. Luckily, the dissents by Harlan and Holmes forge a large part of the path that such an opinion would take. The chapter therefore both builds upon the critiques of formalist legal reasoning offered in the last two chapters and furthers the constructive project of characterizing what a constitutional jurisprudence of Deweyan democratic experimentalism would look like through analyzing one of the most mundane and yet most important constitutional cases in United States history.

The *Lochner* Legacy

The facts and legal issues of the *Lochner* case were indeed horribly mundane for such an infamous and vilified case. Lochner, the owner of a bakery in New York, violated an article of New York's Bakeshop Act because he permitted his employee to work more than sixty hours in one week. The Supreme Court found that the Act's limitation on hours voluntarily worked was unconstitutional because it unlawfully interfered with freedom of contract protected under the Fourteenth Amendment's Due Process Clause. Stated so simply the decision seems innocuous. So why would the "*Lochner* era" in U.S. Supreme Court jurisprudence be so infamous?

The classic answer is found in Lawrence Tribe's *American Constitutional Law.*[2] Therein, Tribe describes the Constitution as a "historically discontinuous composition."[3] That is, the Constitution has had different interpretations, and different meanings, during various periods of United States history. One of the great examples of discontinuity from this perspective is the change from the pivotal "*Lochner* era" where the Court's use of substantive due process to strike down economic regulations was at its apex, to a very different regime after *West Coast Hotel* when the Court backed off strong review of economic regulation under the Due Process Clause, upheld minimum wage legislation, and started approving New Deal laws in a wholesale manner.[4]

The *Lochner* era substantive due process jurisprudence used, according to Tribe, a notion of implied limits founded upon an idea of natural rights. The idea grounding this stance was that "regulation of economic affairs was not impermissible *per se*; it was invalid only where the state moved beyond the sphere of its inherently limited authority by using its powers to help some citizens at the expense of others, rather than to promote genuinely public purposes to benefit the citizenry as a whole."[5] The combination of a realm of economic privacy outside of legitimate governmental regulation attached to a picture of equality that separated legitimate laws from factional grabbing created a notable resistance by members of the Court to many types of legislative acts. As to the judgment of legislative ends, the Court used ostensibly natural law and common law "implied limitation notions." Further, in addition to a legitimate end the Court also required a "real and substantial" relationship between a statute and its objectives. The Court was involved in reviewing the propriety of both the ends and the means chosen.

Often the Court would inquire as to whether purportedly public-minded legislation was a pretense for illegitimate aims. If the Court found pretense, then the legislation would be found unconstitutional. In short, "the Court interpreted its requirement of a substantial means-end relationship so as to invalidate statutes which interfered with private economic transactions unless evolving common law concepts demonstrated a proper fit between the legislation and its asserted objectives."[6] In practice this was a quite stringent analysis.

Tribe argues that *Lochner* serves as the representative case of the era because it is the most characteristic example of this type of review. He argues, further, that the ultimate problem with *Lochner*-style jurisprudence is that the common law and natural law baseline that the Court was using in order to distinguish between private and public realms was unstable.

This instability is exemplified in *Miller v. Schoene* wherein cedar trees were found to be infected with a carrier of fungus which would, if left unabated, destroy the commercial value of a nearby apple orchard.[7] The Supreme Court upheld a statute that ordered the cedar tree owners to cut down the trees to prevent contagion. The Court found the public interest required by due process in the value of the apple orchard. As Tribe puts it, "*Miller* not only indicates that redistribution of property between private parties may be justified in the public interest. The decision also suggests that the state inevitably has a positive role to play, a role whose exercise in *either* direction will benefit some private actors while hurting others. For the Court opined that, if the state had done nothing and permitted disaster to strike the apple orchards, "it would have been none the less a choice.' "[8] Therefore, Tribe concludes that "if one accepted fully the central notion which contributed to *Lochner's* decline—that even judicial enforcement of common-law rules of contract and property represents a governmental choice with discernable consequences for the distribution of suffering, pleasure, and power—then it would be hard to avoid the realization that a judicial choice between invalidating and upholding legislation altering the ground rules of contract and property is nonetheless a positive *choice*, one guided by constitutional language and history but almost never wholly determined by it."[9]

Tribe's analysis offers multiple reasons why *Lochner* might serve as a landmark antiprecedent in constitutional law. Probably the most popular story is that *Lochner* represents a clear case of dogmatic judicial activism and overreaching. That is, the majority opinion shows an activist Court finding ways to impose both its own narrow views of legitimate government activity and an aggrandizing view of the Court's function and abilities. Perhaps the most direct defense of this story is offered by Paul Kens.[10] He finds the case to be a clear example of judicial activism based upon an unexamined attachment to laissez-faire social Darwinism. Further, Kens argues that dogmatic attachment to laissez-faire substantive due process ideology led the Court to ignore multiple reports that documented unsafe conditions in New York bakeries. Indeed, the Court's strong attachment to free-market ideology made acknowledging the existence of alternate ideals of the state, and therefore any empirical needs of the public that were incompatible with their specific assumptions, impossible. This dogmatism is clearly reminiscent of Epstein's stance.

This dogmatic blindness was exacerbated because many members of the Court majority and a large part of the legal profession wrongly saw the judges as "legal monks" who acted in the role of "passive oracles" identifying and applying the law as it is as opposed to constructing it. Further, acting on this conception of the judge's position in government was, in turn, conceived of as showing the Court's commitment to principle and therefore its acting as proper protector of the constitutional order.

Kens claims, though, that this ideological construct could not stand up to the actual facts. Ultimately, the *Lochner* decision came to represent not only a false picture of the respective roles of the Court and the legislature, but also a disagreement over the Court's authority to determine the extent of acceptable state action. The problem, therefore, was that the Court "assumed that it had the right to reign over the legislative domain of the states."[11] This, in turn, shows *Lochner* to be a properly condemned "illustration of the contrademocratic nature of the Court's power of judicial review."[12] Also following this type of analysis, William Marnell concludes that the Court, through a social Darwin based interpretation of the Fourteenth Amendment, made the Constitution into a "comprehensive Bill of Rights for corporations."[13]

A slightly more benign version of the overreaching explanation, but without explicit acknowledgement that the Court's certitude of its central place as protector of the Constitution is questionable, is offered by David Strauss in "Why Was *Lochner* Wrong?"[14] Strauss largely repeats the Tribe analysis, but notes specifically that the standard argument for the case's vilification is seemingly paradoxical in light of current civil rights jurisprudence. In his reading the dominant criticism finds *Lochner* objectionable because the Court enforced "implied" rights through strong judicial review, rights not explicitly mentioned in the text of the Constitution. Therefore, the Court's problem is one of judicial activism.

But this is problematic because the modern Court has recently done much the same thing, though in the realm of civil rights. Such rights as privacy, etc., and now the right of same-sex couples to marry, are under this interpretation equally Court-created rights that are not explicitly mentioned in the Constitution. Yet in the realm of civil rights the Court's cases have not been criticized nearly as harshly, and indeed have often be praised.[15] Given this seeming paradox Strauss finds the implied rights versus activism critique unconvincing. Instead, he claims that "the *Lochner*-era Court acted defensibly in recognizing freedom of contract but indefensibly in exalting it."[16] Strauss concludes that the real failure of the majority opinion was its lack of humility and inability to face the truly difficult and complicated nature of the issues.

A different line of analysis that is also compatible with Tribe's explanation argues that *Lochner* was properly decided in its time, but that in the intervening years factors have changed enough so that it is properly seen as bad law today. One example of such an argument is offered by Jack Balkin.[17] In his terms, *Lochner* was not wrong when decided, but came to be so because facts in the world changed. Bruce Ackerman also supports the "changing correctness" thesis.[18] Howard Gillman also agrees.[19]

Gillman's analysis is particularly interesting in that he offers a meticulous case analysis and locates the origin of liberty of contract ideas in the antislavery movement and the Court's Jacksonian suspicion of class-based or partial legislation. For Gillman, "the decisions and opinions that emerged from state and federal courts during the *Lochner* era represented a serious, principled effort to maintain one of the central distinctions in nineteenth-century constitutional law—the distinction between valid economic legislation, on the one hand, and invalid 'class' legislation on the other—during a period of unprecedented class conflict."[20] Therefore, as opposed to a picture of the justices being willful and aggressive, under this analysis the Court was actually being faithful to precedent and the Framers' intent. The problem with the Bakeshop Act for the Court majority was that labor legislation was thought to be by its very nature class-based and redistributive. Therefore, the Bakeshop Act was contrary to government neutrality. But conditions change. For Gillman the great depression and the rise of modern corporate capitalism ended the ability to believe in the earlier conception of a neutral state. Therefore, "the story of the *Lochner* era is a story about judicial fidelity to crumbling foundations."[21]

Another strand of *Lochner* scholarship argues that the underlying common law assumptions treated as passive and neutral by the majority opinion were active and non-neutral all along. Cass Sunstein offers perhaps the clearest version of this type of argument.[22] Sunstein contrasts *Adkins*, where entitlements are taken as prepolitically given and minimum wage law is described by the Court as an unjustified subsidy to the employee, with *West Coast Hotel* where low wages paid by an employer are seen as being subsidized by society in order to sustain the employee's necessities. Therefore, "the expansion of the police power in *West Coast Hotel* signaled a critical theoretical shift, amounting to a rejection of the *Lochner* Court's conception of the appropriate baseline."[23]

Sunstein draws the conclusion that "whether rights are treated as 'negative' or 'positive' turns out to depend on antecedent assumptions about baselines."[24] Ultimately he believes that the rise of the modern administrative state shows that governmental action outside of common law limits has become so necessary as to make *Lochner*-style analysis obsolete. Along the same lines, Jennifer Nedelsky agrees that "the *Lochner* era opinions show more than an endorsement of Herbert Spencer and his fellow Social Darwinists; they show an impressive continuity with the Federalists' vision of constitutionalism, complete with the rights of property as the central boundary to state power, a suspicion of popular efforts to use democratic power to threaten those rights, and contract as a focus for protecting them."[25] On the other hand, Nedelsky offers the same conclusion as Sunstein—that the common law baseline is now obsolete.

There are also some scholars who argue that the case was decided correctly and it still correct today. Blazing this trail is Richard Epstein. In *Takings: Private Property and the Power of Eminent Domain*, as was noted before, he advocates a return to a *Lochner*-style standard of review especially in cases involving the Takings Clause.[26] His analysis was expanded in *Supreme Neglect: How to Revive Constitutional Protection for Private Property*.[27] Therein Epstein describes the Bakeshop Act as motivated by a goal of eliminating competition and argues that the Act exceeded "any rational conception of police power, for its purpose was not safety, but to alter the competitive balance between competitive forms. The cardinal virtue, therefore, of the much-reviled *Lochner* decision was that it preserved the operation of competitive labor markets from the corrosive effects of differential state regulation. The police power was idle, because there was no market imperfection to cure."[28]

David Bernstein offers a much more detailed version of this argument with a little less free market fundamentalism than is seen in Epstein's work.[29] Bernstein argues against the "prevailing myth" that the problem with *Lochner* is that the justices imposed their own laissez-faire views on the Constitution through overly aggressive interpretation. He sees this story as a recently constructed "morality tale" and a "polemical argument with little factual basis."[30]

According to Bernstein the actual fact of the matter is that *Lochner* was largely ignored until it became a leading anticanon case in the 1980s. But since then, "along with *Dred Scott v. Sandford* and *Plessy v. Ferguson,* *Lochner* has become one of the most reviled Supreme Court cases of all time."[31] Why? He thinks this morality tale was largely created through casebook organization—most importantly, Tribe's treatise *American Constitutional Law*. But, Bernstein claims, scholars "have thoroughly debunked the tale's historical underpinnings."[32]

Lochner v. New York

As stated above, the actual facts of *Lochner* were quite simple and not in dispute. Lochner, the owner of a bakery in New York, violated an article of New York's Bakeshop act because he "wrongfully and unlawfully required and permitted" an employee to work more than sixty hours in one week. The work was voluntary. Therefore, all that was claimed was that the employer permitted the employee to work over sixty hours during one week. The question for the Court was whether the maximum hour limitation was constitutional.

Justice Peckham wrote the majority opinion. The Court found that the language of the Bakeshop Act was the "substantial equivalent" of a law that would require that "no employee shall contract or agree to work" more than ten hours a day. Peckham noted that this keeps an employee by law from earning extra money through extra work if so desired. Because of this,

the statute necessarily interferes with the right of contract between the employer and employees concerning the number of hours in which the latter may labor in the bakery of the employer. The general right to make a contract in relation to his business is part of the liberty of the individual protected by the Fourteenth Amendment of the Federal Constitution. *Allegeyer v. Louisiana*, 165 U.S. 578. Under that provision, no State can deprive any person of life, liberty or property without due process of law. The right to purchase or to sell labor is part of the liberty protected by this amendment unless there are circumstances which exclude the right."[33]

Peckham then noted that states are allowed to limit the right of contract through their "police powers," which relate to "the safety, health, morals and general welfare of the public."[34] Indeed, the Court explicitly accepted that property and liberty rights (and therefore contract rights) are "held on such reasonable conditions as may be imposed by the governing power of the State in the exercise of those powers."[35] If the state is exercising its legitimate police powers then the Fourteenth Amendment does not prohibit such acts. Peckham allowed that the Court has indeed upheld state police powers in borderline cases due to the use of interpretive rules "of a very liberal nature."[36] For instance, a law limiting Utah underground mine workers to eight hours a day was upheld because of the kind of employees and the type of labor, its inherent danger, made it "reasonable and proper" for regulation to be allowed.[37] For that case the Court it was thought important that the law covered only a narrow class of laborers and had an emergency exemption. Peckham also argued that other cases were distinguishable as well. Another case, *Atkin*, had held that a state could control work conditions in its own municipal corporations and *Knoxville Iron Co. v. Harbison* allowed protection for employees cashing "coal orders" at their employer due to specific employee and employer relations.[38] Further, in *Jacobson* the Court allowed for compulsory vaccination for public health reasons.[39]

But, Peckham continued, there must be limits to the police powers, "otherwise the Fourteenth Amendment would have no efficacy, and the legislatures of the States would have unbounded power" to regulate any activity through citing a "mere pretext" of protecting the morals, health or safety of their citizens.[40] The Court's question was therefore, "Is this a fair, reasonable and appropriate exercise of the police power of the State, or is it a unreasonable, unnecessary and arbitrary interference with the right of the individual to his personal liberty or to enter into those contracts in relation to labor which may seem to him appropriate or necessary for the support of himself and his family?"[41] Peckham argued that by framing it this way the majority was not "substituting the judgment of the court for that of the legislature" but rather was deciding whether the law in question is within the legitimate police power of the state and is, therefore, a question of law to be decided by the Court.[42]

The Court found that under this test the Bakeshop Act was mere pretext because bakers as a class were perfectly competent to make contracts, the law was not necessary to protect the safety, morals or welfare of the public, and the trade of baker was not a specifically unhealthy one. Because the law did not show a direct enough relation "as a means to an end" there was "no reasonable foundation for holding this to be a necessary or appropriate health law" and was therefore "an illegal interference with the rights of individuals, both employers and employees, to make contracts regarding labor upon such terms as they may think best, or which they may agree upon with the other parties to such contracts."[43]

Given the possibility of pretext, therefore, *Lochner* substantive due process analysis used the following test: "The purpose of the statute must be determined from the natural and legal effect of the language employed, and whether or not it is repugnant to the Constitution of the United States must be determined from the natural effect of such statutes when put into operation, and not from their proclaimed purpose."[44] Under this test, Peckham, writing for the Court, held that the New York Bakeshop Act was an unconstitutional infringement of contract.

Justice Harlan wrote the first dissent. In it, Harlan started by stating a state's legitimate use of police power is universally recognized and "extends at least to the protection of the lives, the health, and the safety of the public against the injurious exercise by any citizen of his own rights."[45] The state, though, "may not unduly interfere with the right of the citizen to enter into contracts that may be necessary and essential in the enjoyment of the inherent rights belonging to everyone."[46] But he noted that the finding of undue interference is not a simple analysis and, because of this, large discretion is "necessarily vested in the legislature to determine not only what the interests of the public require, but what measures are necessary for the protection of such interests."[47]

The question at issue was what are the outer limits to proper legislative authority? Harlan stated: "Upon this point there is no room for dispute, for the rule is universal that a legislative enactment, Federal or state, is never to be disregarded or held invalid unless it be, beyond question, plainly and palpably in excess of legislative power."[48] Because of this,

if there be doubt as to the validity of the statute, that doubt must therefore be resolved in favor of its validity, and the courts must keep their hands off, leaving the legislature to meet the responsibility for unwise legislation. If the end which the legislature seeks to accomplish be one to which its power extends, and if the means employed to that end, although not the wisest or best, are not plainly and palpably unauthorized by law, then the court cannot interfere. In other words, when the validity of a statute is questioned, the burden of proof, so to speak, is upon those who assert it to be unconstitutional.[49]

Given this analysis, Harlan found plenty of evidence that the New York law can be properly read so as to see the rationality of the belief that working over sixty hours a week baking bread in New York bakeshops could endanger the health of the laborer. He cited empirical studies to that effect. In addition, he saw the statute as a reasonable means to regulate such labor. Next, Harlan found that he could not say that the law was beyond doubt a clear invasion of fundamental rights and because there is "room for debate and for an honest difference of opinion." This was, by itself, enough to decide in favor of the regulation."[50] Finally, Harlan predicted that voiding the statute under the Fourteenth Amendment would cripple the states in the furtherance of their police power duties.

 Holmes filed a separate dissent. Within it he famously claimed that the majority used a controversial economic theory, one that many in the Unites States did not agree with, to decide the case. Holmes then listed many ways in which contracts are interfered with by law every day without any notice such as Sunday laws, usury laws and lottery prohibitions. Further, he noted that the broader idea of a general liberty from interference "so long as he does not interfere with the liberty of others to do the same" is refuted by school laws, the Post Office, and taxes.[51]

In one of the most famous lines in United States constitutional law he then stated, "The Fourteenth Amendment does not enact Mr. Herbert Spencer's Social Statics," and continued:

> But a constitution is not intended to embody a particular economic theory, whether of paternalism and the organic relation of the citizen to the state or of *laissez faire*. It is made for people of fundamentally differing views, and the accident of our finding certain opinions natural or familiar or novel and even shocking ought not to conclude our judgment upon the question whether statutes embodying them conflict with the Constitution of the United States.[52]

Therefore, "general propositions do not decide concrete cases. The decision will depend on a judgment or intuition more subtle than any articulate major premise."[53] Then Holmes offered his alternate test—"the world liberty in the Fourteenth Amendment is perverted when it is held to prevent the natural outcome of a dominant opinion, unless it can be said that a rational and fair man necessarily would admit that the statute proposed would infringe fundamental principles as they have been understood by the traditions of our people and our law."[54] From this judicial stance he concluded that the statute not only passed constitutional muster but that it might be reasonable to allow further legislation in the direction of maximum work hours.

Deciding *Lochner*

In *Lochner*, Peckham, Harlan, and Holmes all disagreed as to the nature of United States constitutional law and how it was to be applied to the Bakeshop Act. The substance of the disagreements are helpful when investigating the relationship of democracy, legislative activity and judicial review in a constitutional democracy. By constructing additional examples of how Epstein, Dworkin, and a practitioner of democratic experimentalism would analyze the case, these issues can be even further clarified.

As can be deduced from the last chapter, Epstein is a fan of Peckham's approach and uses *Lochner* as an example of what he thinks constitutional jurisprudence in the United States should be like. Actually, it goes farther than that. Epstein outs Lochner's *Lochner* in that he would not admit that there are borderline cases nor would he adopt "liberal interpretive standards" as Peckham at least claimed the Court does. While he sees the case as maybe the best example available of the Supreme Court doing its job, he would want an even more resolute Court in place under his theory so that the categories used in *Lochner* could be applied in an all or nothing bright-line manner.

Both dissents, it goes without saying, are anathema to Epstein and represent to him horrible misunderstandings of the place of law and the Court in the United States constitutional system. Harlan's deferential stance is abdication of principle and Holmes's stance is, even worse, explicit rejection of principle in favor of an empirically based and context oriented inquiry full of vague boundaries and way too much deference to "unnecessary" discussion and partisan politics. As with Holmes's takings jurisprudence no doubt Holmes's dissent in *Lochner* must appear morally weak and close to absolute nonsense to Epstein. Therefore, under

Epstein's theory, *Lochner* is correctly decided but still a little fainthearted in its application of the proper principles and understanding of law. Furthermore, as seen in the analysis from Epstein's takings jurisprudence, he has very few worries about judicial supremacy getting in the way of democratic aims.

On the opposite side of the political pole is Ronald Dworkin. That is, Epstein is far right on the U.S. political spectrum and Dworkin resides on the moderate left. Indeed, if it is predictable that Epstein will fall on the right hand side of typical conservative issues, Dworkin is even more predictable in his falling upon the "moderate left" side of any issue of his time. But for Dworkin just like Epstein a properly functioning democracy is fully reliant upon a proper foundational understanding of constitutional law.

In his theory Dworkin famously advocates a theory of essential rights as "trumps," where the individual is expressly protected from the group will, even in the face of policies that are thought to be more beneficial to society as a whole.[55] This conception of rights, of course, creates the ubiquitous and all too familiar problem of antimajoritarianism. Epstein is fine with this because he isn't really that thrilled with democracy and fancies himself a Lockean liberal. Dworkin, on the other hand, claims that despite the antidemocratic appearance of an antimajoritarian source of trumps, judges and constitutional judicial review actually have a foundational role in producing and protecting democracy. Therefore, contra Dewey, democracy as an end requires non-democratic means in order to properly function. Judicial supremacy is thought necessary and, according to him, is a realm of moral principle that expressly excludes "policy" which is more results-driven as it aims at specific goals.[56]

To explain how this translates into law, Dworkin asks us to imagine and to the extent possible emulate an ideal judge, Hercules, the ultimate protector of real democracy. Constitutional law is for Dworkin central to democracy and a strong "moral reading" of this law is "practically indispensable to democracy."[57] As opposed to a democracy based upon majoritarian or statistical premises, where democracy is conceived of as just an aggregation device, Dworkin advocates what he describes as a "communal" or "cooperative" constitutional democracy founded upon the aim of treating all members of the state with "equal concern and respect," as well as having "inherent value" and "personal responsibility."[58]

Legal decisions, when made by Hercules, protect the democratic conditions necessary for a properly structured democracy by utilizing this set of concepts to evaluate the constitutionality of laws. Judges are, therefore, the supreme "guardians of principle."[59] For Dworkin, "the American conception of democracy is whatever form of government the Constitution, according to the best interpretation of that document, establishes. So it begs the question to hold that the Constitution should be amended to bring it closer to some supposedly purer form of democracy."[60] Further, the Constitution is "America's moral sail," and Hercules the judge is the United States' moral interpreter.[61]

What exactly such a communal or cooperative constitutional democracy entails, other than judicial review and a strong moral interpretation of the Constitution based upon the above small set of abstract moral concepts, is not really ever fully described by Dworkin. We know that there must be structural and relational conditions as well as the assumption of personal and individual value. And these conditions include requirements of equality and respect of some type. Further, the communal conception of democracy presupposes a type of collective agency. This requires that the whole community can and must in some way see the law as theirs, as being properly of the people. But beyond this most of the detail goes toward characterizing how Hercules would go about his task.

The "hidden structure" of actual judicial decisions that Hercules follows is a scheme of abstract and substantive moral principles which provide a coherent justification for the application of law in every realm. This, in turn, is best conceived of as "law as integrity." Integrity is a type of principled "coherence" or "consistency" in laws. Such laws are described as the opposite of "checkerboard" laws which, presumably, seem ad hoc. Principled decision is thought more desirable, but this is not because checkerboard laws are by definition less effective; indeed, Dworkin admits that in many cases checkerboard laws might bring about better results. "Principle," though, is the central quality that justifies attachment to law as integrity. Principled legal practice requires a general style of argument that treats democratic community as a distinct type of community, a corporate moral agent where people "accept that their fates are linked."[62] This, in turn, gives legal decisions moral legitimacy because principled integrity creates the reason for legal obligation.

According to Dworkin an understanding of law as integrity is helpfully informed by analogy to the project of writing a chain novel. In creating a chain novel novelists write a novel as a cooperative team. In this hypothetical process, after previous writers have completed earlier chapters in a cooperative novel project in the order they are to be read, the next author writes the following chapter so as to make the novel being constructed the best it can be. Each author is to construct the best novel through testing upon two dimensions. First, there is "fit." This test entails that the next chapter should, as far as possible, "flow" and not leave unexplained major aspects of the text as previously written. Second, if after satisfying the fit requirement there are options left over, the author must construct a chapter that is best "all things considered" or that best "justifies" the previous chapters.

Hercules as the ideal practitioner of law as integrity practices constructive interpretation. What building blocks are found in this construction? Principle only, described as moral principle, rights as trumps, and not policy.

 Dworkin especially abhors pragmatism because pragmatism discounts principle and expressly bases its grounds for decision upon policy choices and consequences. This is a very undesirable position because, according to Dworkin, acting as a judge necessarily requires principled interpretation and construction at the deepest and most philosophical moral level. Indeed, "any judge's opinion is itself a piece of legal philosophy, even when the philosophy is hidden and the visible argument is dominated by citation and lists of fact." In fact, a philosophy of law based upon moral reasoning is the "silent prologue to any decision at law."[63] Hercules knows that only a community based upon law as integrity "can claim the authority of a genuine associative community and can therefore claim moral legitimacy—that its collective decisions are matters of obligation and not bare power—in the name of fraternity."[64] Indeed Dworkin claims that when Hercules "intervenes in the process of government to declare some statute or other act of government unconstitutional, he does this in service of his most conscientious judgment about what democracy really is and what the Constitution, parent and guardian of democracy, really means."[65]

As noted above, Dworkin predictably comes down on the left side in the contemporary political spectrum. Surprisingly, though, when it comes to using Dworkin's jurisprudential philosophy, it has a lot in common with Peckham's majority opinion. First, Dworkin sees the Court's position as that of vigorously protecting the Constitution and its foundational principles. As Peckham does, Dworkin also sees the Supreme Court as the location where definite and principled limits are set to what the legislature may or may not enact. What a democratic process is and what the legislature is allowed to do are for both what the Court properly decides. For both the Court is the proper ultimate protector of individual rights as trumps against social legislation, even if the legislation would make the whole society better off. And both accept the image of the Court as the ultimate forum of principle, a forum that should not involve itself with policy because policy is outside the realm of law proper.

Therefore, the issue in *Lochner* is whether or not the law is properly principled in both fit—dutifully following the proper precedents in a manner that makes them most coherent—and moral vision—holding a proper moral reading of the Constitution. As this is an issue of legal interpretation and not policy, Dworkin agrees that a proper decision by judges of the Court is not a substitution of the personal judgment of the judges for that of the legislature but rather justices acting in their proper role as deciders of foundational issues of law.

From the prevailing scholarship on *Lochner*, it seems as if precedent was on the side of Peckham and the majority of the Court. The majority opinion exemplifies a clear and consistent moral conception of government based upon inalienable rights and common-law foundations. In other words, the majority opinion is in many ways a paradigm of principle. Further, a law that just changes the rules of contract in one discreet area of labor, that of baking, and not more universally, so that only one group of laborers or employees loses their neutral right to contract certainly reads as checkerboard.

As to Harlan's dissent, that is less consistent with Dworkin's theory. While Dworkin certainly could agree that the legislature may often be able to better determine what the interests of the public require, Dworkin would never let the interests of the public as decided upon by the legislature, especially those that legislate public policies rather than principle, trump the individual rights that are deemed constitutionally essential. Determining what is essential is the domain of the Court. Because of this, Harlan's deferential stance toward the legislature reads as dereliction of a justice's duty to both Peckham and Dworkin. Deference is a not a judicial virtue. This, of course, shows just how far Holmes is from Dworkin's ideal judge Hercules. Holmes allows all too much leeway for factional arguments over what Dworkin (and Peckham) think are legal concepts such as contract and liberty. Further, Holmes seems to ridicule principle when he states that "general principles do not decide concrete cases."

Dworkin himself wrote that Hercules "would not have joined the *Lochner* majority" because "he would have rejected the principle of liberty the Supreme Court cited in that case as plainly inconsistent with the American practice and anyway wrong and would have refused to reexamine the New

York legislature's judgment on the issues of policy that then remained."[66] As to why Hercules would find this way he cites the "superior constraint of integrity."[67] He also argues that "overruling was absolutely necessary in order to protect the coherence of constitutional law as a whole."[68]

But from an analysis based upon the scholarly evidence, it seems that this is incorrect and Dworkin's own philosophical tools would have Hercules ruling opposite of Dworkin's personal conclusions. The reasons he gives against the actual *Lochner* decision—that it was inconsistent with United States practice and incoherent, not integral, with the constitutional law of the time—actually seem wrong. Indeed, Tribe, Nedelsky, and Gillman all offer compelling arguments as to why *Lochner* was consistent with precedent, principled and founded upon a coherent moral reading of the Constitution. Indeed, if following Dworkin's chain novel analogy and accepting the requirements of fit and justification, Hercules practicing law as integrity in a principled manner seems required to side with the *Lochner* majority opinion despite what Dworkin would desire in terms of political results.

Democratic Experimentalism and the *Lochner* Decision

Posner reads Holmes's dissent in *Lochner* as a "Deweyan approach." As he puts it, "In Dewey's intellectual universe, invalidating a statute is not just checking a political preference. It is profoundly rather than merely superficially undemocratic" because this gets in the way of "democratic experimentation."[69] Posner is correct. Indeed, Dewey in the 1932 edition of *Ethics* uses *Lochner* as the specific example of the Court contracting state police power in a manner that obstructs democratic process. He continues, "In the case of legislation affecting wages the issue is between the older individualistic principle of freedom in the wage contract, on the one hand; and on the other the more recently affirmed principle that in the interest of social welfare it may be wise for a state to protect its members against exploitation."[70]

This description, it should be noticed, anticipates the ideas adopted by the Court in *West Coast Hotel*, the case that in effect overruled *Lochner* four years later. That Dewey uses *Lochner* as the example of narrow police powers jurisprudence also gives strong evidence against Bernstein's libertarian morality tale wherein a revisionist liberal professor, Tribe, highlights well after the fact a relatively obscure case unnoticed in its own time, and creates a narrative justifying the New Deal with that case at its center.

Elsewhere, there is further evidence that Dewey thought Holmes's dissent in *Lochner* to be important; such as when he observes that Holmes was properly against an absolutist use of the Fourteenth Amendment because that would prevent social experimentation under a delusion of "exactness."[71] And in *Liberalism and Social Action* Dewey notes approvingly that in the *Lochner* opinion Justice Holmes found it necessary to remind his fellow justices that, after all, the *Social Statics* of Herbert Spencer had not been enacted into the American constitution.[72]

Once again, Dewey sees democracy as a way of life that is broadly social before it is seen more narrowly as a political concept. Democratic habits must pervade all of society and not just politics. Democracy also entails pluralistic values and a decentered picture of social institutions. A public is created when social consequences that affect people beyond the immediate group are both noticed and found to be in need of social control. Political democracy, therefore, comes into being where there is a recognized need to control consequences of social activity. Because problems constantly change, the state needs to be continuously re-made. That is, democracy is based upon solving specific problems. It is constructed according to changing demands and is not to be defined in abstraction from these demands. And while democracy employs both scientific knowledge and creativity for communication and solution, recourse to rule by experts or other elites cannot avoid creating an undesirable distance from necessary knowledge of the concrete issues demanding solution. Therefore, ultimate power must always stay with the people and be constructed from the ground up. Because of this, for Deweyan democratic experimentalism it is in the realm of everyday democratic politics that, presumably, most of the experimental possibilities would be worked out.

So, if democratic experimentalism were adopted as a general political practice, obsessing over the interpretive strategies and philosophers of Supreme Court justices would be much less interesting because much less determinative of politics and of the law.

Where traditional pictures of the "rule of law" shared by Peckham, Epstein, and Dworkin fixate on command structures and determinative and foundational rules, in the jurisprudence of democratic experimentalism the presumption is in favor of the revisable choices made by various citizen publics through a decentered and federated structure. This presumption is also shared by the dissents of Harlan and Holmes. Evolutionary learning presumptively happens in local venues. Publics are organized to solve specific problems and are continuously "re-made" in relationship to the social issues needing attention and ultimate power always stays with the people. Indeed, democracy itself is taken as a creative, comparative, and forward-looking project that is only understood through the process of experimentally constructing it democratically.

Under democratic experimentalism a judge could not follow the foundationalist aspects of Peckham's majority opinion. A judge would first look to the record created within the legislative areas and adopt the role of a facilitator of those decisions if at all possible. Rejecting the legislation would be thought unfortunate rather than the primary role of the process. Following from the conception of law as information-producing, the judge would also look to other cases in order to help reason out whether the statute should be upheld or not. Analogous cases are used as valuable evidence, but do not have the morally obligatory quality that they have in Dworkin's system. Other cases are just another type of benchmarking.

Substantively, an experimentalist judge might very well see the Fourteenth Amendment of the Federal Constitution as protecting some contract rights. Indeed, under democratic experimentalism the contemporary distinction between substantive economic rights and civil rights might not be so easy to make. The experimentalist judge, that is, cannot appeal to absolutes or essences so both the contract rights in question as well as the limitation on allowable work hours would have to be investigated through an inquiry into evidence of how such legislation works on the ground and the documented health dangers of working such long hours in New York bakeries. Limits to the right of contract through police powers relating to matters of safety, health, morals, and the general welfare of the public would have to be articulated in terms of identifiable consequences. In addition, of course, the various meanings of these terms would be largely set as far as possible in democratic forums of various types.

On the other hand, there is an emphasis upon evidence and, presumably, if there is no evidence for a regulation and there is significant reputable evidence against it, the Court would have to occupy, however reluctantly, a position that thwarted legislative regulations. And because the experimentalist Court empirically evaluates the evidence for choice of means and ends it could even adopt the "mere pretext" inquiry that Peckham arrived at. Once again, Peckham found that the Bakeshop Act was mere pretext because under his grasp of the facts bakers as a class were competent to make contracts, the law was not necessary to protect the safety, morals, or welfare of the public, and the trade of baker was not a specifically unhealthy one.

But notice here that almost all of this is less a matter of traditional "rule of law as the law of rules" content, and much more an evaluation of factual matters such as was the end legitimate and, if so, was the means chosen proper to serve the end. These are largely matters of empirical fact. How could the Court have known what the facts were from the meager record through which they were offered and the conception of law they were acting on? Peckham seems to be resting his analysis upon his own undisciplined intuitions of the dangers faced within New York bakeries. This, of course, is just an appeal to a priori reason that Peirce critiques as ungrounded.

Under a democratic experimentalist process the empirical record would have been developed starting with records attached to the legislative deliberation that resulted in the regulation. Through the required benchmarking and recordkeeping, the reasons for the law and available evidence for why the specific type of regulation was chosen from other available options would have to be well documented. If, indeed, the conditions were really dangerous there would be evidence to bear that claim out. Further, there would have to be a record of alternate means considered. Even if alternatives had not been thoroughly researched and thought out in the legislative process, bringing the matter to the court system would be information-forcing and, more than likely, information-producing. And as the matter preceded up the court hierarchy presumably the focus upon fact would ensure that the relevant facts are not crowded out by attempts to solve things by arbitrary definitional fiat or the attempt to impose a single-minded substantive theory of justice or legal interpretation upon a contested domain.

Justice Harlan's claim that the finding of undue interference in contract is not simple and, because of this, that discretion is necessarily given to legislative acts in both the determination of ends and means, would be proper to many areas of decision making under democratic experimentalism.

First, the experimentalist aim requires some leeway in order to allow experiments in legislative possibility. As Harlan notes, a bright line prohibition might cripple creative legislative attempts to solve pressing public problems. Second, in most situations the legislature is going to have better democratic pedigree than the court even if law is reconceptualized as itself a democratic means. The institutions that better exemplify the democratic factors should get a presumption of legitimacy over the less democratic ones. Indeed, this might mean that Harlan's statement that "a legislative enactment, Federal or state, is never to be disregarded or held invalid unless it be, beyond question, plainly and palpably in excess of legislative power" could function as a test under democratic experimentalist jurisprudence.

On the other hand, when he writes that, "if the end which the legislature seeks to accomplish be one to which its power extends, and if the means employed to that end, although not the wisest or best, are not plainly and palpably unauthorized by law, then the court cannot interfere," this might be disputed if the record before the Court was really information-rich and offered strong evidence of empirically superior ends or means available or documented harms caused by the regulation. Indeed, this deference can only really be justified due to the fact that Harlan presumes that the Court does not have evidence of this type in order to inform its decision. Here it is important to note that in his dissent Harlan actually cites evidence that the New York law was factually related to the aim of protecting the health of the Bakeshop laborers.

Holmes's dissent has already been described as Deweyan in attitude. It is also pretty close in spirit to democratic experimentalism. Certainly under a regime of democratic experimentalism deduction of a legal result from one controversial conception of economics and contract would be impossible to sustain. Holmes's claim that "a constitution is not intended to embody a particular economic theory" and "is made for people of fundamentally differing views" is therefore accepted. Further, the pragmatist underpinnings of democratic experimentalism ensure agreement with the statement that "general propositions do not decide concrete cases." And the democratic sentiment behind the statement that "the world liberty in the Fourteenth Amendment is perverted when it is held to prevent the natural outcome of a dominant opinion, unless it can be said that a rational and fair man necessarily would admit that the statute proposed would infringe fundamental principles as they have been understood by the traditions of our people and our law" is largely acceptable. This combines great deference to more democratic branches of government with a sense that some fundamental principles are more protected, that some legal practices are still valuable, even when decentered from an absolutely unquestioned foundational role.

But Holmes stops in his *Lochner* dissent before advocating the other essential aspect of democratic experimentalism—the experimentalist demand that democracy proceed with an emphasis upon fact-based inquiry. Indeed, given this dissent, democracy might be seen as a sheer irrational clash of unbounded preferences. This is not the demanding and constructive picture of democracy that democratic experimentalism embraces.

And how does the jurisprudence of democratic experimentalism line up with the scholarly critiques? It does not harmonize with the positive evaluation that Epstein and Bernstein give it. Epstein likes *Lochner*-style review because he not only like the formalist quality of the argumentation, but also because he agrees with the substantive position the Court took on contract rights and the suspicion of democratic legislation the opinion exhibits. *Lochner* preserved markets from state regulation and because Epstein found no market imperfection to cure this was just the Court exercising its proper function.

A Court working along democratic experimentalist lines, it is obvious, has a much different attitude toward democracy. Democracy, contra Epstein's logic, is presumed desirable. And public deliberation upon whether or not to focus upon competition and whether or not to follow common-law conceptions of property, labor, etc., is encouraged as opposed to defined out of bounds through an appeal to formalist economic and constitutional theories. Epstein once again disagrees with Holmes, and once again the disagreement shows off Holmes's experimentalist and democratic judicial virtues. Holmes highlights the controversial nature of the assumptions the Peckham opinion treats as indisputable. Epstein commits exactly the same error but more aggressively due to having the possibility of learning from critiques that followed after *Lochner*.

Tribe's analysis highlights the Court's use of implied limits founded upon an idea of a realm of economic privacy outside of legitimate governmental regulation and a picture of equality that separated legitimate laws from factional grabbing. Further the Court also required a real and substantial relationship between a statute and its objectives. For Tribe the ultimate problem with *Lochner*-style jurisprudence is that the natural law baseline that the Court was using in order to distinguish between private and public realms was incoherent given the needs of modern society. The Court assumed a neutral baseline when actually any choice of baseline stance was exactly that—a choice. And as such the choice must be justified. Sunstein and Nedelsky also offer this critique, finding that the Court's common law baseline assumptions were insupportable due to the rise of the modern administrative state. This is also the import of Gillman's judicial fidelity to crumbling foundations portrait of the *Lochner* decision.

A Court practicing democratic experimentalism does not have the hindrance or help of unquestioned natural law baselines or absolute baselines of any type. The underlying claim of neutrality and all the distinctions made upon it are unavailable as reasons for a constitutional decision. This is not to say that everything is always in flux. There will be, unavoidably, naturalized baselines. As William James noted in *Pragmatism* and Seth Vanetta has more recently highlighted, pragmatism's antifoundational stance is actually in many ways quite conservative in that it always starts by accepting that the majority of our beliefs are held as unquestioned at any time.[73]

Further, the democratic experimentalist judge has no certain principle with which to critique substantive stances. Rather, inquiry and decision making are incremental and evolutionary. Indeed, this is where Sabel and Simon's description of some rights as "destabilization rights" seems too hyperbolic. Any right will both render certain actions more stable, and tend to destabilize other activities. So this is not a unique aspect of rights in democratic experimentalism.

But given the experimentalist nature of legal reasoning, baselines have to be justified when challenged with evidence and are never held as impervious to future revision. The same goes for any rule made by the Court. None get the free ride that a theorist like Epstein wants to give his own favorite assumptions. And given the democratic focus of the inquiry, imposition of a controversial baseline assumption cannot be justified through authoritative appeal to any pre-political essence of contract, law, etc.

The jurisprudence of democratic experimentalism cannot follow its own procedure and at the same time justify its conclusions through appeal to neutral baselines or any unquestioned "certitudes"—all baselines must be justified experimentally and democratically as far as possible. Because of this, a Court imposing its own narrow views of legitimate government activity though an aggrandizing view of the Court's function as "legal monks," who acted in the role of "passive oracles" identifying and applying the law, is incompatible with Deweyan democratic experimentalism.

Closer to what would result substantively is Strauss's conclusion that the fault of *Lochner* was not finding implied rights through the Due Process Clause but rather that the real failure of the majority opinion was its lack of humility and inability to face the truly difficult and complicated nature of the issues. Here, democratic experimentalism offers more information and less conceptual certainty to the Court, encouraging legal professionals to face the real complexity of the issues. Further, an emphasis upon local experimentation would also encourage a broader discussion of the values at stake. Therefore, the antidemocratic failings of judicial activism through uncritical use of controversial natural law or common law base-line assumptions are avoidable through the jurisprudence of democratic experimentalism. While it wouldn't force change, it certainly would not fossilize baselines without empirical evidence. Not only that, but because decisions are made incrementally with awareness of the possibility that further evidence or changed conditions might arise, the critique that the *Lochner* Court tried to fossilize obsolete ideologies into timeless truths is avoided as well.

CHAPTER SIX

Citizens United

That the jurisprudence of democratic experimentalism avoids the antidemocratic flaws of *Lochner* gives some support to its plausibility as a way to approach constitutional law that emphasizes the centrality of democracy. A more recent case that many people also find to be a democracy-thwarting antiprecedent is *Citizens United*. It is indeed a case that implicates democracy quite directly—much more explicitly than *Lochner*.

If *Lochner* showed the Court finding and protecting economic rights to the detriment of democratically passed laws, thereby explicitly limiting the realm of democratic lawmaking through its use of common law assumptions and an avowed suspicion of democratic processes, *Citizens United* purportedly protected economic rights as speech in the name of democratic values. On the other hand, *Citizens United* also found democratically passed legislation that was ostensibly aimed at improving elections unconstitutional because of its implications for political speech. So, the case is a great example of the Court trumping a more democratic branch's legislative act purportedly in order to protect democracy, that is, antidemocratic means being offered up as constitutionally required for democratic ends. Investigating *Citizens United* in relationship to democratic experimentalism can further clarify how different conceptions of law are implicated in and informed by different theories of democracy.

I begin this chapter with an analysis of the *Citizens United* decision, the concurrences and dissent. Then I look at some important critical responses to the decision. Finally, as with the analysis of *Lochner*, I construct an explanation of what a decision based on Deweyan democratic experimentalism. The conclusion is ultimately that because the *Citizens United* Court holds basic unexamined assumptions about law that structured the decision it could not be properly informed. Indeed, the decision highlights a tendency for the Court to treat factually determined issues as issues of "law" and, therefore, issues of conceptual clarification. This is a recurring aspect of the "exclude in order to bind" conception of law exemplified by Scalia's jurisprudence but ubiquitous in legal thought.

Democratic experimentalism, because suspicious of dichotomies such as issues of fact versus law, policy versus principle, or legislation versus judicial judgement, can offer a much better means to a more democratic and experimentally informed decision. Further, because the Court is conceptualized in democratic experimentalism as a collaborator in democratic process, the once and for all quality of current Supreme Court jurisprudence would be largely avoided, therefore allowing the possibility of further learning in complicated areas such as campaign finance—the issue in *Citizens United*.

The *Citizens United* Decision

The Bipartisan Campaign Reform Act of 2002 (BCRA), banned corporations or unions from using general treasury funds to finance "electioneering communications." Electioneering communications were defined as "any broadcast, cable, or satellite communication" that "refers to a clearly identified candidate for Federal office" and is made within thirty days of a primary or sixty days of a general election.[1] An earlier case, *Austin*, had accepted an antidistortion interest in relationship to regulating corporate speech based upon the premise that it might sometimes be necessary and proper under the First Amendment to regulate corporate speech in service of a better functioning democratic election process.[2]

Citizens United brought action against the electioneering ban because it wanted to show *Hillary: The Movie* during the regulated period of time before an election and was worried that it would be considered an electioneering communication. The Court found that *Hillary* was an electioneering communication, indeed the functional equivalent of express political advocacy against Hillary Clinton. The Court also found that any narrower ruling than one on the First Amendment issue of a full ban on electioneering communications funded by corporate or union general treasury funds would ignore the important and unavoidable constitutional matters at issue under the First Amendment and therefore risk chilling important political speech. The Court decided this even though the litigant, Citizens United, expressly offered and seemed to prefer narrower grounds for the decision.

Ultimately, the majority opinion announced that because of the justice's "judicial responsibility" it had to rule on the constitutionality of the regulation.[3] This was due to uncertainty about the propriety of the law, the time it would take for actual applications of the law to clarify its general requirements and limits, the amount of important speech that might be chilled, and the law's effect on "integrity of the election process," which all pointed to the necessity of immediately dealing directly with the constitutional issue.[4] Because they saw a judicial responsibility related to the importance of protecting political speech, "core" First Amendment speech, the Court used the most rigorous standard of "strict scrutiny" to evaluate the constitutionality of the law. This standard required the Court to inquire as to whether the regulation furthered a compelling interest and was narrowly tailored to achieve that interest.[5]

The opinion started by noting that the First Amendment is "premised on mistrust of governmental power," "stands against attempts to disfavor certain subjects or viewpoints," and is generally against preferences for certain speakers. Further, both speech and speakers are protected.[6] The Court offered the broad rule that "the First Amendment does not permit Congress to make these categorical distinctions based on the corporate identity of the speaker and the content of political speech," and from that principle found that the ban on electioneering expenditures by corporations was an unconstitutional restriction of protected speech.[7] The majority ultimately held that "restrictions distinguishing between different speakers" are flatly prohibited due to both the "history" and the "logic" of the First Amendment.[8]

The *Citizens United* Court also found that the regulation at issue created an ongoing chill of core political speech, indeed a virtual ban, and because of this interfered with the "open marketplace" of ideas. Therefore, it overruled the part of the BCRA that disallowed the use of corporate treasury funds for electioneering communications and, further, overruled *Austin*. The ability of a corporation to utilize a Political Action Committee as an alternative under the law for its electioneering was considered both too burdensome legally as well as too removed (because a PAC is a separate legal entity) to remedy this ban. The worry of corporate treasury funds being spent without consent on political positions that stockholders would not approve, therefore using stockholder's money in an improper manner, the Court brushed aside by a reference to procedures of corporate democracy.

The Court then stated, "We now conclude that independent expenditures, including those made by corporations, do not give rise to corruption or the appearance of corruption."[9] Furthermore, Kennedy asserted that "references to massive corporate treasuries should not mask the real operation of the law. Rhetoric ought not obscure reality."[10] Indeed, Kennedy asserted further that even if there is the appearance or actual access to representation through the use of money in elections, this "this will not cause the electorate to lose faith in our democracy," because "by definition an independent expenditure is political speech presented to the electorate that is not coordinated with a candidate."[11] The Court upheld, on the other hand, disclosure requirements arguing that these provide valuable information to the electorate.

Roberts's concurrence offered a slightly different type of argument— claiming that because the "text and purpose" of the First Amendment point the "same direction," therefore "Congress may not prohibit political speech, even if the speaker is a corporation or union."[12] Scalia's concurrence insisted that there was no historical evidence for the allowance of a distinction between speakers under the First Amendment. In fact, he claimed that such regulation was a significant departure from "ancient" First Amendment principles. But maybe most illustrative of Scalia's sympathies was the last line of his concurrence: "Indeed, to exclude or impede corporate speech is to muzzle the principle agents of the modern free economy. We should celebrate rather than condemn the addition of this speech to the public debate."[13] Finally, though he voted with the majority in finding the spending ban unconstitutional, Thomas dissented from the Court's other *Citizens United* finding that disclosure requirements in campaign finance did not chill speech on the grounds that disclosure invites harassment of those who fund unpopular views.

A dissent written by Justice Stevens argued that the majority's analysis was suspect on multiple grounds. Stevens noted that the majority had to go well beyond what the parties had claimed in their briefs or supported in the record to get to their decision. By doing this, he claimed, they not only ignored judicial values of only deciding real cases and controversies, but also made a decision uninformed by a fully developed record (indeed any real record on point at all). He also noted that if the majority really respected the factual basis of their claims they would have remanded to the lower court with the demand for a careful factual inquiry. Stevens thought that the fact that Court majority did not do this was especially worrisome because actual evidence is necessary to verify a real chill in speech as well as to not impede further "legislative experiments" aimed at constructing "democratic integrity."[14]

He also claimed that the majority ignored precedent and cobbled to-gether an opinion that mostly cited the earlier dissents of the various members of the new majority, thus showing that the only real change since *Austin* was a change in members of the Court rather than further factual information or law. In addition, Stevens claimed that the distinction between the speech of natural persons and artificial persons such as corporations is sig-nificant, because corporations are not actual members of society or citizens of "We the People," and cannot vote or run for office.

Stevens also noted that corporations can, due to favorable government legislation, represent great concentration of economic power. Because of this favored yet governmentally constructed position of the corporation in law, corporate speech should be seen as "derivative speech, speech by proxy."[15] In addition, he pointed out that it is unclear who is speaking when a corporation spends money on political communications. It is pre-sumably not the customers, shareholders or the workers that are speak-ing. And the officers and directors are legally obligated to not use corpo-rate money for personal interests. Further, Stevens highlighted the fact that it may be in the best interests of corporations to have these limits legislatively created because otherwise there may be an "escalating arms race" of corporate spending in elections. This escalation could ultimately act like an "election tax" in that corporations would need to spend in or-der to be favored or avoid retaliation after an election.[16]

Stevens also argued that only in a world of infinite time populated by creatures with perfect rationality would the assumption of the majority that more speech is always better speech make any sense. In the real world some speech can crowd out other speech both physically and cognitively. Finally, he pointed out that it is perfectly consistent with the history of American law to regulate corporations in relationship to political speech because the corporation in early American law had been a suspect form of association, and since the Tillman Act of 1907 (which banned all cor-porate contributions to candidates) regulation of campaign speech in re-lationship to corporate money has been accepted.

Critics Dissecting *Citizens United*

As stated at the beginning of this chapter, *Citizens United* is generally thought of as a recent Supreme Court antiprecedent. For instance, Chemerinsky certainly thinks it was wrongly decided. He believes that if nothing else the decision will raise the cost of elections. Further, he agrees with Stevens that there is a real worry of shareholder and union member money going to places they disagree with without their consent and doubts that democratic processes in the private realm will effectually remedy this. He also accepts the plausibility of the fear that highly funded commercial media will drown out less-funded citizen voices. In addition, he agrees that there is no need for corporations and individuals to have the same rights. He also accepts that there might be real distortion interests—for instance, a higher entry level to elections because of the large amounts of money necessary to compete could discourage and exclude some entrants and therefore create a type of chill on speech that the Court seems oblivious to.

Richard Posner also thinks that the *Citizens United* decision was unfortunate and even naive because it evaded the real corruption issue. For him tacit coordination between candidates and corporate advocacy is a genuine problem that the Court was wrong to claim to avoid through legal definition. And, like Chemerinsky, he worries that money differentials might drown out important voices. Furthermore, he claims that the "information addition argument" the Court uses for allowing additional corporate spending is not credible because "almost no information is conveyed by political advertising."[17] On the other hand, Gary Becker's response to Posner's post on the *Becker-Posner Blog* argued that regulating one area of campaign finance without being systematic about the issue just allows other entry areas, and therefore renders the law or the Court's decision questionable as to any real effect at all.

Epstein thinks *Citizens United* is correct. Strangely, he thinks it correct both in terms of First Amendment legal doctrine and in terms of what he calls a "pragmatic" perspective.[18] Even more strangely he allows that a populist take on the First Amendment is available and pulls against his own. Not surprisingly, though, he is once again sure his market-driven version is ultimately correct.

Epstein starts his analysis by allowing that in First Amendment jurisprudence the text does not solve many issues. For instance, he notes that "speech" means really "speech plus" in that is has come to include all kinds of expressive activity. But in the case of *Citizens United*, Epstein offers that this aspect of the analysis is easy because political speech is core-protected speech and the speech at issue was political and not rather of any of the categories of low or marginal speech.[19] So, the issue becomes whether or not there is a justification for regulating corporate advocacy in the realm of core First Amendment speech. For Epstein this brings him back to the classical police powers categories of health, safety, general welfare, or morals that we saw in his takings analysis and evaluation of *Lochner*. He finds none of these categories to be relevant. Therefore, the legislation must be evaluated specifically to its effects upon campaigns.

Epstein then deals with an argument offered by both Stevens and Dworkin—that because a corporation is a state-created entity it has no speech rights. Epstein argues that this is an example of argument that is disallowed because of the doctrine of "unconstitutional conditions." This doctrine holds that even if Congress has the power to allow or prohibit an activity, it cannot use this power to induce a party to waive its constitutional rights so as to be allowed to engage in the activity.[20]

Epstein agrees with Scalia that freedom of speech covers the right to association with others in order to speak together. Furthermore, he states, "the concept of a marketplace of ideas is that of a competitive market which in this context means one of free entry by any and all by whatever strategies or devices that they choose."[21] He even turns to *Lochner*. He starts with an example: "Forbidding individuals to hire labor at below minimum wage rates to distribute leaflets should fall to the First Amendment because such an effort abridges speech, by blocking the necessary and proper means for its realization." Then he notes, "In the earlier *Lochner v. New York* era, the broader protection of freedom of contract had as one of its collateral advantages the additional protection that it afforded to freedom of speech by precluding regulations that inhibited corporate speech, especially on political matters."[22]

His "pragmatic" analysis is offered next. First dealt with is the corruption argument. He thinks that mere "appearance of corruption" is ruled out of possible consideration because the heightened scrutiny that the Court used requires real corruption to even be legally cognizable. And turning to this, he finds no evidence of real corruption. He believes that evidence of corruption would be impossible to find because there is no plausible baseline from which to evaluate a purportedly corrupting influence. That is because changing peoples' ideas is the whole point of political speech.

As to the fear of corporate domination, Epstein thinks that not only are larger companies more at risk for victimization through regulatory retaliation and "milker bills" (bills that try to go after the deep pockets of large corporations via a type of legislative blackmail), but also that fiduciary duties to shareholders make corporate political contributions questionable and possibly a violation of board duties. Further, and perhaps most important, he believes that corporate advocacy of political issues not directly related to business matters risk losing customers and are therefore seen as undesirable by the companies themselves. If anything, Epstein claims that the decision will make unions stronger because they are more focused on their own issues and represent specific constituencies.[23] His conclusion is remarkably positive: "In the end, it is the citizens that will drown out the corporations, as if they wanted to speak, which they do not. Hysterical predictions of transformation are heavily overblown. It will be politics as usual, which is to say that it will be politics as it should be."[24]

In contrast to Epstein's positive analysis, Dworkin described *Citizens United* as a real mistake, indeed claiming in an article entitled "The Decision That Threatens Democracy," in *The New York Review of Books*, May 13, 2010, that the Court's conclusion returns the United States to "a constitutional stone age" driven by "right wing ideology."

But the strength of this conclusion is somewhat surprising given his jurisprudential theory. Looking at the theory as opposed to his own analysis of *Citizens United*, the result seems much more difficult to predict. As earlier explained, Dworkin, in order to analyze a constitutional issue, starts by imagining Hercules, the guardian of the Constitution, deciding the issue. The Constitution is seen as the ultimate "parent and guardian of democracy." Further, there is no recourse to conceptions of democracy outside of the Constitution because whatever the Constitution is in relationship to Hercules' best interpretation is what the word "democracy" means. Through principled and non-checkerboard reading of the law, Hercules constructs a picture of "law as integrity" founded upon principled foundations of communal or cooperative democracy.

It seems from this that Hercules would identify with the appeals to principle made by Kennedy in the majority opinion. The appeal to ancient ideas and the need for fit between precedents would be lauded. The majority members of the *Citizens United* Court certainly see themselves as being the final word upon the Constitution and how it structures the domain of U.S. democracy. Hercules might also agree that treating corporate speech differently than that of a natural person's speech seems too checkerboard to be principled. He might, on the other hand, think it rather checkerboard to treat the speech of fictitious creatures of law as the same as that of flesh and blood citizens.

As opposed to Scalia and Roberts, on the other hand, Dworkin is very suspicious of statements as to the obviousness of the text and purpose of

the First Amendment or the pretense of reading a literal categorical prohibition from one simple sentence as acting like an umpire calling balls
and strikes. Dworkin thinks a judge professing this, let alone a Supreme
Court justice, is either ignorant of the underlying interpretive assumptions determining the judge's own opinion or attempting to disguise a policy decision under false literalism. This is, of course, because for Dworkin
all judicial decision making is interpretive and therefore even the clearest
language is subject to interpretation. But, though interpretation is seen
as necessary, Dworkin notoriously holds to a "right answer thesis" that
claims that for any constitutional issue there is one right answer. In this,
once again, he is like the Court majority in the certainty felt that the Constitution has a determinant and univocal meaning.

Dworkin therefore cannot ultimately agree with Stevens's claim in the
dissent that the majority in *Citizens United* overreached, because practitioners of law as integrity do not value judicial restraint or humility nearly
as highly as they do the integrity of the whole system and getting to the
right answer. This is especially true because Hercules the judge is self-
consciously the ultimate moral protector of the Constitution and, therefore, of democratic values. Further, the dissent's talk of the need for a
more developed record of the facts and the need to allow for legislative
experiments in democratic integrity misunderstands the judge's role as
Dworkin would have it, which is that of guardian of principle, a role which
is not dependent upon the knowledge of specific facts as choices of policy
might necessitate. Worries such as that the decision might create an arms
race of corporate spending are difficult to reach within a purely moral
and principled decision because policy matters are, for Dworkin, thought
irrelevant, indeed anathema, to correct constitutional decision making.

Because the main issues for Dworkin are fit and principle, it is difficult
to know which side of the case Hercules would come down on. On the other
hand, there is no question of where Dworkin stands. In the previously
mentioned *New York Review of Books* article Dworkin stated: "The five
conservative justices, on their own initiative, at the request of no parties
to the suit, declared that corporations and unions have a constitutional
right to spend as much as they wish on television election commercials
specifically supporting or targeting particular candidates." But Dworkin
noted, since the 1907 Tillman Act it has been accepted that corporations
do not have same First Amendment rights as real people. So, therefore
the *Citizens United* majority not only overruled *Austin* and *McConnell*,
but they also repealed "a century of American history and tradition."

Furthermore, the decision "threatens an avalanche of negative political commercials financed by huge corporate wealth." And they already had, in his opinion, too much power.

He then went on to explain that the First Amendment "is drafted in the abstract language of political morality: it guarantees a 'right' of free speech but does not specify the dimensions of that right." To fill in the content requires "interpretation" and if that is "not to be arbitrary or purely partisan it must be guided by principle—by some theory of why speech deserves exemption from government regulation in principle. Otherwise the Constitution's language becomes only a meaningless mantra." Precedent is to be followed but what it means is also determined by theory. Therefore, constitutional interpretation necessarily must start with theoretical inquiry.

Dworkin then surveyed some possible theories. First, there is the need for an informed electorate and therefore as wide and diverse information as possible—the Holmes free marketplace of ideas possibility. The problem here for Dworkin is that corporations have no new ideas of their own, only ideas of managers who could broadcast them as individuals if an outlet through corporate means was not legally available. Therefore, no new information is added. Furthermore, the amplified nature of the doubled opinions of the managers (speaking as individuals and through their corporation) will be misleading. That is, though no new information will be added the purported importance of some information that would be already available will be emphasized possibly in a way that exaggerates and distorts. Plus, in this money-driven process some voices may be overwhelmed by others.

According to Dworkin a second theory of free speech protects "status, dignity, and moral development of individual citizens." He argues that these are not aspects of corporations or considerations that relate to corporate speech at all. A third theory aims at protecting honesty and transparency. Dworkin finds that the Court's ruling does not relate to this at all. But, on the other hand, the Court's ruling, he thinks, does tempt corporations to influence the political process through intimidation. Indeed, Dworkin notes that there was a "very substantial record of undue corporate influence laid before Congress when it adopted the BCRA." All in all, therefore, Dworkin finds *Citizens United* to be unjustifiable and a conservative Court's activist decision based upon simplistic political ideology.

An important analysis of *Citizens United* is found in Robert C. Post's, *Citizens Divided*.[25] Post thinks that majority and the dissent are talking at cross purposes. This is caused by, he claims, a tradition of convoluted First Amendment jurisprudence and justifications. Indeed, he argues that as the jurisprudence stands, campaign finance regulations cannot be reconciled with basic First Amendment principles. His purpose in *Citizens Divided*, therefore, is to construct a more consistent First Amendment framework that will clarify when the regulation of corporate expenditures on political issues is justified under the Constitution.

He starts with the position that the main aim of the First Amendment is "to make possible the value of self-government." This requires, in turn, "public trust that elections select officials who are responsive to public opinion" because "government regulations that maintain this trust advance the constitutional purpose of the First Amendment."[26]

His argument rests upon the claim that there are actually two forms of self-government that need to be acknowledged under the First Amendment. First, "republican representation" and, second, "democratic deliberation." These two forms of self-government have different requirements and different aims: First, "in republican representation, the value of self-determination is realized when the people elect representatives who govern. Second, in democratic deliberation, the value of self-determination is realized when the people actively participate in the formation of public opinion."[27] Therefore, the fundamental question becomes "how our republican tradition may be reconciled with our commitment to discursive democracy."[28]

To show the foundational quality of this framework, Post gives an overview of the history of conceptions of democracy in the United States. He characterizes representation as a democratic tool that is built upon suspicion of democracy. The vote, that is, has to be processed through a representative that is presumably better at making necessary political choices. Direct discursive democracy evolved later and represents more direct rule by public opinion. In republican representation there is the need for "representative integrity"—which is a proper relationship between representatives and constituents. Post argues that *Citizens United* ignores this and rests upon a particularly modern idea of discursive democracy as popular opinion that is omnipresent, always in the making, constantly active, and the real sovereign power while elections are seen rather as intermittent tools for decision making. The "ongoing process of ownership" is what Post labels "democratic legitimation."[29]

This discursive democracy version of democratic deliberation is awkward in relationship to campaign finance, because, "if participation in the ongoing formation of public opinion is to serve as a foundation for democratic self-government, all must have an equal right to participate in the communicative processes by which public opinion is formed."[30] Post claims that in *Citizens United* "the Court applied First Amendment doctrine as though it were a repository of abstract and categorical rules. Because the Court never asked what these rules are designed to accomplish, it could not begin to explain how discursive democracy might be connected to the representative integrity that campaign finance reform seeks to sustain."[31]

The logic of discursive democracy accepts that public opinion is always evolving, ongoing, etc.; therefore, the right to participate or opportunity to participate is essential. Democratic legitimation rests upon the belief that government is potentially responsive to the public's views. Lacking this, citizens are alienated and lack the important experience of ownership. In this, belief is central. That is, democratic legitimation rests upon the trust and confidence of the citizen. Vitally important to this conception of democratic legitimation is not a consensus on what government should do in specific substantive issues, but rather an "identification with *processes* of public opinion formation."[32]

Ultimately, then, given the requirements of discursive democracy, "First Amendment doctrine is structured on the premise that the value of self-governance is most likely to be realized if persons are free to participate in public discourse in the manner they believe will be most effective."[33] Preventing opportunities to participate is constitutionally suspect under this rationale and the Court was right to find regulation of corporate expenditures on electioneering worrisome.

Not only that, but the Court was also correct, according to Post, to find against the antidistortion argument. This is, as Epstein also argued, because in discursive democracy there is no baseline from which the true identity of the public can be identified and that can be used to judge the amount of distortion. Under the discursive democracy perspective, the public is always forming and reforming and never has a single identifiable location of identity. Indeed, "within the framework of discursive democracy, therefore, limiting speech to prevent distortion is equivalent to freezing public opinion and preventing it from changing in response to new ideas and new convictions."[34]

But there are proper limits even within discursive democracy when it comes to speech. First, public discourse is a "distinct and limited" type of speech. And with this Post starts to go at the central arguments of the majority in *Citizens United*: "The scope of public discourse is defined by the constitutional value of democratic legitimation. When democratic legitimation is not at issue in speech, the speech is not constitutionally classified as public discourse. The value of democratic legitimation applies to persons, not to things."[35] Given this principle, "because a corporation cannot experience the value of democratic legitimation, it does not possess an equal right to participate in public discourse."[36] Ultimately, corporate speech is information for persons, for citizens, and not an actual person speaking. Therefore, "at its core, First Amendment doctrine is designed to restrict government regulation of public discourse. By public discourse I refer to the participation of natural persons or their expressive associations in the formation of public opinion."[37]

Because under this analysis corporate speech is only justified as information for citizens and does not attach to a subject that cannot participate in speech from the individual citizen's subjective stance on matters of democratic legitimation, Post thinks a less demanding standard of protection should be allowed. This is especially important because for him this means that "chilling" is less worrisome with corporate speech. Post references *Red Lion Broadcasting* for the principle that it is the right of public and not broadcaster that is most important.[38] Therein, "the Court concluded as a matter of constitutional law that such orderly procedures would produce a more informed public than unregulated communicative laissez-faire."[39] This shows that there is legal precedent that some legal structure to speech opportunities can actually enhance bringing about an informed public. Therefore, "democratic legitimation is not at stake in the speech of ordinary commercial corporations. With regard to such speech, *Belotti* holds that the correct First Amendment value to adopt is that of informed public decision making."[40]

But, more centrally, there is the problem of how all of this this relates to representative democracy. For Post, if properly understood instead of a limit on First Amendment rights, campaign finance reform actually serves and enhances the right of representative democracy. Therefore, "to understand how the First Amendment ought to be applied in the context of campaign finance reform, we must theorize the relationship between discursive democracy, which the First Amendment protects, and representative government, which campaign finance reform seeks to preserve."[41]

He analogizes the project to the accepted space of "managerial authority" within which government may control speech for specific purposes of governmental institutions. Used in relationship to election process this would just require the legislature to show a functional need for the speech regulation. And this is not too difficult, claims Post, because "principles of 'equality of influence' and 'antidistortion' are required within representative government."[42]

Elections, that is, need to be responsive to public opinion. As he puts it, electoral integrity "requires that representatives be responsive to a public opinion whose contents they must in part construct and affect."[43] And here Post diagnoses a blind spot of the Court in that it has not responded to the issue of electoral integrity. Post thinks this is upon what campaign finance regulations should be founded. If it was, it would provide a firm "common ground" for evaluation of regulations.[44] A regulation therefore aiming to "ameliorate the widespread perception that elected representatives are responsive to personal and corporate wealth, but not to public opinion" would be acceptable if properly drafted due to the fact that "electoral integrity is a compelling government interest because without it Americans have no reason to exercise the communicative rights guaranteed by the First Amendment."[45]

This leads to another significant problem with *Citizens United*: "It seemed to imagine electoral integrity as a matter of law, rather than of fact."[46] This was Court hubris because "electoral integrity depends upon how Americans believe their elections actually work" and electoral integrity rests upon "relevant facts of the matter."[47]

Therefore, the current constitutional framework is flawed because the Court ignores the essential aspect of electoral integrity and this is something that is fundamental and central to First Amendment rights rather than balanced against them, and when the Court does acknowledge electoral integrity it incorrectly sees it as a matter of law, not of fact. Yet the issue necessarily requires a fact-based inquiry because the needs evolve with society. Further, 441(b) doesn't regulate public speech but only public information therefore strict scrutiny is inappropriate. And, once again, whether the statute hinders the informational function is an empirical fact. In addition, the speech of ordinary corporations could be regulated as is speech in the managerial domain. Finally, even if the regulation results in loss of information this needs to be set against any gain in electoral integrity. Post concludes, "The thesis of these lectures is that electoral integrity is equally essential to democratic legitimation as the integrity of public discourse. If this thesis is correct, it would follow that courts cannot apply strict scrutiny to protect the integrity of public discourse *at the expense* of electoral integrity."[48]

It is interesting that three important responses to Post's analysis emphasize the importance of a point that Post backs away from when confronted with the implications of his own claims. Frank Michelman largely accepts Post's analysis of the Court's strict scrutiny protocol and also sees the Court as practicing a manner of analysis that tries to review empirical fact as "a matter of law." Because Post's theory is so fact-dependent Michelman sees it as really a critique of the doctrine of strict scrutiny. As he puts it, "Post suggests it is exceptional for a case to turn on findings of facts of public opinion, but need or ought it to be so? Take the *Fisher* case, our paragon of strict scrutiny. Is the very strong presumptive intolerability of any and every racial classification a fixture in the heaven of legal concepts, as the Supreme Court (hubristically?) insists, or do we deal here with a contingent, contextually variable matter of intersubjective social fact?" Therefore, Michelman finds Post's analysis as best seen as a critique of legal formalism.[49]

Nadia Urbinati, in "Free Speech as the Citizen's Right," agrees with Post's analytical framework and postulates an essential "diarchy" in democracy between "will" and "opinion," that is, a diarchy between voting and forming and expressing opinions. As does Post, she argues that we need to protect both. But with Michelman she thinks that this is not to be solved as much through doctrine, or an historical analysis of the concepts, but rather that solutions will emerge from a process of trial and error. She emphasizes that it is crucial that "political representation must attend to the question of the *circumstances of opinion formation*."[50] Once again, this is a fact-based inquiry situated in specific context.

Fact-based analysis is also emphasized by Pamela S. Karlan's response to Post. In "Citizens Deflected: Electoral Integrity and Political Reform," Karlan argues much like Becker had that campaign finance as analyzed in *Citizens United* might better be seen as a symptom of a much bigger problem of institutional design. Therefore, by focusing on a specific symptom the overall problems could go unnoticed and the specific regulations be ineffectual. Further, she worries that as legal doctrine, the concept of "electoral integrity," because so subjective, could be used to justify very contestable regulations. For instance, she thinks the current Court could use this conceptual tool to actually undermine democratic participation.[51]

Perhaps the most direct analysis comes from Laurence Tribe. Interestingly, Tribe accepts the Court's decision in relationship to the specific facts of *Citizens United*. This is because barring a corporation from airing a political documentary near an election, even if better thought of as a feature-length political attack add, was a worrisome censorship of political speech. On the other hand, he thinks that the way that the *Citizens United* majority reached the decision—the reasoning process and legal methodology involved—was an aggressive application of libertarian political dogma.

The manner that this application was achieved required the Court to immensely broaden the issues from the specific facts, even though there were multiple other ways of deciding the case. He labels this Roberts Court tactic "opportunistic overreach." Tribe thinks that the Court is so attached to its one narrow libertarian vision that it does not properly recognize conflicting visions of free speech that foreground equality issues or alternative political views of democracy. Because of its habit of aggressive and opportunistic overreach, Tribe sees the Roberts Court as exhibiting "active vice" rather than the traditionally invoked legal practice of "passive virtue."[52]

But, if the radically activist nature of the opportunist overreach is bad, Tribe thinks the dogmatic application of libertarian views as the "official" theory of the Constitution is even worse. This renders the Court's majority unable to even notice alternative traditions of free speech within the law, such as a tradition that respects principles of "civic equality."[53] For Tribe this dogmatic blindness entrenched the Court on one side of "three dichotomies" found in campaign finance law: trusting versus skeptical views of democracy, "doctrinaire libertarian" versus other approaches to campaign finance law, and fully theorized views versus "incompletely theorized" approaches.[54]

Tribe believes it is not the Court's proper business to decide as philosopher-kings which specific theory of democracy is correct. Rather,

"how to understand the First Amendment, and deciding how it should blend libertarian, egalitarian, and democratic values, is among our most difficult constitutional questions. Yet the Court's majority, in its campaign finance jurisprudence, has treated as an easy (indeed, almost as a self-answering) question, with one set of values trumping all others. In so doing it has reached out to decide issues not squarely before it while implausibly downplaying and at times all but denying, the baleful corruption of American politics by means short of criminal bribery—by means that are lamentable precisely because they are lawful. Faced with weighty normative choices, the wiser path would be for the Court to answer only the narrow question it must resolve to decide the specific controversies presented to it, to be particularly attentive to empirical realities, and—

most of all—to avoid going "all in" on a single, highly contestable theory of democracy and of a single, uncompromisingly skeptical, orientation toward the motives and workings of the political branches."[55]

Democratic Experimentalism and Campaign Finance Regulation

So how would the issues raised in *Citizens United* be evaluated under the jurisprudence of democratic experimentalism? Kennedy's opinion for the majority started with a claim of judicial responsibility. That is, the justices were necessitated out of their duty to the Constitution to decide the issue. First Amendment speech, political speech, might be chilled because of the law and the Court is the ultimate interpreter and protector of constitutional right. Further, Kennedy wrote, the First Amendment was founded upon a mistrust of government, and therefore the presumption follows that there should be no viewpoint or speaker preference in speech legislation. As seen above, this reasoning is almost universally accepted, as it is in basic variations by Epstein, Tribe, and Post. All of it appears to follow quite naturally from the "enforcement of a basic framework" picture of the Constitution, of law, and of the necessity of judicial supremacy. It also is compatible with the save the people from their own excesses role for the Court.

Under democratic experimentalism the judges' duties are somewhat different because of a different conceptualization of the role for the Court. First, instead of a presumption of finding a once and for all categorical rule to set in place because of suspicion of government and a need for an unchanging framework, there is a prior aim at encouraging democratic processes and accountability. This presumption in favor of democracy goes all the way down (or up) to constitutional interpretation. That is, if a Court's interpretation of what the Constitution demands conflicts with that of a more democratically controlled branch, the democratically controlled branch's interpretation is held to be presumptively more legitimate unless strong evidence is available to contradict it.

The presumption, furthermore, is that the legal process under a democratic constitution is preeminently one of experimentation and collaboration rather than that of suspicion, policing, and limiting. A finding by the Court that suspicion and policing is warranted may be necessary given a lack of evidence or proper deliberation in the record before the Court. But this is not thought the default position but rather an unfortunate and

hopefully rare failure of the system. Furthermore, judicial intuition unsupported by empirical fact would not be thought enough to warrant such
judicial policing.

With this change in attitude there is not as much pressure to come to
an absolute position or to claim that one position among a set of available
options is clearly correct. Indeed, instead of starting with a default rule of
suspicion, the Court would look to evidence of democratic pedigree and
empirical effect first in order to evaluate the law. Both would be found
documented as far as possible in a properly constructed record from litigation in the lower courts. These courts would, of course, be encouraged
to create information-rich records that also document the deliberations
over purposes and possibilities driven by local publics. Given this emphasis, Stevens's dissent properly highlights how the Court's majority showed
a disdain for fact when it reached beyond the record available and forced
a decision with very little litigation, therefore limited factual data and an
incompletely developed record of legal analysis from the lower courts.

Given its picture of judicial responsibility and suspicion of legislative
regulation, the Court majority found that because of this potential chill of
core First Amendment speech, political speech, the evaluative standard of
strict scrutiny had to be applied. This meant that the legislation would be
found unconstitutional unless narrowly tailored to further a compelling
governmental interest.

Under democratic experimentalism, given the assumption that publics
are formed for specific issues and that localized knowledge and experimental information is key, if the doctrine of strict scrutiny were followed, both
the evaluation of compelling governmental interest and narrow tailoring
would be seen as fact intensive inquiries that also had to be rooted in knowledge of the specific context.

So, for instance, while corporate domination of small printing presses
in 1776 might not have been worrisome in relationship to electoral integrity, with the scale of modern corporations and modern media an analysis
based solely upon originalist assumptions, Scalia's "exclude in order to
bind" methodology, might be shown laughably ignorant of all the important factual issues involved. Even if a level of scrutiny analysis was accepted,
it would have to be pursued through resort to empirical evidence.

Michelman notes that the doctrinal acceptance of levels of scrutiny
seems to be a way for the Court to try to avoid dealing with the factual
aspects of the issue by artificially converting it into a seemingly legal distinction. He concludes that this renders the levels of scrutiny analysis itself suspect. The democratic experimentalism court sees the attempt to

convert factual analysis into legal dogma as an attempt to return to methods of fixing belief that try to exclude experimental inquiry and therefore resting upon ungrounded appeal to authority or intuition.

This is important to emphasize. For as Becker and Karlan both argued, the law and the Court's decision, whether proper or not, might have inconsequential effects because both were not systemic enough to discourage other routes for financing campaigns. Add to this that Epstein thought the decision ineffectual in that corporations do not want and would not use the First Amendment rights they were given because funding political stances not directly related to the corporation's financial interests risks losing customers and it seems easy to argue that the rush to protect hypothetically chilled corporate speech might have been premature. How does or would the Court know that the means were properly chosen, narrowly tailored, or the end proper to pursue, a compelling governmental interest, without an intensive fact-based investigation? If Becker, Karlan, or Epstein is correct then this raises doubt as to the purported urgent need for a categorical opinion required by the Court majority's picture of judicial responsibility.

For the issue to be properly evaluated under democratic experimentalism the record would be expected to have been well developed in multiple lower courts and therefore information-rich. Further, the justices' appeals to constitutional urgency would themselves have to be founded upon evidence rather than ungrounded intuition. That is, the record would have to offer at least some evidence other than legal hypotheticals that the issue is really an urgent one that the Court must face. Stevens was therefore correct to emphasize that because of the Court's broad ruling, the decision eliminated the possibility of legislative experiments aimed at increasing electoral integrity and possible further knowledge as to what type of campaign finance legislation might be effective for promoting democratic aims (and, of course, what legislation might actually chill political speech).

The *Citizens United* Court majority also found that there is no real antidistortion interest that could justify the regulation. It cited no evidence for or against this conclusion. Epstein argued that this was proper because there is no baseline from which to judge distortion. However, this just sets the problem to be solved because, as opposed to Epstein's analysis, which assumes a naturalized yet questionable "Lockean" baseline, under democratic experimentalism a court cannot assume any natural baseline. But questions don't end just because a neutral baseline cannot be identified. Under Deweyan pragmatism there are no such things to be found. All baselines are constructed for specific purposes and are therefore evaluable in terms of aims and consequence. Testable descriptions of distortion would be expected and evidence would be required, but here none is to be had.

Both the lack of antidistortion evidence and the importance of the corporate offerings for the marketplace of ideas can be disputed. For instance, the Court's picture of a robust "open marketplace of ideas" can be thought naive because of the real possibility of well-funded voices drowning out valuable but lesser funded perspectives. More specifically, Chemerinsky points out that eliminating the funding restrictions might actually raise the amount of money needed for basic entry level for candidates to elections, discouraging otherwise important entrants, therefore actually creating a chill on political speech. This is another possibility that would need a fact-based inquiry.

Indeed, the possibility of other potential market malfunctions seems not to have been emphasized enough in the majority opinion. For instance, both Stevens and Chemerinsky fear that eliminating the regulation might create an arms race of contributions out of proportion to any public benefit. Further, Posner thinks that there is a real corruption issue in tacit coordination between contributors and candidates and Dworkin thinks that the decision gives some people dual sources of advocacy and therefore could distort perceptions as to the real number of people holding a specific view and the strength with which they hold it. Dworkin also thinks that this doubling up doesn't add new information because the persons that utilize corporate funding for their political positions could fund electioneering privately instead and Posner thinks the information argument fails because there is no real information in political ads. Because it didn't face the argument but just evaded it, even doctrinally the Court's analysis of the antidistortion interest was a failure. If, as is more plausible, the antidistortion interest claim is a claim based upon facts and context, then the analysis is even more suspect.

Maybe most startling, and along the same lines, in the Court's opinion Kennedy found that as legally defined the electioneering activities regulated were independent expenditures. He concluded that because by definition they were independent of the candidate, the electorate would not lose confidence in the integrity of the elections.

This seems as if it cannot be solved through verbal definition and that rather evidence, not rhetoric, should control. A Court holding that certain social practices do not give rise to the appearance of corruption without any empirical data appears to be an example of the practice of conceptual hubris. Maybe not real corruption, but certainly the appearance of corruption is a matter of public perception and not something the Court can in any manner decide through judicial fiat.

Post, of course, finds the concept of electoral integrity a First Amendment value that might even require certain campaign finance limits. And these might include some regulation of campaign finance defined as "independent." Urbinati adds that truly protecting such a value would require legislators to attend to the factual circumstances of opinion formation. To a judge that expects to found conclusions upon empirical evidence, Kennedy's analysis looks like an attempt to understand and solve complex real-world issues with a priori verbal definitions—a naive belief in word magic justified through "the rule of law as a law of rules." How exactly could the public's confidence in electoral integrity—a subjective fact—be read off of a legal definition?

In addition, the possibility of corporations spending stockholder money on positions they would disagree with was also not seen as a worrisome issue for the Court because, Kennedy reasoned, stockholders could rely upon procedures of corporate democracy to protect them. This is also an empirical claim if it has any basis at all, but is offered by the Court with no evidence one way or the other.

And as to the other notable aspect of the opinion resting upon corporate organization—finding in some manner that corporations have speech rights, Stevens, Chemerinsky, and Post all found the fact that the Court dismissed or ignored important distinctions between corporations and "we the people" was indefensible.

A Deweyan analysis would see the Court's conflation of natural persons and artificial persons under the general category of "speakers" as a confusion caused by an analogical and historically accidental use of the word "person" by courts to help reason out earlier corporate cases. In other words, the majority fell into bad metaphysics through the (unconscious) assumption that using the same word entails meaning much the same thing. What should be emphasized instead are the actual ends in view. Corporations are functional social institutions (as is law) that are politically and legally engineered to bring about the best possible social results of specific and identifiable types with the least amount of waste. Therefore, they should be seen as subject to reengineering, including the creation of new limits, if changes can plausibly be thought to bring about more desirable social consequences for natural persons and democratic society.

All of this gives support to Tribe's description of the Court majority as practicing aggressive opportunistic overreach attached to libertarian political dogma resulting in the members of the Court majority ignoring alternative traditions and options and therefore treating a difficult case as easy due to judicial blindness. Indeed, it seems that *Citizens United* exhibits many of the vices of *Lochner*.

Of course there is no a priori guarantee that different corporate finance laws will actually inhibit or enhance the effectiveness of election speech. And only a person with a naive idea of neutral baselines from which to evaluate corporate campaign finance regulation—for instance, a stance necessarily ignoring the governmentally engineered aspects of modern corporate law in relationship to acquisition of investment capital, corporate governance, etc.—would be able to think that absence of regulation in the area of corporate political speech is government neutrality. But just because of this inability to appeal to (false) neutrality, courts practicing democratic experimentalism will have to decide each case in a manner that reserves as many options for the other branches to socially experiment with as possible. This is especially true when the record is sparse on fact as was that available to the *Citizens United* Court.

Stevens in his dissent properly emphasizes the need for facts and data, talks of legislative experiments, and seems quite wary of looking at the Supreme Court as the ultimate and properly inflexible word on the Constitution. Under democratic experimentalism the decision would be largely determined by forward-looking aims and goals. Precedent functions as important data, and as important determinants of social expectations, but does not come with any overriding moral obligation. And, once again, a jurisprudence of democratic experimentalism is not nearly as comfortable in placing the judge in the center of constitutional decision making as are members of the current Court.

Further, the jurisprudence would be cognizant of the shifting issues that create the need for various publics, and also be suspicious of any conception of "Law" supposedly able to structure a solution based upon thinking words not things, or to any supposed need for once-and-for-all rules. Therefore, the general trend would be to defer to more empirically effective and democratically sensitive branches of government unless there are strong reasons not to do so. Because of this, the mundane conclusion of this chapter is that under democratic experimentalism in the case of *Citizens United* the general position of the Court would be to defer to Congress and the FEC because of the lack of any real empirical evidence supporting the opposition's stance. On the other hand, the Court might use a narrower argument such as Tribe advocates for in order to allow the showing of *Hillary: The Movie* and encourage further localized experiments in order to develop a more fact-based record of the effects of the law. In any case, though, instead of a once and for all decision, the Court's opinion would be understood as always defeasible in light of further evidence.

CHAPTER SEVEN

Brown and *Obergefell*:
Two Positive Precedents?

E arlier on I had analyzed a set of cases, the majority of which were deemed antiprecedents. In this chapter I analyze two cases generally thought of as examples of the Supreme Court getting it at least substantively right. First will be the greatly celebrated example of the Court's moral leadership, *Brown v. Board of Education*. Second will be the recent case of *Obergefell v. Hodges* wherein the Court majority found a right to marriage for same-sex couples.

While *Brown* is sometimes disputed as to its constitutional foundations or its legal reasoning, it is quite difficult to find dissent as to its substantive result. And when the picture of the need for an antimajoritarian trump on democratic excess is challenged, *Brown* is certain to come up as exhibit number one in support of judicial supremacy.

On the other hand, it is too soon to know exactly what the general opinion on *Obergefell* will be. But it, like *Brown*, can be celebrated as the Court properly protecting the constitutional rights of a politically marginalized and traditionally discriminated against minority. Therefore, these two cases can be thought of as examples where what could be described as the "standard view" of judicial review under the Constitution, as exemplified in this book by Chemerinsky's analysis, is properly followed and at its most successful.

Brown and *Obergefell* are important to face. This is because it is one thing for the jurisprudence of democratic experimentalism to avoid the antiprecedents of American constitutional decisions. Indeed, the mundane result seen in the last chapter is welcome if the only other option is judicial hubris and ignorance. It is quite another thing for it to live up to the most successful examples of the Court protecting democratically attacked rights. When Court leadership is needed a mundane deference might indeed be judicial abdication or lack or moral courage. In this chapter I test the jurisprudence of democratic experimentalism against the reasoning and results of *Brown* and *Obergefell* in order to see whether and how it could have dealt with the pressing issues they involved.

Brown v. Board of Education

Brown overruled the "separate but equal" doctrine found in *Plessy v. Ferguson.*[1] *Plessy* involved a Louisiana statute had that required railways to separate whites and black passengers and provide "equal but separate accommodations for the white and colored races." In its opinion, the Court made a distinction between equality before the law and social equality, and then noted that separations between the races have been generally accepted as legitimate under state police power and do not "necessarily imply the inferiority of either race to the other." Therefore, it continued, "the enforced separation of the races, as applied to the internal commerce of the State, neither abridges the privileges or immunities of the colored man, derives him of his property without due process of law, nor denies him the equal protection of the laws within the meaning of the Fourteenth Amendment."[2] Ultimately the Court found Plessy's argument that the law denied him proper treatment to be based upon a "fallacy":

> We consider the fallacy of the plaintiff's argument to consist in the assumption that the enforced separation of the two races stamps the colored race with a badge of inferiority. If this be so, it is not by reason of anything found in the act, but solely because the colored race chooses to put that construction upon it. The argument necessarily assumes that if, as has been more than once the case and is not unlikely to be so again, the colored race should become the dominant power in the state legislature, and should enact a law in precisely similar terms, it would relegate the white race to an inferior position. We imagine that the white race, at least, would not acquiesce in that assumption. The argument also assumes that social prejudices may be overcome by legislation, and that equal rights cannot be secured to the negro except by an enforced commingling of the two races. We cannot accept this proposition. If the two races are to meet upon terms of social equality, it must be the results of natural affinities, a mutual appreciation of each other's merits, and a voluntary consent of individuals.[3]

Harlan vigorously dissented. He first noted that the law was clearly unjust but that it was a different question as to whether it was unconstitutional. He then noted that a railway is a common carrier and under the law "a sort of public office" and therefore the separation was not a merely a private action.

As to the majority's argument that separation was equal and therefore not an abridgment of rights he wrote, "Everyone knows that the statute in question had its origin in the purpose not so much to exclude white persons from railroad cars occupied by blacks as to exclude colored people from coaches occupied by or assigned to whites."[4] Because of this he argued that "in view of the Constitution, in the eye of the law, there is in this country no superior, dominant, ruling class of citizens. There is no caste here. Our Constitution is color blind, and neither knows nor tolerates classes among citizens."[5] The separate but equal doctrine allows forced segregation and is therefore unlawful because the Constitution does not "permit seeds of race hate to be placed under the sanction of law."[6]

Harlan's dissent was eloquent, but despite his critique the Court's 1896 *Plessy* decision became the framework within which white supremacy was justified in America until 1954 in *Brown v. Board of Education*—that is, fifty-eight years later, when enforced segregation was found inherently unequal by a unanimous Court.[7] *Brown* is commonly regarded and considered a landmark example of the United States Supreme Court protecting minority rights against the democratically expressed wishes of an oppressive majority. And there is no question that it was in its time a very unpopular decision among a large part of the population.

Warren's opinion in *Brown* is, at the very least, clear and concise. He started by describing the constitutional challenge: "Minors of the Negro race, through their legal representatives, seek the aid of the courts in obtaining admission to the public schools of their community on a nonsegregated basis."[8] Each had been denied admission to schools where whites attended "under laws requiring or permitting segregation according to race."[9] The plaintiffs alleged that segregation in public schooling deprive them of the equal protection of the laws under the Fourteenth Amendment. Warren explained that, "under that doctrine, equality of treatment is accorded when the races are provided substantially equal facilities, even though these facilities be separate."[10]

The Court's analysis first found the historical record of aims and intent for the adoption of the Fourteenth Amendment in 1868 inconclusive. Further, the Court noted that the change in status of public schooling in the

United States since its adoption added to the problem of analysis because the civic status of public schooling had expanded dramatically. Because of the inconclusiveness of historical evidence and the drastic change in the position of education in American public life, Warren explained, "we must consider public education in the light of its full development and its present place in American life throughout the Nation."[11] Therefore *Brown* is explicitly not an originalist opinion, but rather one that admits to changing circumstances and, therefore, changing demands of the Court and the Constitution. Warren found that at the time of *Brown* "education is perhaps the most important function of state and local governments," and then continued:

> Compulsory school attendance laws and the great expenditures for education both demonstrate our recognition of the importance of education to our democratic society. It is required in the performance of our most basic public responsibilities, even service in the armed forces. It is the very foundation of good citizenship. Today it is a principal instrument in awakening the child to cultural values, in preparing him for later professional training, and in helping him adjust normally to his environment. In these days, it is doubtful that any child may reasonably be expected to succeed in life if he is denied the support of an education. Such an opportunity, where the state has undertaken to provide it, is a right which must be made available to all on equal terms.[12]

Sweatt v. Painter had earlier found that separated law schools could not be equal because of "qualities which are incapable of objective measurement but which make for greatness in a law school."[13] (This reasoning was also followed the same day as *Sweatt* in *McLaurin v. Oklahoma State Regents.*)[14]

And Warren, continued, the "intangibles" are more important for students at earlier ages, indeed that "to separate them from others of similar age and qualifications solely because of their race generates a feeling of inferiority as to their status in the community that may affect their hearts and minds in a way unlikely ever to be undone."[15] Therefore, intentional segregation has significant effects upon a student's self-image and social opportunities. Importantly, the Court noted that the impact of segregation is greater when sanctioned by law because "the policy of separating the races is usually interpreted as denoting the inferiority of the Negro group."[16] Because of this the Court held that "in the field of public education, the doctrine of 'separate but equal' has no place. Separate educational facilities are inherently unequal. Therefore, we hold that the plaintiffs and others similarly situated for whom the actions have been brought are, by reason of the segregation complained of, deprived of the equal protection of the laws guaranteed by the Fourteenth Amendment."[17] The Court then scheduled further arguments to decide what the proper remedy would be.

After hearing the further arguments, Warren wrote *Brown v. Board of Education 2*. Therein the Court held that implementation of *Brown* should be adjustable to context. Because of the importance of local conditions, regional school authorities have "primary responsibility" for designing a proper integration plan. The same reasoning was accepted for judicial supervision, the conclusion being that the courts closest to schools can best perform proper appraisal of efforts. Lower courts were to be flexible, but were not to allow resistance.

While it was acknowledged that time would be needed for implementation, the Court stated that "the burden rests upon the defendants to establish that such time is necessary in the public interest and is consistent with good faith compliance at the earliest practicable date."[18] Therefore, the cases were remanded to the District Courts in order to bring about the elimination of segregated schools "with all deliberate speed."[19]

Much in *Brown* reflects important aspects of democratic experimentalism. Certainly the remedial order in *Brown 2* exemplifies a lot of the characteristics of democratic experimentalism. The emphasis upon context, flexibility, and local control is all perfectly compatible with the stance advocated here.[20] Missing in the remedial plan, though, is an essential aspect of the information-producing design of democratic experimentalism: an explicit use of benchmarking and, more generally, information pooling. The central aspect of information coordination from higher-level courts is lacking in the *Brown 2* decision.

This information pooling is quite important, because otherwise there is much less potential learning from the focus upon context and experimentation at the lower levels. That is, if there is no coordination between the results of the on the ground experimentation of lower-level courts there is much less opportunity to learn from their experiences. The coordination of the local results at a higher level is therefore properly emphasized as centrally important by many of the theorists working in the area of democratic experimentalism.

For instance, Archon Fung and Erik Olin Wright's variation on democratic experimentalism, "Empowered Participatory Governance," emphasizes the need for "coordinated decentralization," and Burkhard Eberlin emphasizes that recursive revision of plans needs monitoring and peer review of the experimentation attempted.[21] Perhaps Jane Mansbridge puts it best when she argues that the higher-level perspective tends to ignore the part, and the lower level tends to ignore interconnection and therefore what she calls "recombinant participatory democracy" is superior because "it introduces an interaction between levels of government that can be synergistic, creative, and mutually reinforcing."[22] Quite possibly if the Supreme Court had conceptualized its role as a coordinated center of information about lower-level experiments integration in schools could have been more successful.

On the face of it, the first *Brown* decision is much more of a challenge to democratic experimentalism. To better understand whether it really is such a challenge it is helpful to turn to Richard Kluger's epic, *Simple Justice: The History of Brown v. Board of Education and Black America's Struggle for Equality*.[23] A true masterpiece of contextual legal history, Kluger's work shows that *Brown* was the result of a bottom-up, localized quest by the NAACP to use the Court system to both opportunistically and systemically expose legally enforced systems of white supremacy.

His book is full of both interesting trivia, for example the fact that the terminology "all deliberate speed" in *Brown 2* was taken from Justice Frankfurter who himself adopted it from Holmes's 1918 case *Virginia v. West Virginia*, to much more significant and brilliant narratives of the lives of the people involved in the struggles that brought about the *Brown* decisions. His book is also alternately epic, hopeful, and, ultimately, tragic. The exposure of the legal strategies of racial disenfranchisement and harassment, of a Constitution that "politely included slavery" and a legal tradition where, "in the fundamental conflict between human rights and property rights that was implicit in the slave question, the men who cast the mold of basic national policy did not hesitate to select the latter" is devastating.[24] The book is also a great way to get a more nuanced understanding of *Brown* than just a reading of its economically worded decision.

For instance, is *Brown* really the finding of new rights by an activist Court? Is it an example of judicial supremacy and the proper and successful antimajoritarian constitutional policing of democratic excess as Chemerisky and others would have it? Kluger offers this statement in relationship to describing the Court as antimajoritarian moral leader: "In theory, this conception of a judicial breakwater against a tide of potentially rampaging masses was a reassuring one. But in practice the Court worked to institutionalize the hold of the past on the present."[25]

Though Kluger sees the Warren Court as in some ways an exception to this, he also notes that the Court has, ever since *Brown*, been returning to its reactionary ways. Indeed, real tragedy comes in his new chapter 27, "Visible Man: Fifty Years After *Brown*," published twenty-nine years after the original. Therein, the moral victory of *Brown* is described in much less successful terms and is placed in a later context where the Court is seen as at first being diligent in attempting to enforce equal treatment through desegregation and integration, but then as backpedaling through cases such as *Milliken v. Bradley*, *Bakke*, and *Bratz v. Bollinger* where faint-heartedness and a return to formalist analysis ignored the real-world implication of a legacy of white supremacy and racism in favor of the safety of textual analysis.

Judicial triumphalism is not, it is important to point out, the only plausible interpretation of *Brown* available. For instance, it might be claimed that the Warren Court was just undoing damage that an earlier Court did by ignoring the obvious aims and content of the Thirteenth, Fourteenth, and Fifteenth Amendments through legalist evasions. It was, that is, just the judicial undoing of *Plessy*, one of the great antiprecedents in United States Supreme Court History.

To see it not as ringing in anything new, but rather the overturning of the results of judicial supremacy in *Plessy* and the further eroding of democratically mandated constitutional rights in the *Slaughter-House Cases* and the *Civil Rights Cases* of 1883 is quite plausible. And in this case *Brown*, instead of an example of the Court doing what democracy could not, is actually just the Court rectifying its own previous obstruction of the content of constitutional amendments. The *Brown* Court was just overturning the *Plessy* Court's legalistic strategy of ignoring the empirical world and coming up with a priori legal fictions like a standard of "separate but equal" in the face of a tradition of white supremacy, slavery, and oppression of blacks.

This fixation on definition and abstract reasoning focused upon text rather than purpose and empirical context, of course, is exemplified in attempts to construct canons of construction and other formalist devices. Importantly, this type of formalism is not just exemplified in conservative legal thought. For instance, it is (in)famously used in Herbert Weschler's *Harvard Law Review* critique of *Brown*, "Toward Neutral Principles of Constitutional Law." Therein he noted that both sides are under separate but equal in some sense treated equally in that both are separated. He went on, "Given a situation where the state must practically chose between denying the association to those individuals who wish it or imposing it on those who would avoid it, is there a basis in neutral principles for holding that the Constitution demands that the claims for association should prevail?"[26] This is, plainly, a formalism that doesn't understand the implications of enforced segregation in a society based upon caste—and therefore a perverse and systematically blind use of the term "neutral." It is also an interpretive strategy that ignores social facts in favor of "pure" textual analysis.

What Kluger's book shows so clearly is that *Brown* was the result of a bottom-up incremental strategy of litigation adopted by the NAACP in order to expose the empirically obvious but textually avoided recognition of everyday legal enforcement of white supremacy and unequal treatment.

The litigation strategy started with the exposure of unequal access to buses, included attacks on the ubiquitous practice of all-white juries, moved on to the exposure of the multiple inequalities in educational resources, and focused upon graduate school access for strategic purposes (in that it was less threatening to white society as a whole and easier to prove under separate but equal when there was no facility at all for blacks).

As Kluger notes it took years of litigation to just to get out of the state courts.[27] And the bottom-up nature of the challenge actually gave the litigants the chance to develop a factually rich record and to accrue the experience that allowed their legal strategy to evolve. For example, early on the NAACP adopted the "Margold strategy"—that is, a strategy of attacking the "equal" part of separate but equal. This required localized litigation that was heavily fact-based. That litigation, in turn, encouraged a slow evolution to the legal claim that separate is inherently unequal that was ultimately accepted in *Brown*.

This evolution also required the courts to face more empirical evidence than is normal in a constitutional matter. The ultimate NAACP strategy, never fully endorsed by all of its own, was to not only emphasize the fact-based aspects of inequality, but also to incorporate and emphasize social science material. It is sadly telling that many of the lawyers on both sides thought that bringing in social science was "a luxury and irrelevant." Further, those described by Kluger as "legal purists" thought using the social science "something of a gimmick and perhaps beneath the dignity of the profession."[28]

The opposition argued that fact-based inquiry and the results of social sciences should not be included in the cases because the issue involved was "simply a question of law."[29] At its extreme, inclusion of such information would even be described by some participants on both sides as "unjudicial and illegal."[30] Of course the American legal tradition has the contrary precedent of the Brandeis brief wherein a more tradition legal argument is heavily supported by empirical data. But the import of this precedent is still uncertain and its use unpopular, and therefore still has an awkward place in law, where appeals to legal purity and the exclude in order to bind ideology is much more acceptable to its professional practitioners than a conception of law as needing to be information-rich or information-producing. Yet in spite of the pressure to keep the litigation focused upon the "law," *Brown* exemplifies a factually informed and science-rich constitutional law result.

Kluger's chapter, "The Doll Man and Other Experts," shows very clearly how important social science was to *Brown's* result. As the type of analysis offered by Weschler shows, a focus on "law proper" could find neutrality in separate but equal by ignoring empirical fact. Therefore, the NAACP strategy had to find a way to make the Court face social facts rather than legal definitions if there was to be any hope of success.

The disparity in school resources between races was important to document. Another important aim was to show that there is no factual (rational) basis for classification by race. That is, social science and empirical facts were used not only to show the physical and psychological effects of legally enforced segregation but also, and just as importantly, to show the equal learning potential of blacks and whites and therefore change the burden of proof over to the opposite side and force the segregationists to show the reasonable basis for racial restrictions on school admission.[31]

Ultimately doing a good amount of work in the *Brown* decision were the nine "Findings of Fact" from the lower court decision; including a finding that the sanction of law in segregation has real negative impact upon black children.[32] This all finds its place in the *Brown* decision in footnote # 11 that can be seen as "merely a list of seven works by contemporary social scientists" but rather should be seen as maybe the most important evidence in favor of the decision and as also, in its placement as a footnote, an admission of the uncomfortable place that fact and empirical evidence has in constitutional jurisprudence as traditionally conceptualized.

But even so, given all this, isn't *Brown* still an example of an antidemocratic Court protecting important rights from democratic prejudice? Well, as Dewey would have it, a public was formed that exposed the radical disparity between black and white schools. The public then evolved a communicative strategy and tasked multiple social and governmental institutions to advocate for its position.

The litigation strategy was, for instance, only one strategy the NAACP used in its project. (For instance the NAACP was also publishing the *Crisis* as an "organ of propaganda and defense" under the editorship of W. E. B. Du Bois.)[33] The Court, furthermore, was profoundly reluctant to enter the area of controversy and was only moved to do so because of the wide ranging bottom-up community organization work accomplished in the area. Further, if democracy is not to be seen as a mechanical contrivance or a counting of noses but rather as a system of government based upon a combination of equal respect for each individual and self-government, then the practice of white supremacy, even if reflected in elections, was profoundly anti-democratic.

As discussed earlier, Dewey's colleague James H. Tufts emphasized that equality and self-government were both key factors of democracy and ultimately concluded that the "finest and largest meaning of democracy is that all people should share as largely a possible in the best life" and that this is "a view not so much about government itself as about what government is for."[34]

Here the emphasis upon democracy as social before political is important. Harlan's appeal to color-blindness has been emphasized in legal thought because it appeals to the hope for neutral principles and formalist analysis. Maybe better emphasized and less amenable to such an analysis was his further statement that the Constitution would not "tolerate classes among citizens." This might be read as in some circumstances requiring active governmental intervention to dismantle caste and "seeds of race hate." Indeed, for his dissent to make sense the Supreme Court would have had to be able to see race as a social determinant of opportunities and power, otherwise separate but equal becomes perfectly plausible. To understand separate is unequal and see it as race, hate, and white supremacy takes more than thinking just words.

In addition to that, in democratic experimentalism the informational aspects of democracy must also be emphasized. The experimentalism side of democratic experimentalism requires replicable evidence for constitutional analysis. As the litigation experience leading up to *Brown* showed, indeed more clearly as every case went forward, the careful empirical evidence was overwhelmingly on the side of the challengers of segregation. Disparities in funding, qualifications, and access to social opportunities were all blatantly unequal. All those justifying segregation had on their side was an appeal to history and current attitudes of white society. That is, they had an intuition that the races would not successfully integrate and a feeling that it was undesirable. It was a case where the evidence for the losing side was only based upon what would be in Peirce's terminology the methods of authority and the a priori. That this ultimately unsupportable yet intuitively comfortable belief was ruthlessly and "righteously" enforced is also predicted by Peirce's analysis.

Given a Deweyan conception of democracy, *Brown* can be seen as a democratic result. Further, it exemplifies exactly what benchmarking combined with an emphasis upon lower-level experimentation can, at its best, encourage. There was litigation-driven knowledge pooling driven by a public that was experiencing negative externalities from the decisions of others within society. This knowledge pooling was then coordinated and benchmarked at the higher levels. Ultimately the process ended with a decision that "ratcheted up" in that it protected a public that had been discriminated against and did not take anything but unjust caste privilege from those that lost. That is, the only loss was to elements of white supremacy—and these elements were profoundly caste-based as well as exclusionary and therefore antidemocratic.

Further, under this description the Court was not activist. All that changed was that the Court asked for real evidence for why enforced separation should be allowed. But no real evidence was offered. Equality is democratic value, not something forced upon democracy. Wrongly conflating democracy with a mechanical vote is what makes this mistaken stance seem plausible. Of course all the strategies of disenfranchisement utilized by the privileged white caste show clearly how important voting is to democracy. But it does not follow from this that it is all there is to democracy.

Given this analysis it seems better to see the Court not as moral leader, but as clearing an area for greater democracy in light of overwhelming empirical evidence. As a jurisprudence of democratic experimentalism would require, the *Brown* Court's hand was properly forced, it did not morally lead except in a very attenuated form. Actually the Court was forced by the litigants on the side of desegregation to face facts, to be disciplined by the fact, as opposed to escaping into the unbounded freedom of textual analysis and formal reasoning.

Parents Involved

To see the Court's trajectory after *Brown* it is useful to look at the Court's recent *Parents Involved* decision.[35] The decision came after Kluger's added chapter showing the Court receding from *Brown* and returning to a more formalist approach, but it certainly fits that description. Importantly, not only does it show the Court's present direction in school desegregation, but it has also been tagged by Laurence Tribe and Joshua Matz as an important case to analyze because it may foreshadow the future direction of the Roberts Court more generally.[36]

Parents Involved, decided in 2007, was a plurality opinion written by Roberts (the plurality included Scalia, Thomas, and Alito). Kennedy concurred with the result of the decision but not with its reasoning. The case centered upon two public school districts, Seattle and Jefferson County, which had voluntarily adopted student assignment plans that relied in part on race to determine which school a student could attend. The legal question as framed by the plurality was "whether a public school that had not operated legally segregated schools or has been found to be unitary may choose to classify students by race and rely upon that classification in making school assignments."[37]

The Court started by noting that the Seattle school district had never operated segregated schools nor been subject to court-ordered desegregation. The district had voluntarily adopted an enrolment procedure wherein the incoming 9th graders ranked their preference for schools. The District used a set of tiebreakers if the first choice was full. First, the student followed a sibling if enrolled at a specific school. Second, if the school chosen was not within 10 percent of the districts white/nonwhite balance then the student would be assigned to a school where the assignment would help bring the school into balance. After that geographic proximity would be used. The Jefferson County district, in Louisville, Kentucky, did maintain a segregated school system until court-ordered desegregation. The order was dissolved in 2000 because of satisfactory integration. The Jefferson County plan voluntarily adopted since required schools to maintain a minimum 15 percent and maximum 50 percent black enrollment. Students would indicate their first and second choice. If a school had gone over or under the minimum or maximum a student that would contribute to the imbalance would not be assigned to that school. After assignment students could request transfer but could be denied on, among other reasons, those of race.

In the Court's plurality opinion, Roberts explained that when government uses racial classifications the action is analyzed under strict scrutiny review. This means, once again, that the action must be narrowly tailored to achieve a compelling government interest. In school cases Roberts described the Court as recognizing two interests as compelling. First, remedying effects of past intentional discrimination. Second, interest in student body diversity in higher education.[38] Diversity, importantly, was not about race alone but a variety of factors. Further, race could be only included as one factor in a process that was individualized and holistic. In the present case he noted that when race is used it is decisive in a nonindividualized and mechanical way.

Roberts argued that a key limitation of the diversity rationale as accepted by the Court was that it was allowed in the context of higher education.[39] Both of the school districts asserted interests in reducing racial concentration in specific schools as well as education and socialization interests. The plurality opinion did not ultimately decide as to the validity of the aims and results because it found that "the racial classifications employed by the districts are not narrowly tailored to the goal of achieving the educational and social benefits asserted to flow from racial diversity."[40]

According to Roberts there were available means that do not use racial classifications that could achieve the same goals. Further, the goals and the measurements were not narrowly tailored to the ends. "Here the racial balance the districts seek is a defined range set solely by reference to the demographics of the respective school districts." The real problem with the tools utilized by the districts was that "this working backward to achieve a particular type of racial balance, rather than working forward from some demonstration of the level of diversity that provides the benefits, is a fatal flaw under our existing precedent."[41]

He went on to explain that racial balancing as seen in these plans is close to racial proportionality which is not treating them individually. Allowing balancing would therefore get in the way of ultimately eliminating race as a governmental goal. In addition, "To the extent the objective is sufficient diversity so that students see fellow students as individuals rather than solely as members of a racial group, using means that treat students solely as members of a racial group is fundamentally at cross-purposes with that end."[42] Further, the school districts also did not show that they considered other methods to achieve these goals, especially race-neutral alternatives that could achieve the same end. And, possibly most important, "the distinction between segregation by state action and racial imbalance caused by other factors has been central to our jurisprudence," therefore without being justified by the need to remedy past governmental discrimination such programs are much more suspect.[43]

On top of these reasons Roberts also emphasized the institutional limitations of the Supreme Court. Allowing such programs, he argued, shows too much confidence in the Court's ability to distinguish good from harmful

uses of racial criteria and therefore judicial humility is in order. In conclusion, Roberts referenced *Brown* as holding that classification on race
denotes inferiority and then stated, "The way to stop discrimination on
the basis of race is to stop discriminating on the basis of race."[44]

Thomas wrote a concurrence that rested upon the distinction between
segregation and racial imbalance. According to him, segregation is deliberate school segregation on the basis of race. Racial imbalance, on the
other hand, is the failure of schools to meet the demographic makeup of
population. Thomas argued that racial imbalance is not unconstitutional
in and of itself. For him the Court only allows race-based categories if the
schools were segregated by law or to remedy past discrimination when the
state was responsible. Under his analysis neither district's plans fell under
these exceptions.

As with Roberts he argued that strict scrutiny applies to every racial
classification—including purportedly benign ones. Thomas rested his argument heavily upon Harlan's dissent in *Plessy* where the Constitution
was described as "color-blind." Indeed, Thomas argued that the dissent's
views on allowing race categories was the same as offered by the *Plessy*
majority "segregationists." This is because in their deference to local officials, practical consequences, local experience, community consultation,
and knowledge, "segregationists repeatedly cautioned the Court to consider practicalities and not to embrace too theoretical a view of the Fourteenth Amendment."[45] He concluded his analysis by stating that decisions
in this area should not rest upon "faddish social theories," and then stated,
"Beware of elites bearing racial theories."[46]

Kennedy concurred with the Court's result but not with Roberts's reasoning. He started by accepting the need, contra the plurality, to aspire
toward a racially diverse classroom, but noted as well that the solutions
must be lawful. As with Roberts he agreed that the racial classification
schemes of the two school districts were unconstitutional. On the other
hand, he would allow that diversity is a compelling educational goal under strict scrutiny. Here he claimed the tailoring of the programs was not
narrow enough. He wondered why the Seattle plan uses the crude white
versus non-white categories.

Because the issues are complex, Kennedy argued that racial categories can be used, but only with extreme caution. Further, he argued that
the plurality was too dismissive of diversity interests. Harlan's color-blind
Constitution is a noble aspiration, but, "in the real world, it is regrettable to say, it cannot be a universal constitutional principle."[47] Therefore

Kennedy would allow for race-conscious measures as long as they are not based upon mechanical typing. He concluded:

> This Nation has a moral and ethical obligation to fulfill its historic commitment to creating an integrated society that ensures equal opportunity for all its children. A compelling interest exists in avoiding racial isolation, an interest that a school district, in its discretion and expertise, may choose to pursue. Likewise, a district may consider it a compelling interest to achieve a diverse student population. Race may be one component of that diversity, but other demographic factors, plus special talents and needs, should also be considered. What the government is not permitted to do, absent a showing of necessity not made here, is to classify every student on the basis of race and to assign each of them to schools based on that classification.[48]

Stevens's dissent found Roberts's use of *Brown* in the plurality opinion to be cruelly ironic. He noted the lack of level playing field and that exclusions based upon race were historically only one direction. Because of this he argued that the use of strict scrutiny for racial classifications encouraging integration was a strategy the Court adopted in order to avoid seeing the obvious empirical facts about race in American society. His melancholy conclusion: "It is my firm conviction that no Member of the Court that I joined in 1975 would have agreed with today's decision."[49]

Breyer also dissented and was joined by Stevens, Souter, and Ginsburg. He argued that the public interest behind the school district policies was compelling and that the means chosen were narrowly tailored. Breyer referenced *Brown* and its evocation of the central importance of education in American society. He then claimed that under the Court's precedent of *Swann* that school authorities have broad discretion and might legitimately conclude that to prepare students to live in a pluralistic society each school could have a prescribed ratio of black to white students under the discretionary powers of the school districts. Breyer argued that this should be allowed especially in facing extensive educational experiments with various strategies. Indeed, he noted that there are newly arising needs for such programs because of the growing problem of resegregation in American society. Because solutions to the problem are complex he argued that a categorical ruling as the plurality would have it is inappropriate.

He cited evidence that both Seattle and Louisville were in fact highly segregated. Seattle was segregated in part because of school board policies and actions. Not only that, but even though there had not been a Court ordered desegregation plan there had been multiple challenges to seg-regated aspects of the district. These included a 1956 memo, a 1969 NAACP lawsuit, and resulting voluntary school board actions, and an-other NAACP complaint in 1977 that precipitated a formal settlement agreement. And, of course, Louisville's original plan was court-mandated remedial action.

Indeed, Breyer emphasized that the complex histories of each school district's integration efforts belie the false simplicity of any distinction be-tween purposeful segregation and simple racial imbalance. Further, both district plans offered significant reductions in the use of race as a decisive criteria compared with previously upheld cases.

He argued also that Court precedent allows use of race-conscious cri-teria to achieve positive race-related aims and that the strict scrutiny stan-dard can and should change when racial categories seek to include rather than exclude. Therefore, he would have it that in a context where the racial classification doesn't distribute goods normally distributed on merit and is in low supply, where the classification does not stigmatize or ex-clude, where it does not pit races against each other, does not burden one race but benefits all, and does not separate but brings people together, the classification can be analyzed with less suspicion. He also claimed that a lower standard of scrutiny follows when the plans are the results of broad experience, community consultation, and experimental learning.[50]

Finally, Breyer argued that the plurality found the policies not narrowly enough tailored without any example of a more narrowly tailored method that could work. Therefore, "the Constitution does not authorize judges to dictate solutions to these problems. Rather the Constitution creates a democratic political system through which the people themselves must to-gether find answers."[51] He concluded with an appeal to *Brown* as Court's "finest hour" where it helped move toward the promise of true equality, rather than resting in the realm of "fine words on paper."[52]

Parents Involved shows the Court plurality engaging in a clear return to the strategy of analysis exemplified in *Plessy* and forgetting the impor-tant lessons learned in *Brown*. Roberts's statement that "the way to stop discrimination on the basis of race is to stop discriminating on the basis of race" ignores all the social complexity of the matter in favor of a simplistic formalist slogan.

The Court acts as if a history of social and institutional racism instanti-ated deep in social habits could be solved through recitation of a formal tautology. Such a statement starkly shows the same type of formalist legal reasoning the *Plessy* Court used when it claimed that finding stigmatism in separate but equal was a "fallacy." Both moves ignore social fact in favor of textual evasion. The exhaustive litigation leading up to *Brown* forcefully punctured this type of pretension.

But empirical fact, unfortunately, still has an awkward relationship with constitutional law as conceptualized and practiced. Roberts's tautological statement seems to repeat the Plessy pretense of ruling complex social issues through appeal to verbal definition, thereby exemplifying and serving as evidence for Posner's observation that this style of interpretation attempts to think words, not things. But it is worse than that. It is really an attempt to use words to purposefully ignore urgent yet difficult issues. (On the other hand, Roberts's worry that using race-conscious means to construct a color-blind future strikes a Deweyan theme of using means consistent with ends and should not be discounted too casually.)

Thomas's easy distinction between segregation and racial imbalance ignores the causal construction of contemporary racial imbalance in the legal segregation of the past. Furthermore, his attempt to pin the segregationists in *Plessy* to the dissent's reasoning in *Parents Involved* fails because the one side was based upon enforcing caste through separation (with no reason other than caste to justify it) while the other side is attempting to overcome segregation and the remnants of past politically enforced social oppression. Finally, only by ignoring history and social fact could a justice find using the formalist tool of strict scrutiny equally on both types of law "neutral" rather than textual evasion and empirical absurdity.

Kennedy's concurrence is more flexible and less formalist—properly avoiding the categorical strictures so intuitively pleasing to the members of the plurality. He acknowledges the complexity of the issue and accepts the need for flexibility. On the other hand, there is very little empirical support for his acceptance of the claim that though the aim of diversity is compelling the means were not narrowly tailored enough. Here the democratic experimentalist Court's requirement of benchmarking actually could discipline his intuitions. What are the other options? If they were offered in the opinion with the evidence that they, indeed, did serve the purpose without invoking race, who could disagree? Of course without this showing Stevens would question the real usefulness of strict scrutiny as a doctrinal tool for any issue of this demonstrated complexity.

Finally, Breyer's dissent is both information-rich, in that he rooted his analysis in a much more careful description of the two districts, and flexible in its reasoning in that it offers a multi-factor (multi-stranded) analysis instead of a categorical stricture. To look at context, note the type of goods distributed, analyze whether the classification stigmatizes, excludes, or pits races against each other, see who it burdens and benefits is to get at some of the real issues involved. He also allowed that plans that are the results of broad experience, community consultation, and experimental learning should be given more deference.

Within the concurrence of Kennedy and the dissents of Stevens and especially that of Breyer, the components of a decision based upon democratic experimentalism are available, if only heeded. As things stand, though, if *Brown* showed many of the traits of democratic experimentalism, *Parents Involved* exhibits a turn away from empirical fact and toward formalist analysis in a manner very much reminiscent of *Plessy*. Is seems appropriate here to quote Du Bois who, a few years after *Plessy* and a little over fifty years before *Brown* in *The Souls of Black Folk* wrote, "We must not forget that most Americans answer all queries regarding the Negro *a priori*, and that the least that human courtesy can do is to listen to evidence."[53]

Obergefell

A very recent case that might be thought quite similar to *Brown* is *Obergefell v. Hodges*.[54] Therein a sharply divided Court found that a constitutional right to marriage included marriages of same-sex partners. Kennedy wrote the majority opinion. In it he started by explaining that "the Constitution promises liberty to all within its reach, a liberty that includes certain specific rights that allow persons, within a lawful realm, to define and express their identity."[55] Petitioners sought the Court to find that this liberty protected marriage between same-sex partners. In United States law, marriage had been traditionally a matter left to states and many states had defined marriage, and many still did, as between one man and one woman.

The Court reviewed two questions. First, whether the Fourteenth Amendment requires states to license marriages between two people of the same sex. Second, whether the Fourteenth Amendment requires a same-sex marriage licensed and performed in another state to be recognized in state that refuses such recognition.

Once these questions were outlined, the opinion continued, "The annals of human history reveal the transcendent importance of marriage."

Indeed, the Court found that marriage had from "across civilizations" from "the dawn of history" and over "millennia" embodied characteristics such as nobility and dignity, was sacred, offered "unique fulfilment," and was "essential to our most profound hopes and aspirations."[56]

But, the Court acknowledged, though marriage was ancient in origin and essentially important it had evolved as well. For instance, it had evolved from arranged marriages to those of personal commitment. And the status of women within marriage has evolved, therefore changing the legal rights that went with it. These changes, Kennedy noted, "worked deep transformations in its structure."[57] This, he explained, is to be celebrated in that "changed understandings of marriage are characteristic of a Nation where new dimensions of freedom become apparent to new generations, often through perspectives that begin in pleas or protests and then are considered in the political sphere and the judicial process."[58]

This the Court found was exactly the dynamic of society in relationship to its gay and lesbian citizens. Treatment of this group has evolved from them being considered criminal and immoral, and having an illness, to that of being respected and protected. This evolution toward inclusion and respect, of course, has legal implications in relationship to society's basic structure because marriage is such a central social institution. Therefore, "questions about the rights of gays and lesbians soon reached the courts, where the issue could be discussed in the formal discourse of the law."[59] Exemplifying this was the evolution from criminalization to protection in the Supreme Court cases from *Bowers v. Hardwick*, through *Romer v. Evans* to *Lawrence v. Texas*. In marriage the evolution is seen in the Supreme Judicial Court of Massachusetts's *Goodridge v. Department of Public Health* to *United States v. Windsor* where the Supreme Court found the DOMA unconstitutional.

The Court's analysis then turned to constitutional law: "Under the Due Process Clause of the Fourteenth Amendment, no State shall 'deprive any person of life, liberty, or property, without due process of law.'" As explained, the fundamental liberties protected by the Clause include most of the rights enumerated in the Bill of Rights. In addition, liberties protected extend to "certain personal choices central to individual dignity and autonomy, including intimate choices that define personal identity and beliefs."[60] This is because "the identification and protection of fundamental rights is an enduring part of the judicial duty to interpret the Constitution."[61]

Yet, Kennedy continued, the identification of these rights cannot be reduced to a formula. The Court, he explained, should use history and tradition as a source, but it also should use "reasoned judgment." The Court should respect history but "learn from it without allowing the past alone to rule the present."[62] Indeed, "the nature of injustice is that we may not always see it in our own times."[63] Because of this, "when new insight reveals discord between the Constitution's central protections and a received legal stricture, a claim to liberty must be addressed."[64] The Court found it is already established that the right to marry is protected by Constitution under the Due Process Clause. Therefore the question for the Court is whether or not this right includes same-sex couples.

The majority found four "principles and traditions" as the central reasons why marriage is a constitutionally protected right. First, the choice to marry is "inherent in the concept of individual autonomy."[65] Second, marriage "supports a two-person union unlike any other in its importance to the committed individuals."[66] Third, "it safeguards children and families and thus draws meaning from related rights of childrearing, procreation, and education."[67] Fourth, "marriage is a keystone of our social order."[68] In addition to the four principles and traditions, the Court also highlighted that marriage is a civil and public institution that comes with many legal implications. There are "over a thousand provisions of federal law" and these have important implications in the areas of (among others) taxation, inheritance and rules of intestate succession, hospital access and medical decision-making authority, adoption rights; the rights and benefits of survivors, campaign finance restrictions, compensation benefits and health insurance, and, importantly, child custody, support, and visitation rules. Because of being excluded from marriage, these benefits are lost to same-sex couples.

Indeed, this aspect was highlighted in the personal stories of the litigants that Kennedy featured at the beginning of the opinion. James Obergefell's partner, John Arthur, died from ALS. Though married in another state, Obergefell was not allowed by Ohio law to be listed as the surviving spouse in Arthur's death certificate. Co-plaintiffs April DeBoer and Jayne Rowse adopted three children together, but Michigan only allowed opposite-sex couples or individuals to adopt; DeBoer and Rowse could not share legal rights to the children. In emergencies only one would have rights, the other would be legally excluded. And Ijpe DeKoe and Thomas Kostura were married in New York. But in Tennessee their marriage was not recognized. Therefore their marriage had a legal status that varied, "returning and disappearing" as they changed states.[69]

Kennedy went on: "The limitation of marriage to opposite-sex couples may long have seemed natural and just, but its inconsistency with the central meaning of the fundamental right to marry is now manifest."[70] There is a history of wrongful and stigmatizing disapproval. In addition, the denial of marriage rights "works a grave and continuing harm." Therefore, the right to marriage includes same-sex couples.[71]

Kennedy then addressed the question of the Court's decision trumping democratic discourse, a critique the dissents were very insistent about. First, he noted that there had actually been a large amount of democratic deliberation and cited the many referenda, the extensive legislative debates, multiple campaigns, studies, and briefs as well as the exhaustive litigation (and attached a five-page list of cases as an appendix as evidence. The list showed that same-sex marriage had been decided upon thirteen times in United States Courts of Appeals, sixty-one times in United States District Courts and twenty-one times in a state's highest court).[72] He went on: "The Constitution contemplates that democracy is the appropriate process for change, so long as that process does not abridge fundamental rights."[73] If a fundamental right is involved, then the Constitution "withdraws" it from politics and establishes it as a legal principle applied by the Court. In the immediate case he explained that a delay would harm gays and lesbians that want to marry. On the other hand, those that argue against the right and offer as their reason the fear that this will harm the institution of marriage are described by the Court as having offered no evidence in support of the claim.

Kennedy finished his opinion with an emphatic concluding statement:

No union is more profound than marriage, for it embodies the highest ideals of love, fidelity, devotion, sacrifice, and family. In forming a marital union, two people become something greater than once they were. As some of the petitioners demonstrate, marriage embodies a love that may endure even past death. It would misunderstand these men and women to say they disrespect the idea of marriage. Their plea is that they do respect it, respect it so deeply that they seek to find its fulfillment for themselves. Their hope is not to be condemned to live in loneliness, excluded from one of civilization's oldest institutions. They ask for equal dignity in the eyes of the law. The Constitution grants them that right.[74]

Roberts dissented. In his dissent he first allowed that "petitioners make strong arguments rooted in social policy and considerations of fairness."[75] But he did not think this was the same as a constitutional argument, because "this Court is not a legislature," and, "under the Constitution, judges have power to say what the law is, not what it should be."[76] According to his reasoning, the Court was making a policy decision, and not a decision based upon law. He then asserted categorically that "the fundamental right to marry does not include a right to make a State change its definition of marriage. And a State's decision to maintain the meaning of marriage that has persisted in every culture throughout human history can hardly be called irrational."[77] Therefore, the Court's decision was an act of will rather than a legal judgment and had wrongly changed the definition of an institution that "has formed the basis of human society for millennia, for the Kalahari Bushmen and the Han Chinese, The Carthaginians and the Aztecs."[78]

This usurpation of democratic options was, in Roberts's view, the Court replicating the judicial vices of *Lochner*. That is, the Court was projecting its own economic, political, or moral conceptions on to the Constitution and not acting in a properly restrained or neutral manner. The real question for Roberts was what constitutes marriage and who gets to decide.

Roberts claimed that there is a "universal definition of marriage" centered in only one relationship—"the union of a man and a woman."[79] This definition follows from "the nature of things" and is based upon a "vital need," which is "ensuring that children are conceived by a mother and father committed to raising them in the stable conditions of a lifelong relationship."[80] Furthermore, he argued, the Constitution entrusted the definition of marriage to individual states. In turn, every state defined marriage in the "traditional, biologically rooted way."[81] He admitted that some aspects of marriage have changed, but these changes "did not, however, work any transformation in the core structure of marriage as the union between a man and a woman."[82] Until now, "the core meaning of marriage has endured."[83]

Roberts allowed that support for same-sex marriage had "democratic momentum." But, even so, this is not a sufficient reason for the issue to be constitutionalized. Once again, using the Due Process Clause to do so is, for him, indefensible. This is because "allowing unelected federal judges to select which unenumerated rights rank as 'fundamental' and to strike down state laws on the basis of that determination-raises obvious concerns about the judicial role."[84]

Roberts even invoked Holmes's dissent in *Lochner* and saw the Court as not acting with proper restraint and returning to the "unprincipled" approach of *Lochner*. His dissent continued, "Ultimately, only one precedent offers any support for the majority's methodology: *Lochner v. New York*, 198 U.S. 45."[85] Because there, just as in *Obergefell*, the Court converted naked policy preference into a fundamental right under the Due

Process Clause and trumped democratic process. Here he claimed that the Court appealed to a philosophically controversial idea, John Stuart Mill's "harm principle," rather than law. Roberts continued, "But a Justice's commission does not confer any special moral, philosophical, or social insight sufficient to justify imposing those perceptions on fellow citizens under the pretense of 'due process.' "[86]

Following the *Lochner* critique, Roberts returned to his basic argument: "The Court today not only overlooks our country's entire history and tradition but actively repudiates it, preferring to live only in the heady days of the here and now."[87] It allows itself this freedom because, he claimed, the analysis doesn't follow the usual casebook framework for equal protection cases. Furthermore, "in our democracy, debate about the content of the law is not an exhaustion requirement."[88] Indeed, he argued that when the Court jumps in too early, the action closes debate and sullies the opponents. A more modest and restrained role for Court is therefore required. He then concluded: "If you are among the many Americans-of whatever sexual orientation-who favor expanding same-sex marriage, by all means celebrate today's decision. Celebrate the achievement of a desired goal. Celebrate the opportunity for a new expression of commitment to a partner. Celebrate the availability of new benefits. But do not celebrate the Constitution. It had nothing to do with it."[89]

Scalia also dissented. He claimed his dissent was not about the substance of the law, of which he admitted he had little interest, but of the rule of an "unelected committee of nine."[90] As opposed to the Court's activity, he thought the public debate over same-sex marriage "displayed American democracy at its best. Individuals on both sides of the issue passionately, but respectfully, attempted to persuade their fellow citizens to accept their views."[91] On the other hand, under an originalist interpretation, marriage at time of Fourteenth Amendment was unanimously of one man to one woman. Therefore, for Scalia, "that resolves these cases."[92] Because it is not a constitutional right but rather a matter of democratic decision making, he believes that public debate should resolve the issue, not the Court. Indeed, he continued, "a system of government that makes the People subordinate to a committee of nine unelected lawyers does not deserve to be called a democracy."[93] He then repeated claims seen in Roberts's dissent; that the Court showed hubris and acted as legislators.

Thomas's dissent took a different tack and argued that the concept of liberty used by majority was not close to what it is in the Constitution. Constitutional liberty in his analysis is liberty from government, not entitlement to government benefits. The original concept of liberty, he explained, was really just freedom from physical restraint. He found that all the previous marriage cases were about prohibitions on private actions, not rights to entitlements. He argued against substantive due process because it "exalts judges at the expense of the People from whom they derive their authority."[94] He then described the Constitution as backstop for representative government at state level. One other fear he raised is that the Court's decision did not allow the repercussions for religious freedom to be fully understood.

Alito also dissented. He argued, as did the other dissenters, that the Constitution does not answer the question of same-sex marriage. He also sounded the democratic alarm and pointed to the importance of rooting the Court's jurisprudence in history. For Alito, the Court majority's finding of the main purpose of marriage in the well-being of the marrying partners was historically anachronistic. Traditional marriage, "for millennia," was rather linked to procreation in order "to encourage potentially procreative conduct to take place within a lasting unit."[95] States therefore could properly "worry that by officially abandoning the older understanding, they may contribute to marriage's further decay."[96]

He sounded a Burkean theme claiming that no one can predict the ramifications of the holding, and then continued that the Court's decision not only usurps right to democratic process but also marginalizes those with traditional ideals therefore hurting them. This he describes as some type of retaliation: "Recalling the harsh treatment of gays and lesbians in the past, some may think that turnabout is fair play. But if that sentiment prevails, the Nation will experience bitter and lasting wounds"[97] Ultimately, Alito concluded that the Court's lack of restraint will bring about "irremediable corruption of our legal culture's conception of constitutional interpretation."[98]

Obergefell is interesting in that, once again, it focuses attention upon the place of judicial review, and judicial supremacy, in a democracy. The dissents especially sounded the democratic note. For that reason, the analysis of the decision here will start with the dissents. The question asked will be, How do their arguments hold up under a critique informed by Deweyan democratic experimentalism? After that question is answered an *Obergefell* decision based upon democratic experimentalism will be constructed. Fortunately for this chapter much of the structure of what such a decision might look like has already been formulated in Posner's 2014 7th Circuit decision, *Baskin v. Bogan*.

Robert's dissent is interesting in respect to this book because he rested it upon a "core" definition of marriage that he offered as historically universal, as having "formed the basis of human society for millennia" and mixed that with a claim that the reasoning in *Obergefell* exhibited the vices of the great antiprecedent *Lochner*.

As to the first "essential core of marriage" argument, it is difficult to make much out of it. This is because Roberts does no more than attach marriage to claims of "the nature of things" and the welfare of children conceived by a mother and father. Roberts doesn't explain what evidence he uses to identify the nature of things, other than intuition and a very dubious appeal to history. And he doesn't seem to notice the welfare of children that might be adopted and raised in a family based upon a same-sex marriage. Why the child's welfare throughout childhood is essentially attached to the act of conception is not fully explained. Further, how same-sex marriage changes the "core," but allowing women property rights or eliminating the marital rape exemption doesn't, is not explained either.

His appeal to "the nature of things," of course, is one of the reasoning flaws identified in *Lochner*. That is, the majority in *Lochner* treated a theory they found intuitively neutral as if it were written in the nature of things. Holmes rightly called them out on this move—a naturalized concept (a concept that seems to attach to the nature of things but really is just an intuitively comfortable conclusion) is not necessarily true as an absolute natural type. Holmes would surely continue that certitude is not certainty.

Dewey is properly suspicious of such a definitional strategy as well and would refocus the inquiry upon the worldly results of any specific definition. If the welfare of children is a central issue, then Dewey would certainly expect that the Court would care enough to want to be informed as to what legal rule would really best ensure the welfare of children. An "essential core" definition eludes this more difficult task. Of course recourse to naturalistic conceptions of family is especially worrisome to anyone with a historical awareness of the many injustices that appeal to a priori ideas of marriage have justified. In this sense one understands Jane Addams's statement that often it has sometimes been the case that "the elements of tragedy lay in the narrowness of the father's mind."[99] Therefore, for her, the family is able to progress toward more democratic practices as well.[100]

Roberts also falls in to a second *Lochner* mistake. As Tribe describes it, the *Lochner* majority ignored the fact that they were making a choice by acting as if one answer was "the" meaning of the Constitution rather than one possible meaning among others. So when Roberts claims that the majority decision was policy, not law, and that the decision had "nothing to do" with the Constitution, he shows the same overconfidence and judicial hubris that the *Lochner* Court exemplified.

Of course Roberts might be correct that finding a marriage right for same-sex couples in the Constitution is worrisome. But, as with *Brown*, the question is what was lost because of the decision? It is pretty obvious what was gained for same-sex couples. But what exactly was lost? In *Lochner* what was lost was the possibility of broader protections for labor. And this is true whether or not the specific law in *Lochner* was justified. That is, the *Lochner* decision eliminated many possible legislative experiments in labor reform during a dramatically dynamic period in the American economy. In this sense it changed contracting abilities between parties. The law at issue was justified, rightly or wrongly, as a safety measure for the bakers. Nobody was told they could not contract at all—just beyond certain hourly amounts. In *Obergefell*, on the other hand, states were totally excluding a significant part of the population from marriage on what basis? A "core" definition? On the intuitions of hypothetical harms coming only from those doing the excluding? Neither of these grounds is anything more than an a priori appeal to prejudice.

This, of course, brings the analysis back to the Court trumping democratic process. But here, once again, democratic experimentalism offers two further resources for analysis. First, the experimentalism side demands that democratic process itself provide evidence for its conclusions. Second, Deweyan democracy demands much more out of society, politics, and law than the numerical tabulation or a winner-take-all election. It demands a democratic process that respects the parties to the debate, that is, aims at equality of opportunity as well as numerical superiority. Here, Roberts completely ignores the history of prejudice against gays and lesbians and the stigmatism and inequality in social and political treatment that exclusion from marriage entails.

Scalia's dissent also ignored this. His description of the public debate over same-sex marriage as a process that "displayed American democracy at its best" where people on both sides argued "passionately, but respectfully" in an attempt to persuade "their fellow citizens to accept their views" sounds plausible but ignores the harms suffered by members of one side of the debate and the lack of any concrete evidence for the fears animating the other side. Thomas's dissent at least didn't try to create a rosy picture of the "democratic" controversy or evade the draconian result of limiting constitutional liberty rights to original understandings.

But, of course, the virtue of Thomas's argument is that his obedience to originalism shows originalism's extremism to the point of absurdity.

And put next to Alito's dissent, Thomas's dissent highlights how extreme originalism can be as a "conservative" theory of the Constitution. Alito's Burkean analysis offers quite a different conservative analysis. Alito doesn't identify any unchanging core to be protected, but cautions that change should be slow in the face of lasting traditions. However, once again, all Alito can really do is appeal to unknown and uncertain hypothetical harms that might conceivably happen if same-sex couples are found to have a right to marry. This is contrasted with the obvious, important and present harms that same-sex couples were experiencing every day. To privilege the hypothetical harms postulated by the excluding group over the real observable harms being inflicted upon the excluded group reads as another example of words trumping reality. Finally, what Alito imagined as payback toward those arguing against same-sex couples having a right to marry is difficult to figure out. Does he imagine an attempt to outlaw opposite-sex marriages? Systemic legal oppression of heterosexuals? His worry in this area seems nothing short of absurd.

As to Kennedy's majority opinion, it combines wide-ranging rhetorical flourishes in much the way Roberts does, but with the opposite results. The "dawn of history" "transcendent importance" over a "millennia" is a little exaggerated. Indeed, in this sense it is interesting to contrast it with Warren's sober and confident wording in *Brown*.

That being said, Kennedy's description of American conceptions of law and justice as learning and evolving, becoming apparent to new generations, "often through perspectives that begin in pleas or protests and then are considered in the political sphere and the judicial process" sets a properly evolutionary and fallibilist tone compatible with democratic experimentalism.

But then by describing the evolution as one were when it gets to the courts, "where the issue could be discussed in the formal discourse of the law," the underlying formalist bias comes out. This formalist bias is, of course, uncomfortably combined with a conception of evolutionary learning. Therefore, Kennedy has recourse to "reasoned judgment." But what exactly constitutes reasoned judgment in this context is difficult to pin down.

Kennedy offered a four-part analysis as to why marriage is constitutionally protected; it is inherent in individual autonomy, uniquely supports two-person unions, safeguards children and families, and is a "keystone" of American social order. Furthermore, marriage gives legal rights and privileges unavailable otherwise. Kennedy then noted that the history of discrimination against gays and lesbians was now seen as unjustifiable and that continuing exclusion of same-sex couples from marriage allows continuing harms to be legally enforced.

As to the dissenters' universal outcry of the Court's trumping of democratic process he offered two justifications for deciding the issue: first, that democracy works within the limits of fundamental rights; and, second, that the issue had been extensively litigated so the reasons for and against were properly developed for the Court. Of course the exhaustive record does fit in with the jurisprudence of democratic experimentalism. Furthermore, a stranded or multi-factor analysis is much more in line with the theory advocated in this book as well. Even Kennedy's vocabulary of "withdrawing" a right from politics is permissible if combined with a caveat such as "withdrawn from politics and presumptively enforced pending substantial evidence to the contrary." The Court, that is, is never truly final because interpreting the Constitution is seen as a collaborative and evolving project. Otherwise, core definitions of constitutional rights and of marriage might have withdrawn from political remedy discriminatory aspects of earlier marriage law thought at the time timeless and unchanging.

It is informative to contrast the soaring rhetoric and morally charged reasoning in *Obergefell* with the sober and empirically based reasoning in Posner's earlier 2014 7th Circuit decision on the same subject, *Baskin v. Bogan*.[101]

Indiana and Wisconsin had appealed from lower court cases invalidating their bans on recognizing same-sex marriages. Posner argued that the case raised two main issues. First, discrimination against homosexuals. Second, the welfare of American children. The second was central because this was the reasoning both states offered for not recognizing or allowing same-sex marriages. That is, both states centered their arguments for justification of state regulation and support of heterosexual marriage on the need to discourage accidental births and encourage proper care of children.

Posner noted that under the Supreme Court's equal protection jurisprudence, and given the legal claim made in the state cases being analyzed, courts should not replace legislative judgment with their own, but must use a very deferential rational basis test. But even when rational basis analysis is used the court expects some reasons. If the classification proceeds "along suspect lines" or infringes fundamental rights, then an even higher standard of review is invoked. Suspect lines are found where legal discrimination is against a minority that has been historically discriminated against.

Instead of following the Supreme Court's legal terminology and conceptual framework verbatim, Posner's evaluation followed a cost/benefit standard. This alternate framework rested upon the following basic framework: if the law is found to be suspect, then it is presumptively unconstitutional unless a compelling showing of the benefits of law clearly outweigh harms to victims.

Posner's opinion then proceeded to avoid further discussion of what these types of scrutiny levels amount to by focusing on the arguments offered by states to see if the reasons they offered could first pass the lower rational basis test, indeed if there were any real reasons offered at all.

He formulated the analysis in terms of four questions. First, "does the challenged practice involve discrimination, rooted in a history of prejudice, against some identifiable group of persons, resulting in unequal treatment harmful to them?"[102] He found this incontrovertible because of the obvious historical discrimination. Second, is this unequal treatment based upon immutable characteristic that isn't relevant to participation in society? He answered this yes as well. Third, does the discrimination, even if the first two aspects are true confer important offsetting benefits on society as a whole? Here Posner found no offsetting benefits. One reason offered was that allowing same-sex marriage harms marriage itself as a social institution. Posner found the states could offer no real evidence as to the harm involved. Indeed, he found that there are indeed plenty of harms attached to the legal issues, but they all follow from the ban and accrue to those excluded. The ban results in stigmatism and legal and financial hardships for same-sex couples and their children. Posner then proceeded to reason that even if the third cost/benefit factor is acceptable the law might be over or underinclusive. That is, is it overinclusive because the benefits could be brought about with less harm to the group or underinclusive because the law could apply to other groups equally? Posner found the laws involved clearly underinclusive because the reasons offered for not recognizing same-sex marriage would apply equally to other marriages allowed in both states. For instance, both states allowed marriage between people unable to procreate because of old age.

Wisconsin offered three other arguments. The first was an argument from the importance of tradition. Posner responded that a tradition can be good or bad, and if it is clearly harmful and has no evidence of benefit to the contrary then it should not count as really a reason at all. The second argument was an appeal to unforeseen consequences. Posner didn't waste much time refuting this Alito or Burke-like stance but rather wrote that this was true of all Supreme Court decisions and therefore cuts both ways. The third argument was to democratic process. Here he responded that the purpose of constitutional law is to protect minorities, indeed that "minorities trampled on by the democratic process have recourse to the courts; the recourse is called constitutional law."[103]

Posner explained that he thought his unequal treatment framework was better than current Court doctrine because it focuses on costs and benefits rather than "fit." Fit as the Supreme Court uses it doesn't, indeed really cannot, notice the severity or importance of the harm inflicted. And this, of course, is a significant aspect of the issue of equal protection. Especially understanding of the tailoring of a law requires knowing what harms are involved. Indeed, why would the Court be worrying about the issues unless there were significant costs and/or benefits? Therefore, the problem with current Supreme Court doctrine is, as is often the case it seems, its own framework renders the Court unable to admit to looking at, or strategically allows the justices to actually not look at, the most important factors for making the decision.

Importantly, Posner's opinion in *Baskin v. Bogan* is notably clear of legal jargon. Once he is free of explaining the basic legal framework almost the whole opinion is based upon science-based sources for support of the cost-benefit analysis. Indeed, Posner's judicial reasoning in *Baskin v. Bogan* shows a clear preference toward empirical support over legal form. In this, his opinion exemplifies a jurisprudence that is disciplined, even bound, by fact rather than form.

Just like Warren's opinion in *Brown*, Posner's decision is sober, information-rich, direct, and does not turn to verbal definitions to decide fact-rich questions. Yes, this type of opinion does not allow great confidence that difficult constitutional cases can be decided in a casebook-style manner as Roberts expressly desired in *Obergefell*. But it is not the case that the decision is untethered, unlawful, impure, lawless, etc. Instead it is a careful opinion based upon looking at the distribution of legal burdens and benefits and judging the law in the face of how the known legal and empirical facts line up with the purported justification. This is just fine if a judge is conceived as a member of a cooperative enterprise in the ongoing construction of constitutional democracy rather than as a type of constitutional conceptual border police.

Furthermore, because the issue was decided upon equal protection grounds, Posner did not have to postulate a non-enumerated right under the Due Process Clause. Finally, under the equal protection claim it is virtually impossible to see the marriage ban as requiring and enforcing anything other than absolute inequality in that there wasn't even the possibility of a "separate but equal" evasion. One group had the right, the other group was absolutely excluded.

Because of this the rhetorical flourishes and high-sounding moralisms on both sides of *Obergefell* might have been avoided, thereby in turn avoiding or at least discouraging the ubiquitous claim of Court activism. All that the opinion really does is change which side of the issue faces the burden of proving the acceptability of the regulation. Certainly when one side is excluded from a desired good by another side that has that good shifting the burden of proof to those doing the excluding would be often justified. Instead of hoping for an a priori decision justifying each of the justice's a priori intuitions, a decent respect for the people involved and the known and knowable relevant facts should control.

Posner's opinion was bound by the harms and blatant inequalities involved in the marriage ban which, when all were braided together, weighed overwhelmingly in favor of a finding of unequal treatment. This was activist and unlawful only if dubious formalist hopes are allowed to trump the overwhelming empirical evidence. As with *Brown*, Posner's opinion in *Baskin v. Bogan* was forced by overwhelming fact. Once again, it is undemocratic to accept laws that enforce caste. Posner's opinion exemplified how using a jurisprudence of democratic experimentalism attached to the requirements of Deweyan democracy could arrive at the substantive if not the formal doctrinal result in *Obergefell*. It would be interesting indeed to see what arguments the dissenters in *Obergefell* could offer against this result.

CHAPTER EIGHT

From Social Contract Theory to Sociable Contract Theory

E ven if the jurisprudence of democratic experimentalism can successfully avoid justifying the results of Supreme Court antiprecedents
such as *Lochner* and would support the decisions that are thought successful such as *Brown*, isn't the Constitution a foundational contract that
sets up the basic ground rules within which democratic processes must
function? Further, wouldn't following the evolutionary, democratic, and
experimental aspects of democratic experimentalism be incompatible
with a political system built upon a written social contract?

This chapter offers a critique of standard contract doctrine and offers
an alternate conception of social contract theory, "sociable contract theory," that is compatible with the theory of Deweyan democratic experimentalism constitutional interpretation offered in this book. Indeed, both
the sociable or cooperative aspects of democracy and the idea of a social
contract as dynamic have been argued for before, however tentatively, by
some of Dewey's colleagues. James H. Tufts, for instance, emphasizes the
importance of cooperation in his book, *The Ethics of Cooperation*.[1] And
Frank J. Goodnow, in *Social Reform and the Constitution*, highlights the
fact that taking the idea of a social compact as static rather than dynamic
is not necessary but is rather a particular and contingent historical development.[2] It is also a theory that answers both the above questions in
a manner compatible both with democratic experimentalism and constitutional law.

The chapter will start by centering the critique on the philosophical theory of John Rawls. This is appropriate in part because Rawls's *Theory of Justice* has been the dominant text in contemporary political thought for over

forty years. It is also appropriate because his theory of justice as described
by Rawls himself is founded upon the social contract tradition.

Given the central import of contract in his analysis it is surprising how
little investigation of the concept of contract there has been in social contract and Rawls scholarship. It seems as if contract has often been taken
as a given, indeed maybe even as a natural type. To highlight this critical blind spot, I will emphasize the scholarship of Grant Gilmore, Ian R.
MacNeil, and the recent work of Ronald J. Gilson, Charles F. Sabel, and
Robert E. Scott. This scholarship challenges the idea that there is a non-
controversial conception of a contract.

The hope is that by questioning the notion that there is an easily identified core to the concept of contract and by noting some of the problems
with contract more focus will be put on the investigation of contract in
the context of social contract theory. I will then move on to constructing an alternative to social contract theory that might be called "sociable
contract theory." This theory differs from standard social contract theory
in that it encompasses some pragmatic themes such as the importance of
context, fallibilism, social learning, and experimentation. This quality of
the "sociable contract," in turn, shows how constitutional law can be conceptualized as compatible with democratic experimentalism.

Rawls's Contract

In *A Theory of Justice*, John Rawls aims to elaborate a systemic moral
conception of justice through the use of social contract theory. The centrality of social contract thought to the project is clearly stated in chapter 1 where he writes:

> My aim is to present a conception of justice which generalizes and carries to a
> higher level of abstraction the familiar theory of the social contract as found,
> say, in Locke, Rousseau, and Kant. In order to do this we are not to think of
> the original contract as one to enter a particular society or to set up a particular
> form of government. Rather, the guiding idea is that the principles of justice
> for the basic structure of society are the object of the original agreement. They
> are the principles that free and rational persons concerned to further their own
> interests would accept in an initial position of equality as defining the funda-
> mental terms of their association. These principles are to regulate all further
> agreements; they specify the kinds of social cooperation that can be entered

into and the forms of government that can be established. This way of regarding the principles of justice I shall call justice as fairness.[3]

He then reiterates the foundational aspect of his contractual project by describing the situation as where "a group of persons must decide once and for all what is to count among them as just and unjust."[4] Further, he explains that the idea of contract is important in that

> the merit of the contract terminology is that it conveys the idea that principles of justice may be conceived as principles that would be chosen by rational persons, and that in this way conceptions of justice may be explained and justified. The theory of justice is a part, perhaps the most significant part, of the theory of rational choice. Furthermore, principles of justice deal with conflicting claims upon the advantages won by social cooperation; they apply to the relations among several persons or groups. The word "contract" suggests this plurality as well as the condition that the appropriate division of advantages must be in accordance with principles acceptable to all parties. The condition of publicity for principles of justice is also connoted by the contract phraseology. Thus, if these principles are the outcomes of an agreement, citizens have a knowledge of the principles that others follow. It is characteristic of contract theories to stress the public nature of political principles. Finally, there is the long tradition of the contract doctrine. Expressing the tie with this line of thought helps to define ideas and accords with natural piety.[5]

These contract themes are repeated throughout his writings. For instance, in his *Collected Papers*, in the 1958 version of "Justice as Fairness" he states that "however mistaken the notion of the social contract may be as a history, and however far it may overreach itself as a general theory of social and political obligation, it does express, suitably interpreted, an essential part of the concept of justice."[6] In the 1968 article, "Distributive Justice: Some Addenda" he states that "the fundamental idea of the doctrine of the social contract, of which justice as fairness is simply an elaboration, is that this decision should be made in an initial contractual situation in which fair representation is given to each individual as a moral person."[7] In the same article he describes "the core of the contract view" as "the idea that since the essence of society is a plurality of distinct individuals, the plurality of persons must be conceived as choosing together before one another their common conception of justice."[8] And in "The Law of Peoples," social contract doctrine is described as "universal" in reach and therefore valid between peoples.[9]

It is unclear as to whether or not Rawls thinks social contract theory is based upon a literal use of contract or is rather a theory constructed upon analogy to contract. What is clear is that contract terminology is doing a lot of work for the Rawlsian system. Indeed, for Rawls at least the idea of contract was central to his project. And from the above sections it is possible to highlight some notable aspects of Rawls's description of the contract. It "conveys the idea" the principles of justice would be chosen by rational persons, facing a situation of conflicting claims yet where cooperation is advantageous. It also rests upon a proper division of advantages under conditions of publicity and shared knowledge. A central aspect is that the contract is foundational. From a carefully constructed original position persons decide "once and for all" upon a basic framework of justice that determines the rules for all further transactions in their society. The concept of justice offered is non-changing, and new, perhaps unimagined aspects of future human society do not and it seems cannot essentially change the concept of justice or the framework derived from it. This means the concept is clearly non-evolutionary. (So are and must be, it seems, his conceptions of the person, rationality, etc., which must be settled on in advance in order to perform their function.) Therefore, the system rests upon an analytical framework that does not change radically given a new context, a new invention, or any type of incremental learning. Majority rule, indeed any democratic choice, is completely and "once and for all" constrained.[10]

What Is a Contract?

Because some conception of contract is central and indeed foundational to the Rawlsian project, and to much other theorizing on constitutional law as well, it would seem imperative to investigate the concept in order to see if it can properly carry the analytical load required of it. Perhaps a good place to start when trying to understand contract is in legal thought. Surely with multiple hundreds of contracts classes being taught to 1Ls every year in law school there is some clarity on the nature of contract.

What exactly are the essential elements of a contract? This is not as easy to answer as it might be thought. In *Introduction to the Law of Contract*, P. S. Atiyah states, "Broadly speaking, the law of contract is that part of the law which deals with obligations which are self-imposed." Therefore, as in Rawls's theory, some type of consent is central. But Atiyah immediately hedges this in the same paragraph noting that in reality "many of the obligations recognized by the law of contract cannot be realistically thought of as self-imposed.[11]

That the basic aspects of contract are not as simple as hoped for may explain the fact that Atiyah's introduction to contract is 495 pages long. Oliver Wendell Holmes Jr's investigation of contract in *The Common Law* is just a tiny bit under one hundred pages so in sheer bulk if nothing else is much more concise than Atiyah. Holmes sees modern contract as embodying the great move from subjective to objective perhaps better than any other area of law. Indeed, for him contract can be summed up simply as a legal event having the necessary elements of promise, acceptance and consideration (consideration being normally thought of as a benefit conferred or burden incurred but also thought of as more a requirement of evidence).[12] If these three simple elements are objectively present, as judged from the parties' "overt" behavior reasonably construed, then there is a legally enforceable contract. By legally enforceable what is meant is that either the parties perform the contract as made or breach and pay damages, specific performance being a very rare and undesirable exception.[13]

Grant Gilmore in *The Death of Contract* offers an analysis of the concept of contract that would suggest that Holmes's idea of contract is an artificial construct and that the real area of contract law has no essential core to it. Indeed, according to him, "the common law had done very nicely for several centuries without anyone realizing that there was such a thing as the law of contracts."[14] Gilmore attributes the formal qualities of modern contract law to some of the most important of American legal theorists; Langdell, Williston, Corbin and, of course, Holmes. But he notes that belief in contract as a legal concept that could be given any formal coherence was brief and disintegrating by the time of Corbin's treatise on contracts in 1950. Gilmore explains this disintegration as caused by the fact that the classical idea of contract was "a theoretical construct which, having little or nothing to do with the real world, would not—or could not—change as the real world changed."[15]

In his analysis Gilmore notes that contract was the subject matter of the first casebook, that authored by Christopher Columbus Langdell. Of course, Langdell is the paradigmatic legal formalist. Gilmore characterizes Langdell's take on contract as "dogmatic rather than reasoned."[16] But ultimately it is claimed that Langdell "did little more than launch the idea that there was—or should be—such a thing as a general theory of contract. The theory itself was pieced together by his successors."[17] Gilmore calls the finished conception of contract from this tradition "the Holmes-Williston construct" thereby highlighting those he thought most responsible for the theory.

Gilmore further describes the concept of contract offered by these legal greats, and in this he mostly credits Holmes, as largely designed to reduce social liability between persons. Under this construct, which is based upon the idea of only two possible legal results, either performance or payment of damages, courts enforcing the contract act as detached referees instead of using concepts of equity, fairness or the like. Individuals, in turn, get to pursue their own specific interests with a minimum of social interference.

Gilmore argues that this theory of contract was attached to, and reflected, "liberal" liassez-faire economic theory. Because of this, he thought that from the perspective of his time, 1974, that "as we look back on the nineteenth century theories, we are struck most of all, I think, by the narrow scope of social duty which they implicitly assumed."[18] In his later 1977 work, *The Ages of American Law*, Gilmore notes that the infamous formalist conservative Supreme Court of the early twentieth century, now often known as the *Lochner* Court, used this narrow picture of contract to strike down social legislation. As he characterizes the Court's reasoning, "if a ten year old child wants to work twelve hours a day in a textile mill, by what warrant is the legislature empowered to deprive the child's parents of their right to enter into such a contract on his behalf?"[19]

But Gilmore is less worried about the narrow picture of social duty the theory rests upon than he is of the extreme formalism of the construct. For him, "the basic idea of the Langdellian revolution seems to have been that there really is such a thing as the one true rule of law, universal and unchanging, always and everywhere the same—a sort of mystical absolute."[20] And, the mystical absolute of the "Langdellian revolution" was best seen in one area: "For a riot of pure doctrine, nothing could have been better than Contract."[21] Yet, unfortunately for the Langdell legal world, "the general theory of contract was never as neat and tidy and all-of-a-piece in the real world as it was made to appear in casebook and treatise and Restatement." Indeed, "the apparent unity of doctrine was achieved through what might be called an extremely selective handling of the case material."[22]

The Holmes-Williston theory of contract was, according to Gilmore, an "ivory tower abstraction" whose "natural habitat was law schools."[23] Further, it was a product of an irrational faith in the eternal truths of the legal categories of their time.[24] But, "the trouble was that businessmen, adapting to changing circumstance, kept doing things differently."[25] For Gilmore, investigation of "case law undergrounds" shows a much less univocal situation. Courts have moved away from formalism and to various alternate constructions in order to, ironically in the context of this chapter, "promote the ends of justice."[26] Gilmore argues that contract as a legal concept is being reabsorbed into tort and suggests that this might create a subject called "contort." Ultimately, though, his real conclusion is that contract is a concept with anything but a clear and uncontroversial content. And though the formalist ideal was popular, it failed in practice. Hence, the death of contract.

This story is supported and enriched by Ian MacNeil's *The New Social Contract: An Inquiry into Modern Contractual Relations*. MacNeil starts, somewhat humorously, with a state of nature theory in which he treats social organization as necessarily prior and foundational to a theory of contract. This, of course, is in direct contrast to the standard social contract tradition that uses a contract to escape from the state of nature as variously construed. As he puts it in his origin story, "in the beginning was society." But this is, he claims, a "forgotten fact" or "lapse of memory we deliberately impose" because of "our heroin-like addiction to discrete transactions." But, he continues, "surely it is some kind of madness . . . to carve out of the body of society its economic heart, yet to expect to examine it as an independent and functioning organ."[27] He emphasizes to the contrary that "contract without social structure and stability is . . . rationally unthinkable" and that the "fundamental root, the base of contract is society."[28]

While ignoring the context necessary for contracting is very problematic for MacNeil, he thinks an even worse distortion comes from thinking of contract as limited to the notion of legally enforced promise. The problem here is that according to him "in many circumstances promise is neither the most effective nor the most important exchange-projector in contractual relations."[29] In his conception of contract, instead of promise determining exchange, factors more determinant might be at various times and in different contexts, such things as positions in a bureaucracy, custom, status, habit, or even previous contracting and markets which then serve to validate expectations that similar exchanges will occur in the future.

MacNeil is particularly motivated to disabuse contract theorists from privileging so-called discrete contracting as the central case of contract. A discrete contract is one in which no relation exists between the parties apart from the simple exchange of goods. Its paradigm, according to

MacNeil, is the transaction of neoclassical microeconomics. But for him it is important to note that "every contract, even such a theoretical transaction, involves relations apart from the exchange of goods itself. Thus every contract is necessarily partially a relational contract, that is, one involving relations other than a discrete exchange."[30] Given this fact it is seen that "the discrete transaction is *entirely* fictional."[31] This is because "even the purest discrete model necessarily does postulate a social matrix. It must provide at a minimum: (1) a means of communication understandable to both parties; (2) a system of order so that the parties exchange instead of trying to kill and steal; (3) in typical modern application, a system of money; and finally (4) in the case of exchanges promised, an effective mechanism to enforce promises."[32] MacNeil then highlights that, "in the purest of discrete transactions, those of neoclassical microeconomics, we have a kind of neutral external god providing these social benefits for no apparent reason and demanding no return."[33]

This costless external god regulating the contract is, of course, a somewhat metaphysical requirement necessary for the ideal discrete contract to function. But there are many more such assumptions animating this conceptual universe of discrete contract. Some further assumptions that he identifies are the following: discrete transactions are "nonprimary relations," they "involve only a small part of the personality," are "very limited in scope," they are "nonunique in personal terms," the "communications are limited" and "formal."[34] Further, in this contract universe, "no contractual solidarity exists except for that external god providing social stability, enforcement of promises, and other basic requirements."[35] If there is a breach then the costless external god enforces the remedy (all the results having been previously agreed upon).

Importantly, all issues in the contract have been brought into the present—indeed the all-important task for a discrete contract is to "presentiate."[36] This is because in the truly discrete contract all planning is necessarily done in advance and therefore no future cooperation beyond the explicit terms of the contract is required, all contingencies have been planned for and both benefits and burdens are fully allocated by contract and obligation only comes from the promises. Finally, each party to the contract enters for purely selfish reasons therefore "the discrete transaction tends to focus on the divisiveness and selfishness inherent in exchange."[37]

Of course this concept of contract is absolutely artificial. It is, therefore, an example of "ideal theory" if there ever was one. Real contracts, MacNeil emphasizes, tend to be more relational, involve large numbers of people and range over a longer time frame. Contracts indeed need high levels of specificity. But they also need to instill relational patterns and flexibility.

Further, sources of contractual solidarity are both internal and external and encompass "complex webs of interdependence."[38] When planning there is the constant factor that much is not easy to make discrete. Instead, often focus is less on "substance" of exchange as on "planning the structures and processes."[39] Because of the relational aspects, "tacit assumptions abound."

Finally, changes must be dealt with mutually. This often includes sharing and dividing benefits and burdens. If one of the desired aspects of contract is its discreteness, this is often lost because in relational contracts (which all contracts are to a greater or lesser extent), "many of the factors found in relations—for example, the need for future cooperation—create high levels of interdependence in which the interests of each party become the interests of other parties."[40] In this picture, not all aspects of the contract can be presentiated. And because interdependent relationships create dependence, power becomes a greater issue. Further, this issue of power is not one that can be solved in a presentiated manner because it is essentially a dynamic and changing type of power.

When looking to the social context, MacNeil sees the contract resting, as shown in his originating story above, upon prior prescriptive social norms or standards of conduct. Contract itself will change in different contexts and cultures. Conceptions and practices of contract must be fitted to the society it is practiced within. Many of these social practices and norms "put boundaries on power."[41] These include limits on the power of government and that of contract. Indeed, for him legal or state power is not always the top in social importance. More important than government in many cases are "custom, socially reinforced habit, morality, a host of institutional behavioral patterns, and the like."[42]

This is not to say that what MacNeil calls common contract norms cannot change previously existing social attitudes. Norms can "emerge from the patterns of basic contractual behavior."[43] For instance, role integrity as a technique of social control is seen as common to contracting practices. This is because expectations of role integrity are useful as an attempt to reduce conflicts between short term and long term goals. Contracting norms also rest upon a type of mutuality in that all agree there are mutual gains but there must also be a decision as to how such gains will be divided.

Another norm is the "effectuation of consent." As MacNeil describes this, "classical contract law . . . endeavored to bring all the relation within the realm of consent. It did this through stretching the term . . . and through an imaginative array of fictions."[44] Really in modern contract he believes consent only plays a "triggering role." But in any case it is still a norm that comes with the practice of contracting. And, finally, another important set of norms relate to the creation and restraint of power. Indeed, "the very ideas of consent, of contractual planning, of contractual solidarity, and of the linking norms, all presuppose ability to create changes in power relations."[45] So as with the social contract, legal contracts are about both the creation of power and its limitation and therefore bring in tow norms about how such power functions.

But given the complexity of contracts in the real world, why does the idealization of the discrete contract still remain intuitively plausible? For MacNeil, this is because the discrete picture of contract focuses upon two of common contract norms; "implementation of planning and effectuation of consent."[46] These are important goals but focusing upon them to the detriment of all the others is distorting to the understanding of the actual practice of contracting. Actually, "even the simplest transactions go far beyond the capacity of bounded rationality to encompass everything in one grand moment of consent."[47]

MacNeil then asks, "What explains its success . . . particularly in capturing Western economic and social thinking?"[48] His response is that it offers a very seductive image of precision. But he finds this image of precision to be quite dangerous. This is because due to the idealization of consent, precision and discreteness, when discrete and relational issues conflict there is no theory available that is able to notice the relational aspects. The discrete assumptions occupy the whole theoretical field and distort theoretical understanding of the contractual domain.

Finally, the work on contract by Ronald J. Gilson, Charles F. Sabel, and Robert E. Scott have developed in three recent articles echoes and adds to the results of Gilmore and MacNeil. Gilson, Sabel, and Scott's version of contract is first offered in "Contracting for Innovation: Vertical Disintegration and Interfirm Collaboration." These authors are less concerned than Gilmore or MacNeil are with critiquing classical ideas of contract and more focused upon contemporary needs of contracting. But, though they are not as interested in critiquing classical ideas of contract, an underlying claim motivating their work is that with the unavoidable systemic uncertainty in contemporary business practices, traditional ideas of contract are unhelpful and sometimes obstructive (this is especially true if courts apply the traditional ideas formally and uncritically).

According to their understanding, industry practices between firms in areas reliant upon innovation show new forms of agreement have been created because of the great and unavoidable uncertainties and complexities of collaboration for such innovation. What is seen instead of the classic contract is "a process of iterative collaboration and co-design."[49] This process is fostered by a "rich braiding" of more traditional and explicit contractual obligations with "implicit" obligations of a type that are unenforceable under traditional contract doctrine.[50] This new type of contracting for innovation is necessary, because "the inability of the parties to specify ex ante the nature of the product to be produced or its performance characteristics means that the terms of performance will be determined by the very governance process the contract creates."[51] This process, though, creates interdependencies and vulnerabilities that in turn motivate innovations in contract necessary to support the new collaborative structures.

This new collaborative structure is seen in the system of "iterated co-design." Therein, firms developing a product together conduct a thorough process of benchmarking. Then provisional designs are produced and developed. In this process, "the exchanges of information required for benchmarking, simultaneous engineering, and error detection and correction increase the mutual transparency of the actors to each other."[52] But this also places firms in positions of risk because the process also creates multiple opportunities for strategic profit seeking, for instance by holding out at a particularly vulnerable moment for the other party. So within this context, the parties have to create governance mechanisms that will function in lieu of the risk-allocation aspects of conventional contracts. Ideally, if the governance mechanism functions as intended, this type of contract creates mutual trust and "coordination cascades."[53]

The question is how to make a contract that fosters innovation and creates warranted trust and punishes unfair and dishonest behavior given that the process and results are full of uncertainties. Gilson, Sabel, and Scott note that traditional contracts can encourage specific investments and encourage mutually beneficial exchange. Yet fully specified contractual terms that encourage parties to make investments may undermine the ex post efficiency of the transaction if completion is compelled when one party still benefits though circumstances have changed to the point that the overall result is a net loss for the parties jointly. Here transaction costs frustrate mutual aims. Further information costs come from trying to (using MacNeil's term) presentiate and make explicit as many contingencies as possible in the written contract. There are also costs associated with proving any issue relevant to the contract.

These are just the problems in the more traditional picture of discrete contract. If instead parties are contracting for collaborative innovation, then they incur further demands. For example, there must be ways to encourage the sharing of information, where this includes information about technical capacity, ability to collaborate and each party's capacity to deal with the disagreements that the authors think will inevitably arise when the full characteristics of the results of the contract cannot be specified in advance.

Sharing of information requires asymmetric investments and therefore generates interdependency and continuous uncertainty. This, in turn, makes planning more difficult because the uncertainty is continuous, and therefore the optimal tradeoff between ex ante and ex post advantages is unknown.

For Gilson, Sabel, and Scott, this makes the central question in contract enforcement not the traditional "have the discrete terms of the contract been fulfilled?" but rather "whether one's counterparty acts opportunistically—that is, takes advantage of the collaborative process to capture a larger share of the jointly created surplus."[54] Therefore, the "key challenge" in creating the contract for innovation is how to "support the cooperative effort by constraining the strategic behavior made possible by ex ante specific investment in the collaborative project."[55] In more detail this means that the aim is to create an enforceable agreement that "(1) induces efficient, transaction-specific investment by both parties; (2) establishes a framework for iterative collaboration and adjustment of the parties' obligations under conditions of continuing uncertainty-responding, that is, to coordination cascades; and (3) limits the risk of opportunism that could undermine the incentive to make relation-specific investments in the first place."[56] The authors believe that their theory does all three through a braiding of formal and informal terms and nested options.

For information and collaboration one tool is the use of various organizational processes or protocols understood to provide "explicit mechanisms with respect to collaboration and dispute resolution."[57] These processes should be designed in order to encourage and develop trust between parties. One example of this is the "contract referee mechanism." This is designed to avoid and mitigate "noisy signals" that might lead one party to see problems with the other's performance through an explicit commitment to share supervision of management decisions via a committee of referees appointed from both firms. The argument is that the contract referee mechanism and other information sharing aspects do a lot of work toward building trust by making the process quite transparent therefore screening out blatant opportunism. Further, the iterative nature of the braided contract builds up switching costs. In such iterated relationships there are also the possibility of reputational sanctions. This possibility is heightened because the procedural aspects create opportunities to observe character.

The unique feature of contracts as conceptualized in this newly flexible manner is that they "use the process of collaboration to generate new information in two ways-to create the innovative product and to bind each party to the other in a process of symmetrical investments so that neither one has a hold-up advantage over the other at any point in time."[58] The problem in terms of contract theory and its general acceptance in legal practice is that formal contracting based upon more traditional assumptions may "crowd out" more relational behavior. Indeed, due to this crowding out, "the presence of formal contract and the potential for high-powered sanctions *degrade* the information about the nature of the counterparties and the nature of their interactions."[59] Parties change their behavior to everybody's detriment because of their understanding of nature and requirements of contract.

The example of this given by the authors is that of the problem of late parents at daycare. To discourage tardiness in the picking up of children a day care center imposed fines upon late parents. This strategy, under traditional contract assumptions, should encourage prompter parents. It actually produced the opposite effect in that parents were tardy more often. The authors conclude that the strategy backfired because the idea of a formal fine "crowded out" a reputational norm of punctuality.

More generally the "high-powered" sanctions required of standard contract law may signal lack of trust to both parties. They also may crowd out information that would support reciprocity if trust were aimed at more directly. This they term the "breacher-status" problem where a mistake can bring sanction rather than coordination and readjustment. Instead, "braiding uses formal contracts to create governance processes which support iterative joint efforts with low-powered enforcement techniques that partially protect the commitment to collaborate, but do not control the course or the outcome of the collaboration."[60]

They find that two components of the braiding are of central importance: (1) commitment to project with information sharing and (2) explicit procedures for resolving disputes. This creates a sociable and so-
cializing context. Firms aiming for cooperation in the project of product
innovation "write contracts in which they manifestly intend to establish a
deeply collaborative relation, where little or none existed before, through
a combination of formal and informal elements."[61]

From the Social Contract to the Sociable Contract

Gilson, Sabel, and Scott use their analysis of contract to critique Coase's
influential work on firms. Therein he argues that choice between market
or firm rests upon which of the two reduces transaction costs more in any
given setting. According to them, this "dichotomy of hierarchy and contract cannot survive," because, first, "there are no governance tasks done
only by firms or only by the market," and second, "there are entire classes
of governance mechanisms that simply cannot be usefully categorized
as either hierarchy or contract." For them, empirical observation shows
instead a world of federated structures of various types. And therefore,
"firms do not have essences." Instead, "the firm in every epoch takes the
shape necessary for the most pressing of the prevailing governance problems: risk in the last century, uncertainty at the start of this one."[62]

This is a very profound conclusion following from their investigation of
contract. What if this same version of contract is projected back into social contract thinking and the state? Many of the assumptions that Rawls's
use of the contract would have to be questioned. More broadly, what if a
conception of a "sociable contract theory" as opposed to social contract
theory could be constructed? What would this look like?

Starting with Gilmore, the first move would be to question working
with a concept (whether treated literally or as an analogy) that is so ob-
viously out of line with real-world practices. Pragmatists, of course, see
untested ideas and idealisms of various types as abstractions that tend to
obstruct constructive analysis. Gilmore gives us great reason to suspect
that contract is one of the most seductive of such ideas. As he puts it,
classical contract was a "mystical absolute," and an "ivory tower abstraction" that courts had in the end to ignore in order to "promote the ends of
justice." These are strong words with a conclusion that is extremely ironic
in the context of trying to derive justice from contract.

MacNeil's work adds to Gilmore's critique by emphasizing the social context of contracting. Indeed, as opposed to the standard social contract story where contract is seen as the tool to remedy the defects of the state of nature, in MacNeil's story human social habits of a particular kind are a necessary foundation only within which contract can function.

He emphasizes not only the need for specific prescriptive social habits for contract to flourish, but also emphasizes the highly artificial and extremely metaphysically demanding nature of the assumptions animating standard pictures of discrete contract. First there is the need to "presentiate." That is, there is the ideal in contract that every contingency be already thought out in advance. This is, of course, the demand for a god-like view from nowhere. In social contract theory this is analogous to the demand for a once and for all version of contract. MacNeil's image of the discrete contract resting upon the costless and neutral external god ready to investigate, adjudicate and enforce further highlights the fictitious nature of standard conceptions of contracting. Here the sociable nature of all contracts becomes apparent because outside of economic theory contracts have to be socially enforced, and this enforcement necessarily rests upon social habits and institutions. The sociable nature of the contract is further emphasized when MacNeil moves to his version of real contract, in that these are relational and both rest upon and create "complex webs of interdependence."

Between Gilmore and MacNeil then, we get a critique of ideas of discrete contract that emphasizes its metaphysical qualities in the sense both of not corresponding to real activities or real-world possibilities. We also get an emphasis upon the social context and requirements of contract. Gilson, Sabel, and Scott allow a new aspect to be highlighted in addition to this—that of contracts actually designed to enhance sociability and innovation. They investigate agreements between firms that do business in areas that require rapid innovation and sophisticated knowledge sharing in the face of uncertainty. What they find is that through properly formed contracts that are aimed at enhancing trust, that emphasize communication and governance mechanisms that encourage mutual decision making, contracts of their expressly non-traditional type actually can encourage collaboration, "coordination cascades," and sociability.

These contracts, though, not only rely upon a different set of assumptions but they also rely upon a reengineering of the enforcement structure. That is, whereas in a traditional contract damages are triggered by a breach of the express terms and which is then remedied in a cash transfer,

in the sociable contract what triggers damages is unfair or dishonest behavior that is usually made visible through the governance procedures internal to the contract. Further, the A or B quality of the Holmes-Williston
contract attached to performance or breach is not thought conducive to
creating coordination. The sociable contract has internal dispute avoid-
ance and resolution mechanisms and aims to use "lower-powered" damages in service of encouraging parties to the contract to internally solve
the contractual impasse.

It is also telling to note what Gilson, Sabel, and Scott are most troubled
by. Their biggest fear is that the standard ideal of the discrete contract will
"crowd out" the more desirable aspects of the sociable contract. That is,
the positive innovative and sociable aspects they identify in contracts for
innovation might not be possible if parties blindly act under the formalist
assumptions animating discrete transactions. This is a place where ivy tower
abstractions might actively frustrate better real-world possibilities. If this is
the case, instead of reasoning from the idea of such a contract the real issue
becomes whether or not the use of such an idea is even justified.[63]

"Sociable contract theory" will encompass these insights and have at
minimum the following attributes. First, it will not construct arguments
from any conception of an agreement that rests upon patently artificial or
blatantly impossible assumptions. This is not to say that all "ideal theory"
is to be eliminated. But in the quest for the least controversial set of assumptions upon which to rest a social contract theory, the assumptions
should not be absurdly artificial or demanding (i.e., no requirements of
costless gods or views from nowhere or totally presocial human beings).
Second, a quest for either legitimate political obligation or foundational
theories of justice should not be expected to produce once and for all
solutions. Even as a constructed ideal from which to critique government such as advocated by Rawls, change through time should not be
abstracted away.[64] This is important because with the addition of time to
the sociable contract fallibilism and evolution come into play. This makes
possible a third aspect of sociable contract theory—the ability of contracting through time to actually construct more sociable social habits.
Once it is realized that some conceptions of contract encourage sociability, and that others largely define the possibility out, and as a result
leave each human being looking only for arms-length discrete moments
of mutually beneficial exploitation, a bland appeal to "contract" as if it
is a natural type or well-defined concept becomes highly questionable.
Fourth, because of the possibility of new habits and innovation within the

contracting environment and the possibility of a feedback loop between these results and the greater social environment, the hope for a static and foundational starting point, the hope for a "priority of game rules to the game" is out of the question. This means that context cannot be fully abstracted away. This leads to the fifth and final point. Sociable contract theory really does start from where we are here and now and yet does not try to ossify the intuitions we have at present. There is no state of nature to appeal to nor timeless natural laws. This means, further, that there is no way to deal with social power once and for all.

If power is dynamic, and new types and constellations of power might come up unexpectedly and at any time, the only hope is to have flexible governance mechanisms and good social habits in place in order to deal with them (even possibly innovate in relation to them). Allocation of power has been one of the most central aspects of social contract theory. But the once and for all version of contract has attempted, as it seems it must, to treat power as a known type of entity that divides into discrete categories. If power is, to the contrary, fluid and changing—if it evolves and mutates, then the proper social contract might need to be able to adjust accordingly. But this leads to one of the most important of pragmatic ideas—contracting in light of an unfinished and open universe. Put in more banal terms, if there can be contracts for innovation between firms for business, why could there not be sociable contracts for governmental innovation between citizens?

Why not a sociable Constitution? A sociable Constitution would have to give up the hope that everything was "presentiated" in the original act of creating a constitution. It seems undeniably naive to think that the founding fathers had the time or ability to presentiate much at all of the future needs that the constitutional government they created would have to face. The social context that enabled a constitution to be created would have to be seen as prior and constitutive of the constitutional moment. This just simply restates the Deweyan claim that the social is prior to and constitutive of the political. Instead of an individualism of suspicion the sociable aim of government would be emphasized and aimed at. This, of course, would explain the centrality in contemporary society of public education as a governmental function.

Forward-looking experimental construction of and for democratic relations grounded in the world would be the aim, not the protection of some fictional isolated pre-social and rights bearing abstraction. A priori assumptions such as these Hobbesian creatures would be discounted in favor of empirical investigation. This would include the a priori assumptions of constitutional doctrine. The hope for once and for all foundations or historical grounding would also be discounted in favor of a fallibilist and meliorist methodology. The Constitution would be conceptualized as a document that was meant to encourage learning and social progress through rich social braiding. This offers a hint at how to conceptualize social contract theory so as to see the United States Constitution as such a forward-looking document. As stated above, if power is not static but creative and changing, and if governmental challenges are not changeless and eternal, then a static Constitution is not up to the challenge. Given sociable contract theory, a jurisprudence of democratic experimentalism offers a more desirable methodology for constitutional interpretation.

Conclusion

This treatise has outlined various democratic challenges to and possibilities of constitutional law in the hope of constructing a theory of an emphatically democratic constitution. It takes the greatest democratic challenge to be the virtually unquestioned belief in the need for judicial supremacy in constitutional interpretation combined with a lack of an alternative vision.

The first chapter identified and critiqued one dominant explanation for judicial supremacy in constitutional law. This is the "protection from the tyranny of the majority" story. It was examined in the form offered by Erwin Chemerinsky in *The Case Against the Supreme Court*. It was argued that while Chemerinsky holds to this theory, his analysis actually highlights the failure of the United States Supreme Court to live up to the theory through a long, indeed overwhelming, list of antiprecedents. An alternate possibility was then offered, that of "popular constitutionalism," thereby raising a strong question as to why the narrow perspective offered by protection from majority theories, and more broadly of judicial supremacy theories, go largely unchallenged.

 Using the pragmatist theories of John Dewey and an outline of Charles Sanders Peirce's ways of fixation of belief, the argument progressed by next proposing the construction of a democratic and experimental conception of constitutional law labeled "democratic experimentalism." This conception requires law to be practiced as a democratic means because of Dewey's demand—a demand accepted as valid in this treatise—that democracy can only be properly pursued through democratic means. To supplement this demand an outline of various explicit demands Dewey makes of democratic practice were then outlined.

The democratic aims outlined were seen to be informed most generally by an overriding requirement of pragmatism—that of experimentalist procedure. Knowledge, that is, is instrumental and tested by effects in the world. Following from this, a picture of law as democratic means with a broader social conception of experimental democracy was constructed.

Various examples of contemporary scholarship that include experimentalist methodology combined with democratic aims were outlined and critiqued. Each offered important clues how experimentalist and democratic practices could be used in law. But, regardless of their experimental content, most of them, such as those offered by Cass Sunstein or Roberto Unger, do not live up to Dewey's strong demands for a truly democratic politics.

On the other hand, through utilization of the democratic experimentalism scholarship of Michael Dorf and Charles Sabel (among others), it was argued that a plausible picture of law as a democratic means can be constructed. This pragmatic reconstruction of constitutional law, it was argued, satisfies the stringent demands Dewey makes of democratic practice. Most importantly, such a conception of law shows that rather than the ubiquitous foundational picture of constitutional law as giving final and foundational rules to democracy, a jurisprudence of democratic experimentalism can offer an experimental version of constitutional law that is democratic "all the way down."

A jurisprudence of democratic experimentalism, a jurisprudence that emphasizes a decentered conception of law based upon localized rule-making, and sees the role of the court system as more about coordination and information pooling than ultimate and foundational rulemaking, not only greatly broadens the levels of democratic practice within law, but also allows for the conception of a much more information-rich jurisprudence. Indeed, it is opposed to strategies that try to exclude as much information as possible.

As was shown, information-excluding strategies are ubiquitous in legal thought and practice. Justice Scalia's public meaning originalism was taken as a prime example of this strategy. But Scalia is not alone in wanting to exclude many reasons, and a lot of information, as extra-legal. For example, Ronald Dworkin does the same. Of course Scalia and Dworkin disagree on what reasons are essentially legal and which are not, but both think there is a proper line to draw between the legal, which are legitimate to cognize, and the extra-legal or illegitimate reasons the Court should not notice, no matter how empirically vital to the issue.

As opposed to this exclusionary strategy, two other strategies were identified. First, legal decision making in the constitutional area could include as much information as available. Lately this strategy has been exemplified in Richard Posner's recent work on judging. This, it was claimed, is a great improvement on the exclusionary strategy. Under democratic experimentalism there is the even more hopeful possibility that courts could be set up to actually help to encourage the production of relevant information and alternate possibilities on governance.

Using Scalia's information-excluding opinion in the gun-rights case *District of Columbia v. Heller*, and Posner's information including Second Amendment opinion, *Baskin v. Bogan*, it was argued that information-rich jurisprudence offers a much more effective and sensitive jurisprudential strategy in constitutional interpretation. Indeed, Posner's decision has information-producing or -forcing aspects that align it quite nicely with democratic experimentalism.

The analysis then moved onto a historically interesting as well as currently volatile area of "regulatory takings" through an investigation of Oliver Wendell Holmes's foundational case in the area, *Pennsylvania Coal Co. v. Mahon*, Antonin Scalia's controversial *Lucas v. South Carolina Coastal Council* and the stark takings theory of Richard Epstein. Epstein's theory, a key theory for the modern resurrection of takings jurisprudence, was outlined and utilized as an example of formalist and deductivist legal reasoning.

Epstein emphasizes the importance of bright-line rules and critiques Holmes's *Mahon* "matter of degree" style of reasoning as incoherent and theoretically weak. As opposed to this, the argument offered here critiqued Epstein's assumptions, showing them to be empirically and formally weak. Indeed, his argument is only as strong as every individual link in his argument, and many of the links are controversial and easy to dispute. In contrast, the basic reasoning shown in Holmes's opinion exemplifies a stronger braided style of argument as Peirce advocated for and as would be required under a jurisprudence of democratic experimentalism.

From takings the analysis moved on to one of the central cases in United States constitutional law, *Lochner*, and an analysis of what exactly constitutes "Lochnering"—considered to be about as undesirable a type of legal reasoning as can be. "Lochnering" is, indeed, an almost universal term of derision in constitutional analysis. For instance, in his *Obergefell* dissent, Roberts critiqued the majority opinion by claiming that it replicates the mistakes of *Lochner*.

In this treatise, via analysis of critical literature on the case, it was argued that *Lochner* usefully highlights how conceptions of law and democracy inextricably implicate each other. The theories of Richard Epstein and Ronald Dworkin were used as helpful examples to illustrate this inextricability. Ultimately, the conclusion was that the theories of both Ronald Dworkin and Richard Epstein replicate the undesirable antidemocratic features of *Lochner*, as, ironically, does Roberts's dissent in *Obergefell*. The important and famous dissents in *Lochner* written by Holmes and Harlan, on the other hand, exemplify democratic virtues that foreshadow the jurisprudence of democratic experimentalism.

This result, in turn, led to an analysis of *Citizens United*—an example of a case where the Supreme Court overruled a law created by democratically elected representatives in the name of democratic process. In particular, the evaluations of Epstein, Dworkin, and Robert C. Post were highlighted. What was concluded is that just as the fact-based and experimental outlook of democratic experimentalism would have helped the Court avoid the dogmatic and authoritarian stance that the majority exemplified in *Lochner*, it would have also saved the Court from the legalistic dogmatism that the *Citizens United* opinion unfortunately exemplifies. As opposed to covertly and ineptly converting intensely fact-based issues into purported issues of legal definition, a Court informed by democratic experimentalism could have grappled with the ambiguities and empirical difficulties that the legal question of election finance actually required.

The results up to this point were encouraging. A Court practicing democratic experimentalism would have avoided various mistakes exemplified in many of the Courts great antiprecedents. But what of *Brown* and *Obergefell*, two decisions thought of as positive precedents? *Brown* famously overruled the "separate but equal" doctrine of *Plessy v. Ferguson*. *Obergefell* found a constitutional right to same-sex marriage.

Surprisingly, *Brown* was shown to be an information-rich decision that exemplifies much that is required of democratic experimentalism. *Obergefell*, on the other hand, was presented as arriving at the correct legal conclusion, but through a roundabout way that could have been better justified if the Court used the fact-based jurisprudence of democratic experimentalism. Posner's opinion, *Baskin v. Bogan* was offered as a better option in that it was based upon real identifiable harms that discrimination against same-sex couples caused.

Finally, "sociable contract theory" was offered to conceptually frame the evolutionary and non-foundational qualities of a constitutional regime based upon democratic experimentalism. Many constitutional law theories rest upon a foundational conception of the social contract. For instance, John Rawls's theory of justice rests upon a contractual idea whereby once and for all principles regulate all further political decisions within a society. From this a conception of constitutional law as a foundational a static framework follows quite easily.

In this treatise a different ideal for constitutional law was constructed— that of a "sociable contract." Using the work of Grant Gilmore, Ian R. MacNeil, Ronald J. Gilson, Charles F. Sabel, and Robert E. Scott, it was argued that an evolutionary, flexible, and more empirically accurate conception of contract could inform the understanding of constitutional law in a manner that is harmonious with the demand of democratic experimentalism.

A static, foundational constitution protected by a set of robed legal dictators is difficult to justify if the aim is to truly be self-governed. No matter how much you plate it in gold, it is still a cage. Democratic experimentalism was offered as a possibility wherein law becomes not the cage within which democracy functions, but rather a flexible and evolving tool engaged in the construction of ever more democratic practices.

Edward Levi, in speaking about university administration, said that we need to "develop new institutions weak enough to be free, but in which ideas can be developed which are strong enough to change the world."[1] This statement applies just as aptly to constitutional law. No matter how euphemistically one describes a cage, it is still a cage. And no matter how educated in legal reasoning the justices are, handing final decision making off to them is ultimately an abdication of democracy. Much better to emphasize democratic self-rule and ways of making decision making more informed, more intelligent. Constitutional law needs to be weak enough to be free, to evolve and to be able to learn from experimentation in the world. Strength and rigidity are not synonymous, indeed, the dogmatism in contemporary constitutional law is really a sign of weakness and an appeal to the fact-avoidant, often even resistant, methods of tenacity, authority, and the a priori that Peirce rightly critiqued. A stronger constitution would be more experimental, more empirical, information-rich, and more democratic. It would, that is, instantiate law as a democratic means.

Acknowledgments

M any of the ideas and arguments here were developed in earlier form in the pages of *Contemporary Pragmatism*, *Pragmatism Today*, and *Etica & Politica*. I am thankful to all those involved in these projects. I am especially thankful to Brill for allowing me to publish as the last chapter of this book in only slightly edited form my *Contemporary Pragmatism* article, "From Sociable Contract Theory to Sociable Contract Theory" (© Editions Rodopi B. V., Amsterdam 2014). It is great to have these publishers offer such effective venues to work out issues in pragmatism and legal theory. It is also a real help to have teachers, friends, and colleagues such as Connie Bostic, Mellissa Burchard, Tom Burke, Edgar W. Butler, Patricia J. Butler, Grace Campbell, Alessandro Capone, Don Carson, Amy Cohen, Erin Dickey, Michael Eldridge, Jacob Goodson, Sydney Green, Blake Hobby, Fred Kellogg, Douglas Lind, Keya Maitra, Jacob Mey, Gregory Pappas, David Peifer, Richard Posner, Shane Ralston, Charles Sabel, Jay Schulkin, Alice Sebrell, John Shook, William Simon, Michael Sullivan, Fred Turner, Seth Vannetta, and Gordon Wilson. Of course this just names a few of the people who have helped on this project and there are many more that deserve to be listed. I would also like to thank Joe Urgo and UNC–Asheville for generously supporting my academic projects. Finally, I owe a debt of gratitude to everybody at the Black Mountain College Museum + Arts Center for helping me understand in practice what ground-level democracy aspires to (and to expect both successes and failures in pursuit of such an ambitious goal). This book was helped by the anonymous reviews of earlier drafts in the editing process and I would like to thank the reviewers for their efforts. Their suggestions did add significantly to the finished work. I would also like to thank Christie Henry, Susan Karani, and Holly Smith at the University of Chicago Press for taking over the advocacy and editing of this volume after the unexpected passing of Christopher L. Rhodes. This volume is especially dedicated to Chris. His support at the early stages was so positive and enthusiastic that, though I only knew him a short while, he made a great impression on me. I hope that the finished work in some small way does honor to his belief in the project.

Notes

Introduction

1. This is the thesis argued quite effectively for in John Henry Schlegel, *American Legal Realism and Empirical Social Science* (Chapel Hill: University of North Carolina Press, 1995), 226, 253. Schlegel argues that though there have been movements in American law that emphasized empirical science, they have always been conducted from the position of insiders "occupying a fort." This results in a discounting of empirical methodology to traditional legal practices.

2. Karl N. Llewellyn, *The Bramble Bush* (Oxford: Oxford University Press, 2008), 40–41.

Chapter One

1. *Buck v. Bell*, 274 U.S. 200 (1927).

2. Erwin Chemerinsky, *The Case Against the Supreme Court* (New York: Viking Penguin, 2014), 1–4, 15–16.

3. Ibid., 5.

4. Ibid., 10.

5. Ibid., 6–7.

6. Ibid., 10.

7. Ibid., 10.

8. Charles A. Beard, *An Economic Interpretation of the Constitution of the United States* (New York: Macmillan, 1913), 156.

9. Gerald Rosenberg finds along these lines that while there is no real evidence for the U.S. Supreme Court having the ability to promote social change, there is evidence that the Court can be effective as an obstacle to change. Gerald N. Rosenberg, *The Hollow Hope: Can Courts Bring About Social Change?* (Chicago: University of Chicago Press, 2008), 5, 71.

10. Chemerinsky, *The Case Against*, 292.

11. Ibid., 284.

12. Ibid., 284.

13. Ibid., 276. *Obergefell v. Hodges*, 576 U.S. ____ (2015) found that same-sex couples had a constitutional right to marriage.

14. Chemerinsky, *The Case Against*, 298.

15. John Hart Ely, *Democracy and Distrust: A Theory of Judicial Review* (Cambridge, MA: Harvard University Press, 1980), 100. Alexander M. Bickel, *The Least Dangerous Branch: The Supreme Court at the Bar of Politics* (New Haven, CT: Yale University Press, 1962), 27–28.

16. Ran Hirschl, *Towards Juristocracy: The Origins and Consequences of the New Constitutionalism* (Cambridge, MA: Harvard University Press, 2004).

17. Ibid., 16.

18. Ibid., 43.

19. Richard D. Parker, in *"Here, the People Rule": A Constitutional Populist Manifesto* (Cambridge, MA: Harvard University Press, 1998), 56–58.

20. Ibid., 80.

21. Ibid., 96.

22. Ibid., 114.

23. Ibid., 53.

24. Ibid., 73.

25. Ibid., 91.

26. Ibid., 214.

27. Ibid., 217.

28. Ibid., 229.

29. Ibid., 247.

30. Mark Tushnet, *Taking the Constitution Away from the Courts* (Princeton, NJ: Princeton University Press, 1999), ix.

31. Ibid., 179.

32. Ibid., 182.

33. Ibid., 192.

34. Sidney Hook finds the idea of a legislative override in the letters of John Marshall. He also thinks that unless the Court's vote is unanimous it should not override the legislative branch of the federal government. Sidney Hook, *Paradoxes of Freedom* (Buffalo, NY: Prometheus, 1987). 73, 102.

35. Nathan Houser and Christian Kloesel, eds., *The Essential Peirce, Volume 1 (1867–1893)* (Bloomington: Indiana University Press, 1992) 114.

36. Ibid., 114–15.

37. Ibid., 115.

38. Ibid., 117.

39. Ibid., 118.

40. Ibid., 117.

41. Ibid., 119.

42. Ibid., 121.

43. Ibid., 29.

44. Ibid., 132.

45. Cheryl Misak, *The American Pragmatists* (Oxford: Oxford University Press, 2013), 17–18.

46. Richard J. Bernstein, *The Pragmatic Turn* (Cambridge: Polity, 2010), 36, also Misak, *American Pragmatists*, 37. As Peirce emphasizes, and Nicholas Rescher takes pains to point out, this is a self-corrective process. Nicholas Rescher, *Realistic Pragmatism: An Introduction to Pragmatic Philosophy* (New York: State University of New York Press, 2000), 99.

47. Charles Morris, *The Pragmatic Movement in American Philosophy* (New York: George Braziller, 1970).

48. Hilary Putnam, "A Reconsideration of Deweyan Democracy," in *Pragmatism in Law and Society*, ed. M. Brint and W. Weavers (Boulder: Westview Press, 1991), 227.

49. Misak, *American Pragmatists*, 244, Hilary Putnam, "Pragmatism and Moral Objectivity," in *Words and Life,* ed. James Conant (Cambridge, MA: Harvard University Press, 1994), 172.

50. Michael Sullivan. *Legal Pragmatism: Community, Rights and Democracy* (Bloomington: Indiana University Press, 2007), 73.

51. Dewey, LW 13, 273. (All references to Dewey's work will be to the scholarly edition edited by Jo Ann Boydston and published at Southern Illinois Press. The convention used will be as follows: for the early works, "EW;" for the middle works, "EW"; and for the later works, "LW," followed by volume number and then page number.)

52. Dewey, LW 13, 187.

53. Ibid.

54. Ibid., 155, 156.

55. Dewey, LW 11, 298.

56. Dewey, LW 14, 229–30.

57. Dewey, LW 11, 298.

58. Jane Addams, *Democracy and Social Ethics* (New York: Macmillan, 1920), 11–12.

Chapter Two

1. Alfonso J. Damico calls this the traditional "juridical conception of society." Alfonso J. Damico, *Individualism and Community: The Social and Political Thought of John Dewey* (Gainesville: University Presses of Florida, 1978), 54. A clear analysis of this assumption is found in Henry S. Richardson, *Democratic Autonomy: Public Reasoning about the Ends of Policy* (Oxford: Oxford University Press, 2002), 9. Richardson notes that if the claim is that judicial review over

democratic process is needed to curb democratic excesses this is an empirical claim and therefore one that would require testing, and should not be accepted upon anything other than such evidence. Of course there are arguments as seen in the last chapter to the effect that the constitution should be interpreted democratically rather than by judges. Finally, there is the legitimate worry that judicial review encourages legislatures to evade their democratic responsibility to legislate by drafting vague laws and letting the courts clarify a meaning according to their own lights. Hook, *Paradoxes*, 92. This worry, of course, can be extended to the citizens evading their responsibilities as well due to a hope that the courts will decide. On the other hand, Michael Sullivan argues quite eloquently for these seemingly anti-democratic aspects of law being important for democratic ends. Sullivan, *Legal Pragmatism*, 3.

2. As Judith Green emphasizes, for Dewey democracy is constructed through the use of "directional indicators we must continually throw before ourselves and retrospectively redetail as we reflect on the active processes of transformative experience they help to guide." Judith M. Green, *Pragmatism and Social Hope: Deepening Democracy in Global Contexts* (New York: Columbia University Press, 2008), 90.

3. John Dewey, LW 2, 325.

4. Dewey, LW 13, 187.

5. James H. Tufts, *Our Democracy: Its Origins and Its Tasks* (New York: Henry Holt, 1917), 221, 268.

6. This belief is eloquently expressed by Cornel West; "To focus solely on elec-toral politics as the site of democratic life is myopic. Such a focus fails to appreciate the crucial role of the underlying moral commitments and visions and fortifica-tions of the soul that empower and inspire a democratic way of living in the world." Cornell West, *Democracy Matters: Winning the Fight against Imperialism* (New York: Penguin, 2004), 15. Though this conception of democracy might seem radi-cal, it is important to note that even "conservative" civic republican advocates of democracy make the same claim. Jean Bethke Elshtain, *Democracy on Trial* (New York: Basic Books, 1995), 80.

7. Gregory Fernando Pappas, *John Dewey's Ethics: Democracy as Experience* (Bloomington: Indiana University Press, 2008), 225. Indeed, Pappas argues that de-liberation needs to be anchored to experimental evidence because the democratic ideal is not just to convince each other but, rather, "the idea is not to talk merely to convince each other. The ideal is also for everyone to have the willingness to concede to the authority of a communal judgment that is the result of transacting with the world and learning from it." Gregory Fernando Pappas, "What Would John Dewey Say about Deliberative Democracy and Democratic Experimental-ism?" *Contemporary Pragmatism* 9 (2012): 67.

8. John R. Shook, *Dewey's Social Philosophy: Democracy as Education* (New York: Palgrave Macmillan, 2014), 70.

9. A nice treatment of Dewey's conception of this process in relationship to democratic experimentalism is offered in Amy J. Cohen, "Producing Publics: Dewey, Democratic Experimentalism, and the Idea of Communication," *Contemporary Pragmatism* 9 (2012): 143, 147. As an example of the manner in which democracy as characterized here must go "all the way down," Michael Magee argues that the individual person as such is constructed through membership in various subcommunities so that pluralistic options are actually essentially important for the construction of free individuals as individuals. Michael Magee, *Emancipating Pragmatism: Emerson, Jazz and Experimental Writing* (Tuscaloosa: University of Alabama Press, 2004), 24, 103. In this Magee agrees with Cornel West's picture of American democracy as best thought of in terms of a jazzlike composition. West, *Democracy Matters,* 62. One way to explain this is to claim that both individuals and social groups can make up for blind spots and lack of imagination by cooperating with others, therefore gaining critique, comparative insights, and broader experience.

10. Dewey, LW 2, 244–45. For good discussions of Dewey's idea of a public see Erick MacGilvray, "Dewey's Public," *Contemporary Pragmatism* 7 (2010): 31, 33, and James Bohman, "Participation through Publics: Did Dewey Answer Lippmann?," *Contemporary Pragmatism* 7 (2010): 49, 50. See also William H. Simon, "Afterward—Part II: New Governance Anxieties: A Deweyan Response," *Wisconsin Law Review* (2010): 727–29, for a discussion of Dewey's conception of publics in relationship to new governance.

11. Dewey, LW 2, 255.

12. Ibid., 256. Sor-Hoon Tan explains one motivation behind this statement: "To fully appreciate Dewey's conceptual reconstruction, the political forms of social and ethical democracy are not to be equated with specific modes of government as we know it. Even assuming that democratic forms of government have to be 'systems of laws and administration' might be allowing what *is* too much constraint over what *can be*. This is no mere utopian claim; the awareness of such a possibility is a safeguard against the facile assumption that the solution to every political problem must be some law or government agency or action. Dewey insists on the plurality of political forms, and he repeatedly cautions readers against prejudging which political forms would work best." Sor-Hoon Tan, *Confucian Democracy: A Deweyan Reconstruction* (Albany: State University of New York Press, 2004), 124.

13. Dewey, LW 2, 264. On the other side of this is the creation of a constitution that fits the project at hand. An example of this, possibly, is the Indian constitution. Interestingly, Ambedkar, the Chairman of the Drafting Committee of the Indian Constitution, and a highly influential person on its formation, was a student of Dewey and had a strong influence on his thought. See Keya Maitra, "Ambedkar and the Constitution of India: A Deweyan Experiment," *Contemporary Pragmatism* 9 (2012): 301, 309.

14. What exactly experimentalism entails is an important topic. Chis Ansell argues that it is best thought along the lines of design experiment and not along

the lines of positivist conception of science. Chris Ansell, "What Is a 'Democratic Experiment'?," *Contemporary Pragmatism* 9 (2012), 152. Charlene Haddock Seigfreid argues against the positivist model of science and contends that Jane Addams led Dewey to see democracy as a way of life involving everyday experimental habits of mind and character and the willingness to learn from mistakes. Indeed, even objectivity is defined as "a characteristic of a community's practice of science rather than of an individual's." Charlene Haddock Seigfried, *Pragmatism and Feminism: Reweaving the Social Fabric* (Chicago: University of Chicago Press, 1996), 189, also 22, 58, 160, 200.

15. Hilary Putnam, *Renewing Philosophy* (Cambridge, MA: Harvard University Press, 1992), 186.

16. Dewey, LW 13, 175.

17. As Pappas puts it, "A community of inquiry that is not centered and guided by the unique problem at hand usually deteriorates into mere conflict of ideologies without the fullness of interaction required for learning. Moreover, this leads to an oversimplification of concrete social problems and often to a faulty solution." Gregory Fernando Pappas, *John Dewey's Ethics: Democracy as Experience* (Bloomington: Indiana University Press, 2008), 241.

18. Indeed, it is surprising the number of claims to the effect that Dewey underestimates the kind and amount of social conflict. First, Dewey does not feel the need to "prove" there is social conflict—this is accepted as a given. Second, Dewey does not claim that all conflict is, in the end, eliminable. What is claimed is that if it is eliminable in a manner that harmonizes interests, his proposed form of government is best placed to find the solution. Melvin L. Rogers, *The Undiscovered Dewey: Religion, Morality, and the Ethos of Democracy* (New York: Columbia University Press, 2009), 4. Rogers claims that Dewey was perfectly aware of the inability to control everything and argues for a humble view of what can be controlled combined with an awareness of the dangers attached to human intervention. See also Sidney Hook, *John Dewey: An Intellectual Portrait* (Westport, CT: Greenwood, 1971), 48.

19. Damico puts it this way—the argument of a rule of experts proves too much because "if the masses are as irredeemable intellectually as this theory asserts, democracy is impossible." Damico, *Individuality and Community*, 107.

20. Dewey, LW 2, 364. Jay Schulkin offers a possible model for how expert knowledge can combine with the ultimate placement of democratic authority in the citizenry in the use of "informed consent" in the medical profession. Methods analogous to this might inform democratic decision making. Jay Schulkin, *Naturalism and Pragmatism* (New York: Palgrave Macmillan, 2012), 118.

21. Robert Westbrook, *John Dewey and American Democracy* (Ithaca, NY: Cornell University Press, 1991), xvi.

22. Sullivan, *Legal Pragmatism*, 85.

23. Dewey, MW 15, 69.

24. Ibid., 68.

25. Ibid., 71.

26. Ibid., 73.

27. Ibid., 75.

28. Dewey, LW 3, 188–89.

29. Ibid., 190.

30. 18 N.Y.S.2d 821 (1940).

31. Dewey, LW 14, 237.

32. Ibid., 243.

33. Dewey, EW 4, 73.

34. Ibid., 79.

35. Ibid., 87.

36. Dewey, LW 12, 106.

37. Dewey, LW 3, 327.

38. Ibid., 327.

39. Dewey, EW 4, 40.

40. Ibid., 40–41.

41. Dewey, LW 17, 102. There are, of course, possible reasons to think of a legal system itself as part of the social and political multiplicity. Henry Richardson notes that even if law loses any essential uniqueness that could underlie a "separation of powers" doctrine, having a legal system among governmental agencies might help keep alive a "balance of powers" necessary in order to avoid too much centralization of power. Richardson, *Democratic Autonomy*, 143.

42. Dewey, LW 14, 115.

43. Ibid., 117.

44. Ibid.

45. Ibid., 118.

46. Dmitri Shalin notes that Dewey considered the advocates of natural rights theory in his time to be dogmatists and reactionaries. See Dmitri N. Shalin, *Pragmatism & Democracy: Studies in History, Social Theory, and Progressive Politics* (New Brunswick, NJ: Transaction, 2011), 268.

47. Dewey, MW 7, 63.

48. Dewey, MW 10, 212.

49. Ibid., 214.

50. Dewey, MW 7, 59.

51. Ibid.

52. Of course this allows an important distinction between the natural and the naturalized. Feminist thought especially has highlighted the manner in which custom can be naturalized to the point of smuggling in strongly biased perceptions as neutral and objective. As Dewey's friend and fellow democratic philosopher put it, "Of course, it is always difficult to see the wrong in a familiar thing; it is almost a test of moral insight to be able to see that an affair of familiar intercourse and

daily living may also be wrong." Jane Addams, *Newer Ideals of Peace* (New York: Macmillan, 1907), 155.

53. Dewey, LW 2, 22.

54. Ibid., 38.

55. Dewey, LW 14, 117.

56. Ibid.

57. Thurman W. Arnold, *The Symbols of Government* (New Haven, CT: Yale University Press, 1935). Therein he portrays most appeals to the Constitution and the Supreme Court as fearful and uncertain prayers because though the appeal is not based on reliable reasons, the faith is unquestioned, p. 230–31.

58. Edward Steven Robinson, *Law and the Lawyers* (New York: Macmillian, 1935), p. 21, 28, 275.

59. Cass Sunstein, *Designing Democracy: What Constitutions Do* (Oxford: Oxford University Press, 2001), *Infotopia: How Many Minds Produce Knowledge* (Oxford: Oxford University Press, 2006), and *Republic.com 2.0* (Cambridge: Cambridge University Press, 2007).

60. Sunstein, *Designing Democracy*, 43.

61. Roberto Mangabeira Unger, *Democracy Realized: The Progressive Alternative* (London: Verso, 1998). Also Roberto Mangabeira Unger, *What Should Legal Analysis Become?* (London: Verso, 1996).

62. Unger, *Democracy Realized*, 5.

63. Ibid., 22.

64. Ibid., 24.

65. Jack Knight and James Johnson, *The Priority of Democracy: The Political Consequences of Pragmatism* (New York: Russell Sage Foundation, 2011), 5.

66. Ibid., 7.

67. Ibid., 23.

68. Ibid., 171.

69. This is not universally accepted, of course. For instance, it is contrary to Karl Llewellyn's explicit claim that "law not only is a machine for dispute resolution, but it is also a machine for choice from among experiments." Karl N. Llewellyn, *The Bramble Bush* (Oxford: Oxford University Press, 2008), 126.

70. Ibid., 172.

71. Ibid., 174.

72. Christopher K. Ansell, *Pragmatist Democracy: Evolutionary Learning as Public Philosophy* 18 (Oxford: Oxford University Press, 2011).

73. Ibid., 131.

74. Ibid., 11.

75. Ibid., 89.

76. Ibid., 30.

77. Ibid., 32.

78. William H. Simon, "Solving Problems vs. Claiming Rights: The Pragmatist Challenge to Legal Liberalism," *William & Mary Law Review* 46 (2004): 127–212,

also, William H. Simon, "Toyota Jurisprudence: Legal Theory and Rolling Rule Regimes," in *Law and New Governance in the EU and the US*, ed. Grianne de Burca and Joanne Scott (Oxford: Hart, 2006).

79. Michael Dorf and Charles Sabel, "A Constitution of Democratic Experimentalism," *Columbia Law Review* 98 (1998): 267. In order to avoid the impression that democratic experimentalism is being embraced as without potential problems of its own, the following are some essays that are critical of its stance (many of the critiques offered in these articles will be investigated in later chapters): Lisa T. Alexander, "Stakeholder Participation in New Governance: Lessons from Chicago's Public Housing Reform Movement," *Georgetown Journal on Poverty Law Policy* 16 (2009): 117; Benjamin J. Beaton, "Walking the Federalist Tightrope: A National Policy of State Experimentation for Health Information Technology," *Columbia Law Review* 108 (2008): 1670; Christie Ford, "New Governance in the Teeth of Human Frailty: Lessons from Financial Regulation," *Wisconsin Law Review* 2010 (2010): 441; Alana Klein, "Judging as Nudging: New Governance Approaches for the Enforcement of Constitutional Social and Economic Rights," *Columbia Human Rights Law Review* 39 (2008): 351; and David A. Super, "Laboratories of Destitution: Democratic Experimentalism and the Failure of Antipoverty Law," *University of Pennsylvania Law Review* 157 (2009): 541.

80. Dorf and Sabel, "A Constitution of Democratic Experimentalism," 284–85.

81. Ibid., 285.

82. Ibid., 286.

83. Ibid., 286.

84. Ibid., 287.

85. Ibid.

86. Ibid., 345.

87. Ibid., 355. Mark Tushnet worries that localized deliberation, while it does allow the utilization of non-expert local knowledge, also risks "domination by the articulate." Of course one response to this is that at least it would be the domination of the locally articulate rather than the professionalized articulate. Another factor that might help avoid this type of domination is the emphasis put upon benchmarking and other sources of information. Mark Tushnet, *The New Constitutional Order* (Princeton, NJ: Princeton University Press, 2003), 168, 170.

88. This emphasis upon publicly available information is reminiscent of Louis Brandeis's idea that sunlight is the best of disinfectants. An interesting take on this is offered by Mary Graham in her *Democracy by Disclosure*, wherein she shows the salutary work that publicity can do, but also worries that too much information, and information improperly communicated can have negative effects. Mary Graham, *Democracy by Disclosure: The Rise of Technopopulism* (Washington: Brookings Institution Press, 2002), 3, 142.

89. Dorf and Sabel, "A Constitution of Democratic Experimentalism," 288.

90. Ibid., 389.

91. Ibid.

92. Ibid., 397.

93. Ibid., 401. For an investigation of courts already functioning in this manner, see Michael C. Dorf and Charles F. Sabel, "Drug Treatment Courts and Emergent Experimentalist Government," *Vanderbilt Law Review* 53, (2000): 831. See also Michael C. Dorf, "Legal Indeterminacy and Institutional Design," *New York University Law Review* 78 (2003): 945. Of course the role of the lawyer would have to be reconceptualized as well, changing, possibly, from traditional litigator to another type of "problem solving" agent. For a discussion of this see Douglas NeJaime, "When New Governance Fails," *Ohio State Law Journal* 70 (2009): 337–48.

Chapter Three

1. Mark Joseph Stern, "Listen to a Conservative Judge Brutally Destroy Arguments against Gay Marriage," *Slate*, August 27, 2014. Accessed January 10, 2015. http://www.slate.com/blogs/outward/2014/08/27/listen_to_judge_richard_posner _destroy_arguments_against_gay_marriage.html.

2. Posner Same-Sex Marriage Opinion. Unanimous. Listed as 14–2386 to 14–2388, 14–2526.

3. Mark Joseph Stern followed up with a new article titled "Judge Posner's Gay Marriage Opinion Is a Witty, Deeply Moral Masterpiece," *Slate*, September 5, 2014. Accessed January 10, 2015. http://www.slate.com/blogs/outward/2014/09/05 /judge_richard_posner_s_gay_marriage_opinion_is_witty_moral_and_brilliant.html.

4. *District of Columbia v. Heller*, 554 U.S. 570 (2008).

5. Ibid., 3.

6. Ibid., 4.

7. Ibid., 10.

8. Ibid., 20.

9. Ibid., 53.

10. Ibid., 56–57, citations omitted.

11. Ibid., 2.

12. Ibid., 5.

13. Ibid., 9.

14. Ibid., 10.

15. See Rory K. Little, "*Heller* and Constitutional Interpretation: Originalism's Last Gasp," *Hastings Law Journal* 60 (2009): 1417–1419; and Saul Cornell, "Originalism on Trial: The Use and Abuse of History in *District of Columbia v. Heller*," *Ohio State Law Journal* 69 (2008): 626, Cornell claims that the *Heller* decision actually demonstrates that "plain meaning originalism has no coherent, historical methodology. It is little more than the old law-office history dressed up in the latest legal-academy fashions."

16. Mark Tushnet, "*Heller* and the New Originalism," *Ohio State Law Journal* 69 (2008): 610, 619.

17. Samuel Issacharaoff, "Pragmatic Originalism?" *New York University Journal of Law & Liberty* 4 (2009): 530–31.

18. Reva B. Siegal, "*Heller* and Originalism's Dead Hand—In Theory and Practice." *UCLA Law Review* 56 (2009): 1399–1402.

19. See, for example, Josh Blackman, "The Constitutionality of Social Cost," *Harvard Journal of Law & Public Policy* 34 (2011): 956.

20. Richard A. Posner, "In Defense of Looseness," *New Republic*, August 27, 2008. Accessed January 12, 2015. http://www.newrepublic.com/article/books/defense-looseness.

21. For example, Richard A. Epstein, "A Structural Interpretation of the Second Amendment: Why *Heller* Is (Probably) Wrong on Originalist Grounds," *Syracuse Law Review* 59 (2008): 171–83. And for an originalist critique see Nelson Lund, "The Second Amendment, *Heller*, and Originalist Jurisprudence," *UCLA Law Review* 56 (2009): 1343.

22. *McDonald v. City of Chicago*, 561 U.S. 3025 (2010).

23. Ibid., 14.

24. Ibid., 51, 56.

25. Antonin Scalia, *A Matter of Interpretation* (Princeton, NJ: Princeton University Press, 1997), 9.

26. Ibid., 13.

27. Ibid., 14.

28. Ibid., 17.

29. Ibid., 22.

30. Ibid., 25.

31. Ibid., 39.

32. Ibid., 40.

33. Ibid., 41.

34. Ibid., 41.

35. Ibid., 43.

36. Ibid., 45.

37. Ibid., 45–46.

38. Scalia, "The Rule of Law as a Law of Rules, *University of Chicago Law Review* 56 (1989): 1176.

39. Ibid.

40. Ibid., 1178.

41. Ibid.

42. Ibid.

43. Ibid., 1179.

44. Ibid., 1180.

45. Ibid.

46. Ibid., 1182.

47. Ibid., 1183.

48. Scalia, *Matter of Interpretation*, 140.

49. Scalia, "The Rule of Law," 1184.

50. Indeed Posner explicitly accepted my terminology of "information producing" for his jurisprudence as opposed to Scalia's exclusionary model in his recent book *Reflections on Judging*. Richard A. Posner, *Reflections on Judging* (Cambridge, MA: Harvard University Press, 2013), 235.

51. Richard A. Posner, *How Judges Think* (Cambridge MA: Harvard University Press, 2008), 3. Posner is aware that his critique might not work in civil law jurisdiction where codified law and a professionalized and careerist judiciary are involved.

52. "Hearing on the Nomination of John Roberts to Be Chief Justice of the Supreme Court before the Senate Judiciary Committee," 109 Cong., 1st Sess. 56 (Sept. 12, 2005). Posner states that no judge really believes this and therefore that this statement is "a blow to Roberts's reputation for candor." Posner, *How Judges Think.*, 81.

53. Ibid., 41.

54. Ibid., 42.

55. Ibid., 42.

56. Ibid., 248, 244.

57. Ibid., 47.

58. Ibid., 9.

59. Ibid., 79.

60. Ibid., 77.

61. Ibid., 13.

62. Ibid., 104. This claim was made quite forcefully by Edward H. Levi in his classic *An Introduction to Legal Reasoning*, where he notes in relationship to the British unwritten constitution that "the influence of constitution worship" combined with a written constitution can give "great freedom to a court," so much so that through going back to the text the court can give itself "a freedom greater than it would have had if no such document existed." Edward H. Levi, *An Introduction to Legal Reasoning* (Chicago: University of Chicago Press, 1949), 59.

63. Breyer's "active liberty" is exemplified in his *Heller* dissent, critiqued by Posner as ideology posing as pragmatism in *How Judges Think*, and detailed in various legal realms in Stephen Breyer, *Active Liberty: Interpreting Our Democratic Constitution* (New York: Vintage, 2005).

64. Posner, *How Judges Think*, 202.

65. Ibid., 198, 202.

66. Ibid., 201. Posner makes the further point that if it is found that legislative amendment is feasible then it may be used to fix mistakes following from other interpretive strategies, such as loose construction, as well as the results of strict construction.

67. Ibid., 202.

68. Ibid., 19.

69. Ibid., 73.

70. Ibid., 61.

71. Ibid., 7–9.

72. Ibid., 61.

73. Ibid., 61. Mark Tushnet makes this point in his article "*Heller* and the Critique of Judgment," *Supreme Court Review*, vol. 2009 (2008): 82. Therein he makes the argument that legal training develops an implicit "legal judgment" that is very much habitual. Therefore, "put simply, training socializes people into understanding what it means to be a good lawyer. Some possibilities, conceptually available, are taken off the table through socialization."

74. Posner, *How Judges Think*, 241.

75. Ibid., 1.

76. Ibid., 198.

77. Ibid., 86.

78. Ibid., 44.

79. Ibid., 13.

80. Dorf and Sabel, "A Constitution of Democratic Experimentalism," 267–473.

81. Ibid., 400.

82. Ibid., 397.

83. Ibid., 401.

84. Posner, *How Judges Think,* 249–53.

85. *Moore v. Madigan,* 3. In *Reflections on Judging*, Posner derides this type of multi-page historical analysis as needless complexity and "verbosity masquerading as precision." Posner, *Reflections on Judging*, 118.

86. *Moore v. Madigan*, 7.

87. Ibid., 5.

88. Ibid., 8.

89. Ibid., 13.

90. Ibid., 15.

91. Ibid., 15.

92. Ibid., 15.

93. Ibid., 16.

94. Ibid., 16–17.

95. Ibid., 18–19.

96. Ibid., 20.

97. Ibid., 21. Williams's dissent focuses much more of its energy on the historical analysis of the Second Amendment's meaning. But the conclusion is the same— the nine pages of historical analysis end inconclusively. Then the argument turns to strength of justification especially if in "core" of right protected and appeals to common sense for the conclusion that the Illinois law as passed would protect individuals. Tellingly, though, the dissent also devotes ten pages to an empirical analysis. Ultimately the disagreement between the court's majority and Williams

rests upon the proper level of deference. That is, Williams argues that Posner did not defer enough to legislature and references Brandeis's advocacy of the states as laboratories for experimentation. So, even though the argument in dissent is more grounded in historical analysis, it too is notable for advocating for experimentation and evidence. As opposed to the type of analysis offered by Scalia in *Heller* and followed by Alito in *McDonald*, both Posner and Williams at least grapple with the actual world—and therefore think things not words.

Chapter Four

1. Holmes was also involved in some notable cases that are, in hindsight, thought of as mistakes. Of course there is *Buck v. Bell*, mentioned earlier, with its notorious acceptance of eugenics to limit reproduction of "imbeciles." For a survey of his less popular cases see chap. 5 in Albert W. Alschuler, *Law without Values: The Life, Work, and Legacy of Justice Holmes* (Chicago: University of Chicago Press, 2000).

2. Suzanna Sherry, "Property Is the New Privacy: The Coming Constitutional Revolution," *Harvard Law Review* 128 (2015): 1452.

3. William Michael Treanor, "Jam for Justice Holmes: Reassessing the Significance of *Mahon*," *Georgetown Law Journal* 86 (1998): 814.

4. Bruce A. Ackerman, *Property and the Constitution* (New Haven, CT: Yale University Press, 1977), 156.

5. Mark Tushnet, *The New Constitutional Order* (Princeton, NJ: Princeton University Press, 2003), 61.

6. Frederic R. Kellogg, *Oliver Wendell Holmes, Jr., Legal Theory, and Judicial Restraint* (Cambridge: Cambridge University Press, 2007), 139.

7. Richard A. Epstein, *Supreme Neglect: How to Revive Constitutional Protection of Private Property* (Oxford: Oxford University Press, 2008), 107, 114. Two other central works of scholarship in the area, though more sympathetic with Holmes's jurisprudence, also find the area to be close to incoherent. Joseph L. Sax, "Takings and the Police Power," *Yale Law Journal* 74 (1964): 36; and Frank I. Michelman, "Property, Utility, and Fairness: Comments on the Ethical Foundations of 'Just Compensation' Law," *Harvard Law Review* 80 (1967): 1173. See Sherry, "Property Is the New Privacy," for an overview of this movement and Epstein's central pace in it. As she puts it, his 1985 book on takings was the "movement's first manifesto." Epstein's latest version of this argument is found in *The Classical Liberal Constitution* (Cambridge, MA: Harvard University Press, 2014).

8. "But when meaning giving takes the form of the a priori preference for sharp and definitive theories, it should not be considered thorough-mindedly practical—as it is, all too often, in today's intellectual climate. Rather this form of theory pursuit is itself a *tender-minded* indulgence . . . a flight from the complexity of the

world, driven by the kind of fear that underlies the absolutist quest for certainty." Thomas Grey, "What Good Is Legal Pragmatism?," in *Pragmatism in Law and Society*, ed. Michael Brint and William Weaver (Boulder: Westview Press, 1991), 22.

9. By far the best exposition of the fact is in the first chapter of William A. Fischel's *Regulatory Takings*. William A. Fischel, *Regulatory Takings: Law, Economics, and Politics* (Cambridge, MA: Harvard University Press, 1995).

10. *Pennsylvania Coal Co. v. Mahon*, 260 U.S. 393 (1922), 413. As shown in a useful analysis offered by Treanor, property under substantive due process before *Mahon* was analyzed under three distinct rationales: (1) police powers, (2) businesses affected with public interests, and (3) eminent domain. The first area was "classic police power" relating to public health, safety, or morals. Under this category, a regulation that barred activity that endangered public health, safety, or morals would withstand constitutional scrutiny if the legislature's goal was the protection of public health, safety, or morals and the means chosen in the legislation were suited to achieve the goal. If so, then regulation was valid. Regulation of a nuisance would fit under this category. The classic statement of this position is in *Mugler v. Kansas*: "A prohibition simply upon the use of property for purposes that are declared, by valid legislation, to be injurious to the health, morals, or safety of the community, cannot, in any sense, be deemed a taking or an appropriation of property for the public benefit." *Lochner*, according to Treanor, is the same type of case as *Mugler*, "as each turned on whether a regulation fell within the police power." This type of analysis "turned on the use of a formalist, categorical rule." The second area is that of businesses affected with a public interest. In *Munn* the Court held that regulation of rates charged by "businesses affected with a public interest" was constitutionally permissible. As Treanor explains, "With respect to businesses affected with a public interest, it was the regulation that was presumptively permissible. The limit to state power was that the regulation could not deny a reasonable rate of return. If it did, however, compensation was the remedy." The problem under this category, though, was not only with figuring out reasonable rate of return but also what businesses were affected with a public interest. The third area was that of eminent domain. Here the original rule was that there had to be a physical seizure before compensation was owed. Treanor, "Jam for Justice," 839.

11. *Mahon*, 413.

12. Ibid., 414.

13. Ibid.

14. Ibid., 415.

15. Ibid.

16. Ibid.

17. Ibid., 416.

18. Ibid.

19. Ibid., 417.

20. Ibid.

21. Ibid., 419.

22. Ibid., 422.

23. *Penn Central Transportation Co. v. New York City*, 438 U.S. 104 (1978).

24. Ibid., 124.

25. Ibid., citations omitted.

26. Ibid., 125.

27. Ibid., 130–31.

28. Ibid., 139.

29. Ibid., 139–40.

30. Ibid., 140.

31. Ibid., 147–48.

32. Ibid., 152–53. Citations omitted.

33. *Pruneyard Shopping Center v. Robins*, 447 U.S. 74 (1980).

34. Ibid., 83.

35. *Munn v. Illinois*, 94 U.U. 113 (1877).

36. Pruneyard, 94.

37. *Keystone Bituminous v. DeBenedictus*, 480 U.S. 470 (1987), 473–74, citations omitted.

38. *Keystone*, 484.

39. Ibid., 487–98, *Mugler v. Kansas*, 123 U.S. 623 (1887).

40. *Miller v. Scheone*, 276 U.S. 272 (1928).

41. *Keystone*, 492, citing *Agins* at 260–61.

42. *Penn Central* 130–31, *Andrus* at 65–66.

43. *Keystone*, 500–501.

44. Ibid., 507–8.

45. Ibid., 513.

46. Ibid., 520.

47. *Lucas v. South Carolina Coastal Council*, 505 U.S. 1003 (1992), 1014–1015.

48. Ibid., 1015.

49. Ibid., 1018.

50. Ibid.

51. Ibid., 1019.

52. Ibid., 1029.

53. Ibid., 1036–1037.

54. Ibid., 1039.

55. Ibid., 1046.

56. Ibid., 1051.

57. Ibid., 1055.

58. Ibid, 1063.

59. Ibid., 1069.

60. Ibid., 1075–1076.

61. Richard A. Epstein, *"Pennsylvania Coal v. Mahon*: The Erratic Takings Jurisprudence of Justice Holmes," 86 *Georgetown Law Journal* 875 (1998): 891.

62. Ibid., 888.

63. Ibid, 894.

64. Ibid., 883–84.

65. Ibid., 887.

66. Ibid., 888.

67. Richard A. Epstein, *Design for Liberty: Private Property, Public Administration, and the Rule of Law* (Cambridge, MA: Harvard University Press: 2011), 106.

68. Epstein, "Pennsylvania Coal," 876.

69. Richard A. Epstein, *Takings: Private Property and the Power of Eminent Domain* (Cambridge, MA: Harvard University Press, 1985), 18.

70. Ibid., 13.

71. Ibid., 58.

72. Ibid., 95.

73. Ibid., 111.

74. Ibid.

75. Ibid., 128.

76. Ibid., 129.

77. Ibid., 266.

78. See, for instance, the problem of the "tragedy of the anticommons." Michael Heller, *The Gridlock Economy: How Too Much Ownership Wrecks Markets, Stops Innovation, and Costs Lives* (New York: Basic Books, 2008). As Suzanna Sherry put it correctly, Epstein seems too often to exhibit "a willful lack of engagement with the real world." Sherry, "Property Is the New Privacy," 1461.

79. R. H. Coase, *The Firm, the Market, and the Law* (Chicago: University of Chicago Press, 1988), 7, 9.

80. Jeremy Waldron, *The Dignity of Legislation* (Cambridge: Cambridge University Press, 1999), 82.

81. Daniel J. Boorstin, *The Mysterious Science of the Law* (Gloucester: Peter Smith, 1974).

82. Carol M. Rose, *"Mahon* Reconstructed: Why the Takings Issue Is Still a Muddle," *Southern California Law Review* 57 (1984): 591. She gets this term from M. Cunliffe, in *The Right to Property: A Theme in American History* (1973) 11, 21.

83. Rose, *"Mahon* Reconstructed," 594.

84. Charles A. Reich, "The New Property," *Yale Law Journal* 73 (1964): 733. See also Thomas C. Grey, "The Disintegration of Property," in *Nomos XXII: Property*, ed. J. Roland Pennock and John W. Chapman (New York: New York University Press, 1980), 69. Therein Grey argues that the concept of property is so fragmented as to be incoherent. And in what surely is the definitive treatment of property in the United States in Stuart Banner concludes: "Property is not an end in itself but rather

a means to many other ends. Because we have never had unanimity on how to priori-
tize those other ends, we have never had unanimity on an understanding of property. Our conceptions of property have always been molded to serve our own particular purposes." Stuart Banner, *American Property: A History of How, Why, and
What We Own* (Cambridge, MA: Harvard University Press, 2011), 290.

85. Richard H. Thaler and Cass R. Sunstein, *Nudge: Improving Decisions about
Health, Wealth, and Happiness* (New Haven, CT: Yale University Press, 2008),
26–27.

86. Fischel, *Regulatory Takings*, 104.

87. *Tyson & Bro. v. Banton*, 273 U.S. 418, 445–47 (1927). See also *Truax v. Cor-
rigan*, 157 U.S. 312 (1921) where Holmes warns in his dissent of the "dangers of
a delusive exactness" in Fourteenth Amendment issues that could get in the way
of social experimentation and therefore the Court should stay out unless the legislature goes beyond constitution's obvious meaning, and *Springer v. Philippine
Islands*, 277 U.S. 183 (1928).

88. *Missouri Pacific Railway Company v. Nebraska*, 217 U.S. 196 (1910).

89. Robert Brauneis describes Holmes as rejecting both the "vested rights tradition" and that of conceptual essentialism. The vested rights tradition holds that
because a right has been given, it has been "vested," and therefore it is unjust to
take it away. The obvious problem with the vested rights tradition is that there
is no non-controversial version of it, because "if one asked the only truly uncontroversial form of the question, 'Does this law create a new obligation in respect
to a transaction already past,?' every statute turned out to be retrospective." If
this version of rights protection is accepted, it seems quite clear that "government
hardly could go on." Of course the other option, the ahistorical approach attached
to conceptual essences is anathema to both the discounting of categorical sche-
matization and the evolutionary historical approach understanding exemplified in
Holmes's scholarship; indeed, if this ahistorical conceptual approach is accepted
the "path" of the law becomes largely irrelevant. Most important for Brauneis
is that Holmes's analysis rests largely upon measuring the degree of legal change
from culturally embedded "structural habits." Like habits, the principles are not
innate or natural, but are contingently acquired or developed over time; they are
features of a particular legal culture or tradition. On the other hand, like habits,
they may become so settled and involuntary in application that they seem natural
and are difficult to discard." Robert Brauneis, "The Foundation of Our 'Regulatory Takings Jurisprudence'": The Myth and Meaning of Justice Holmes' Opinion
in *Pennsylvania Coal v. Mahon*," *Yale Law Journal* 106 (1996): 627, 646. See also,
Robert Brauneis, "Treanor's *Mahon*," *Georgetown Law Journal* 86 (1998).

90. As quoted in Louis Menand, *The Metaphysical Club* (New York: Farrar,
Straus and Giroux, 2001), 64.

91. Jeremy Waldron, *The Dignity of Legislation*. His more recent book where
he directly critiques Epstein's conflation of property rights and the Rule of Law

is Jeremy Waldron, *The Rule of Law and the Measure of Property* (Cambridge: Cambridge University Press, 2012).

92. Richard A. Posner, *The Essential Holmes* (Chicago: University of Chicago Press, 1992), 23, 181.

93. Pds.lib.harvard.edu/pds/view/42978053. Accessed February 28, 2013.

Chapter Five

1. *Lochner v. New York*, 198 U.S. 45 (1905).

2. Lawrence Tribe, *American Constitutional Law* (New York: Foundation Press, 1988), 564.

3. Ibid., 1.

4. *West Coast Hotel v. Parrish*, 300 U.S. 379 (1937).

5. Tribe, *American Constitutional Law*, 564.

6. Ibid., 569.

7. *Miller v. Schoene*, 276 U.S. 272 (1928).

8. Tribe, *American Constitutional Law*, 577.

9. Ibid, 584.

10. Paul Kens, *Lochner v. New York: Economic Reglation on Trial* (Lawrence: University Press of Kansas, 1998).

11. Ibid., 100.

12. Ibid., 180.

13. William H. Marnell, *Man-Made Morals: Four Philosophies that Shaped America* (New York: Anchor Books, 1966), 257.

14. David A. Strauss, "Why Was *Lochner* Wrong?" *University of Chicago Law Review* 70 (2003): 373–86.

15. This analysis is supported by Sunstein's narrative tracing such an "activist" stance both forward through *Roe v. Wade* (1973) and backward to *Dredd Scott v. Sandford*. Cass R. Sunstein, *Radicals in Robes: Why Extreme Right-Wing Courts Are Wrong for America* (New York: Basic Books, 2005), 82–86.

16. Strauss, "Why Was *Lochner* Wrong?," 375.

17. Jack M. Balkin, "'Wrong the Day It Was Decided': Lochner and Constitutional Historicism," *Boston University Law Review* 85 (2005), 677–725.

18. Bruce Ackerman, *We the People 1: Foundations* (Cambridge, MA: Harvard University Press, 1991), 64–65.

19. Howard Gillman, *The Constitution Besieged: The Rise and Demise of Lochner Era Police Powers Jurisprudence* (Durham, NC: Duke University Press, 1993).

20. Ibid., 10.

21. Ibid., 205.

22. Cass R. Sunstein, "*Lochner's* Legacy," *Columbia Law Review* 87 (1987), 873–919.

23. Ibid., 880.

24. Ibid., 889.

25. Jennifer Nedelsky, *Private Property and the Limits of American Constitutionalism: The Madisonian Framework and Its Legacy* (Chicago: University of Chicago Press, 1990), 228.

26. Richard A. Epstein, *Takings: Private Property and the Power of eminent Domain* (Cambridge, MA: Harvard university Press, 1985).

27. Richard A. Epstein, *Supreme Neglect: How to Revive Constitutional Protection for Private Property* (Oxford: Oxford University Press, 2008).

28. Ibid., 166.

29. David E. Bersnstein, "*Lochner v. New York*: A Centennial Retrospective," *Washington University Law Quarterly* 85 (2005): 1469–1528.

30. Ibid., 1472.

31. Ibid., 1473.

32. Ibid., 1473.

33. *Lochner*, 53.

34. Ibid.

35. Ibid.

36. Ibid., 54.

37. *Holden v. Hardy*, 169 U.S. 366 (1898).

38. *Atkin v. Kansas*, 191 U.S. 207 (1903), *Knoxville Iron Co. v. Harbison*, 183 U.S. 13 (1901).

39. *Jacobson v. Massachusetts*, 197 U.S. 11 (1905).

40. *Lochner*, 56.

41. Ibid.

42. Ibid., 56–57.

43. Ibid., 58, 61.

44. Ibid., 64.

45. Ibid., 65.

46. Ibid.

47. Ibid., 66.

48. Ibid., 68.

49. Ibid.

50. Ibid., 72.

51. Ibid., 75.

52. Ibid., 75–76.

53. Ibid., 76.

54. Ibid.

55. Ronald Dworkin, *Taking Rights Seriously* (Cambridge, MA: Harvard University Press, 1978), xi.

56. "I call a 'principle' a standard that is to be observed, not because it will advance or secure an economic, political, or social situation deemed desirable,

but because it is a requirement of justice or fairness or some other dimension of morality." Ibid., 22. Principle in this sense is against legal pragmatism which in his opinion focuses solely upon policy.

57. Ronald Dworkin, *Freedom's Law* (Cambridge, MA: Harvard University Press, 1996), 6.

58. Ibid., 17. Also, Ronald Dworkin, *Is Democracy Possible Here?* (Princeton, NJ: Princeton University Press, 2008), 9–11, 133.

59. Ibid., 31.

60. Ibid., 75.

61. Ibid., 38.

62. Dworkin, *Law's Empire*, 187–88, 211.

63. Ibid., 90.

64. Ibid., 214.

65. Ibid., 399.

66. Ibid., 398.

67. Dworkin, *Freedom's Law*, p. 82–88.

68. Ibid., 125.

69. Posner, *Law, Pragmatism*, and *Democracy.* (Cambridge, MA: Harvard University Press, 2005) 122.

70. Dewey, LW 7, 414–15.

71. Dewey, LW 3, 180.

72. Dewey, LW 11, 16.

73. Seth Vannatta, *Conservatism and Pragmatism: In Law, Politics and Ethics* (New York: Palgrave MacMillan, 2014), 207.

Chapter Six

1. *Citizens United v. Federal Election Commission*, 558 _____ (2010).

2. *Austin v. Michigan Chamber of Commerce*, 494 U.S. 652 (1990).

3. *Citizens United*, 16.

4. Ibid., 16–17.

5. Ibid., 23.

6. Ibid., 6.

7. Ibid., 49.

8. Ibid., 24–25.

9. Ibid., 9.

10. Ibid., 40.

11. Ibid., 44.

12. Ibid., 5.

13. Ibid., 9.

14. Ibid., 56, 59–60.

15. Ibid., 77.

16. Ibid., 78.

17. *The Becker/Posner Blog*, April 8, 2012.

18. Richard A. Epstein, "*Citizens United v. FEC*: The Constitutional Right that Big Corporations Should Have but Do Not Want," *Harvard Journal of Law & Public Policy* 34 (2011): 640.

19. Ibid., 643.

20. Ibid., 647.

21. Ibid., 648.

22. Ibid., 650.

23. Ibid., 659.

24. Ibid., 661.

25. Robert C. Post, *Citizens Divided* (Cambridge, MA: Harvard University Press, 2014).

26. Ibid., 4.

27. Ibid., 5.

28. Ibid., 6.

29. Ibid., 36.

30. Ibid., 37.

31. Ibid., 43.

32. Ibid., 50.

33. Ibid., 51.

34. Ibid., In an important response to Post, Lawrence Lessig argues that the antidistortion analysis is actually based upon a founding generation conception of corruption as improper dependence—an institutional virtue related to republican representation. Here the worry becomes the power of money intended to effect (and distort) the chain of representation between "representative" and citizens. Lawrence Lessig, "Out-Posting Post" response essay to Post, *Citizens Divided*, 101.

35. Post, *Citizens Divided*, 68.

36. Ibid., 69.

37. Ibid., 73.

38. *Red Lion Broadcasting Co. v. FCC*, 395 U.S. 367 (1969).

39. Post, *Citizens Divided*, 78.

40. Ibid., 79. *First National Bank of Boston v. Belotti*, 435 U.S. 765 (1978).

41. Post, *Citizens Divided*, 59.

42. Ibid.

43. Ibid., 61.

44. Ibid., 62.

45. Ibid., 62–63.

46. Ibid.

47. Ibid., 64–65.

48. Ibid., 159.

49. Frank Michelman, "Legitimacy, Strict Scrutiny, and the Case Against the Supreme Court," response essay to Post, *Citizens Divided*, 123. *Fisher v. University of Texas*, 570 U.S. _____ (2013).

50. Nadia Urbinati, "Free Speech as the Citizen's Right," response essay to Post, *Citizens Divided*, 139.

51. Pamala S. Karlan, "Citizens Deflected: Electoral Integrity and Political Reform," response to Post, *Citizens Divided*, 143.

52. Laurence H. Tribe, "Dividing *Citizens United*: The Case v. The Controversy." (March 9, 2015), 14. Available at SSRN: http://ssrn.com/abstract=2575865. Accessed June 3, 2015, 14.

53. Ibid., 17.

54. Ibid., 25. This concept is most clearly offered in Cass R. Sunstein, "Incompletely Theorized Agreements," *Harvard Law Review* 108 (1995), 1733.

55. Tribe, "Dividing Citizens United," 30.

Chapter Seven

1. *Plessy v. Ferguson*, 163 U.S. 537 (1896).

2. Ibid., 548.

3. Ibid., 551.

4. Ibid., 557.

5. Ibid., 559.

6. Ibid., 560.

7. *Brown v. Board of Education of Topeka*, 347 U.S. 483 (1954) and 349 U.S. 294 (1955).

8. Ibid., 487.

9. Ibid., 488.

10. Ibid.

11. Ibid., 492–93.

12. Ibid., 493.

13. *Sweatt v. Painter*, 339 U.S. 629 (1950).

14. *McLaurin v. Oklahoma State Regents*, 339 U.S. 637 (1950).

15. *Brown*, 494.

16. Ibid.

17. Ibid., 495.

18. Ibid., 348.

19. Ibid., 349.

20. Therefore, the sensitivity and "call to look at context" as a method of noting previously ignored features of the issue is properly emphasized by Martha Minow and Elizabeth Spelling. Martha Minow and Elizabeth V. Spelman, In Context," *Southern California Law Review* 63 (1990): 1998.

21. Archon Fung and Erik Olin Wright, "Thinking about Empowered Participatory Governance," in *Deepening Democracy: Institutional Innovations in Empowered Participatory Governance*, ed. Archon Fung and Erik Olin Wright (London: Verso 2003), 5, 21; and Burkhard Eberlin, "Experimentalist Governance in the European Energy Sector," in *Experimentalist Governance in the European Union: Towards a New Architecture*, ed. Charles F. Sabel and Jonathan Zeitlin (Oxford: Oxford University Press, 2010), 64–65.

22. Jane Mansbridge, "Practice-Thought-Practice," in *Deepening Democracy*, ed. Fung and Wright, 178. Charles Sabel emphasizes this as well. Charles Sabel, "The Institutional Configuration of Deweyan Democracy," *Contemporary Pragmatism* 9 (2012): 45.

23. Richard Kluger, *Simple Justice: The History of Brown v. Board of Education and Black America's Struggle for Equality* (New York: Vintage, 2004).

24. Ibid., 746, 33.

25. Ibid., 205.

26. Herbert Wechsler, "Toward Neutral Principles of Constitutional Law," *Harvard Law Review* 73 (1959): 34.

27. Kluger, *Simple Justice*, 451.

28. Ibid., 321, 400.

29. Ibid., 405.

30. Ibid., 708–10.

31. Ibid., 523.

32. Ibid., 425.

33. W. E. B. Du Bois, *Writings* (New York: The Library of America, 1986), 710.

34. James H. Tufts, *Our Democracy: Its Origins and its Tasks* (New York: Henry Holt, 1917), 211.

35. *Parents Involved in Community Schools v. Seattle School District No. 1* (551 U.S. _____ (2007).

36. Laurence Tribe and Joshua Matz, *Uncertain Justice: The Roberts Court and the Constitution* (New York: Henry Holt, 2014), 20.

37. *Parents Involved*, 2.

38. *Grutter v. Bollinger*, 539 U.S 328 (2003)

39. *Parents Involved*, 16.

40. Ibid., 18.

41. Ibid., 21.

42. Ibid., 25.

43. Ibid., 28.

44. Ibid., 40–41.

45. Ibid., 32.

46. Ibid., 35.

47. Ibid., 8.

48. Ibid., 18.

49. Ibid., 6.

50. Ibid., 35.

51. Ibid., 62.

52. Ibid., 67.

53. Du Bois, *Writings*, 431.

54. *Obergefell v. Hodges* (576 U.S. ____ 2015).

55. Ibid., 1–2.

56. Ibid., 3.

57. Ibid., 7.

58. Ibid.

59. Ibid., 8.

60. Ibid.10 (citations omitted).

61. Ibid.

62. Ibid., 11.

63. Ibid.

64. Ibid.

65. Ibid., 12.

66. Ibid., 13.

67. Ibid., 14.

68. Ibid., 16.

69. Ibid., 6.

70. Ibid., 17.

71. Ibid., 22.

72. Ibid., 29–33.

73. Ibid., 24.

74. Ibid., 28.

75. Ibid., 1.

76. Ibid., 2.

77. Ibid.

78. Ibid., 3.

79. Ibid., 4.

80. Ibid., 5.

81. Ibid., 6.

82. Ibid, 8.

83. Ibid.

84. Ibid. 11.

85. Ibid., 19.

86. Ibid., 22.

87. Ibid.

88. Ibid., 25.

89. Ibid., 29.

90. Ibid., 2.

91. Ibid.
92. Ibid., 4.
93. Ibid., 5.
94. Ibid., 2.
95. Ibid., 4.
96. Ibid., 5.
97. Ibid., 7.
98. Ibid., 8.
99. Jane Addams, *Democracy and Social Ethics* (New York: MacMillan, 1920), 81.
100. Ibid., 78. This is also emphasized by Charlene Haddock Seigfried. Seigfreid, *Pragmatism and Feminism*, 247.
101. *Baskin v. Bogan* 7th Circuit, decided September 4, 2014.
102. Baskin, 4.
103. Ibid., 37.

Chapter Eight

1. James H. Tufts, *The Ethics of Cooperation* (Boston: Houghton Mifflin, 1918).
2. Frank J. Goodnow, *Social Reform and the Constitution* (New York: MacMillan, 1911), 2.
3. John Rawls, *A Theory of Justice* (Cambridge, MA: Harvard University Press, 1971), 11.
4. Ibid., 12
5. Ibid., 16.
6. John Rawls, *Collected Papers* (Cambridge, MA: Harvard University Press, 1999), 71.
7. Ibid., 173.
8. Ibid.
9. Ibid., 530, 550. See also John Rawls, *The Law of Peoples* (Cambridge, MA: Harvard University Press, 1999), 5, 58.
10. Michael J. Sandel's analysis is perhaps more definitive of this aspect of Rawls's theory. Michael J. Sandel, *Democracy's Discontent: America in Search of a Public Philosophy* (Cambridge, MA: Harvard University Press, 1996), 28.
11. P. S. Atiyah, *An Introduction to the Law of Contract* (Oxford: Oxford University Press, 4th ed., 1989), 2.
12. Oliver Wendell Holmes, Jr., *The Common Law* (Boston: Little, Brown, and Company, 1881), 253. Cherelstein reduces consideration to "something of value." The need for consideration was acute enough for social contract theorists when showing the parallels between legal contract and social contract attempts were made to find it therein. Marvin A. Chirelstein, *Concepts and Case Analysis in the*

Law of Contracts (Westbury, NY: The Foundation Press, 1990), 13. So, for example Chipman found that the surrender of specific rights was the consideration involved. N. Chipman, *Sketches of the Principles of Government* (Rutland, VT, 1793), 110–11.

13. Holmes, *The Common Law*, 300–301.

14. Grant Gilmore, *The Death of Contract* (Columbus: Ohio State University Press, 1974), 5.

15. Ibid., 8.

16. Ibid., 14.

17. Ibid., 15.

18. Ibid., 104.

19. Grant Gilmore, *The Ages of American Law* (New Haven, CT: Yale University Press, 1977), 63.

20. Gilmore, *Death of Contract*, 106–7.

21. Ibid., 107.

22. Ibid., 61.

23. Ibid., 19.

24. Gilmore, *Ages of American Law*, 46.

25. Gilmore, *Death of Contract*, 37.

26. Ibid., 81.

27. Ian R. MacNeil, *The New Social Contract: An Inquiry into Modern Contractual Relations* (New Haven, CT: Yale University Press, 1980), 1.

28. Ibid.

29. Ibid., 7.

30. Ibid., 10.

31. Ibid., 11.

32. Ibid.

33. Ibid.

34. Ibid., 13.

35. Ibid., 14.

36. Ibid., 19.

37. Ibid., 18.

38. Ibid., 23.

39. Ibid., 24.

40. Ibid., 30.

41. Ibid., 37.

42. Ibid.

43. Ibid., 39.

44. Ibid., 49.

45. Ibid., 56.

46. Ibid., 60.

47. Ibid., 62.

48. Ibid., 63.

49. Ronald J. Gilson, Charles F. Sabel, and Robert E. Scott, "Contracting for Innovation: Vertical Disintegration and Interfirm Collaboration," *Columbia Law Review* 109 (2009): 433.

50. Ibid., 435.

51. Ibid.

52. Ibid., 448.

53. Ibid., 449.

54. Ibid., 455.

55. Ibid.

56. Ibid., 472.

57. Ibid., 479.

58. Ibid., 488.

59. Ronald J. Gilson, Charles F. Sabel, and Robert E. Scott, "Braiding: The Interaction of Formal and Informal Contracting in Theory, Practice, and Doctrine," *Columbia Law Review* 110 (2010): 1399.

60. Ibid., 1403.

61. Ibid., 1404.

62. Gilson, Sabel, and Scott, "Contracting for Innovation," 501.

63. As Gough puts it, "the real question is not so much that of the exact terms in which the analogy is expressed as whether the analogy itself is justifiable." J. W. Gough, *The Social Contract: A Critical Study of Its Development* (Oxford: Oxford University Press, 1957), 6.

64. Interestingly here it may be that Kant's formulation is able to handle changing conditions better than Rawls because it is less foundationalist.

Conclusion

1. Edward H. Levi, *Point of View: Talks on Education* (Chicago: University of Chicago Press, 1969), 162.

Bibliography

Ackerman, Bruce A. *Property and the Constitution*. New Haven, CT: Yale University Press, 1977.

———. *We the People 1: Foundations*. Cambridge, MA: Harvard University Press, 1991.

Addams, Jane. *Democracy and Social Ethics*. New York: Macmillan, 1920.

———. *Newer Ideals of Peace*. New York: Macmillan, 1907.

Alexander, Lisa T. "Stakeholder Participation in New Governance: Lessons from Chicago's Public Housing Reform Movement." *Georgetown Journal on Poverty Law Policy* 16 (2009): 117–85.

Alschuler, Albert W. *Law without Values: The Life, Work, and Legacy of Justice Holmes*. Chicago: University of Chicago Press, 2000.

Ansell, Chris. *Pragmatist Democracy: Evolutionary Learning as Public Philosophy*. Oxford: Oxford University Press, 2011.

———. "What Is a 'Democratic Experiment'?" *Contemporary Pragmatism* 9 (2012): 159–80.

Arnold, Thurman W. *The Symbols of Government*. New Haven, CT: Yale University Press, 1935.

Atiyah, P. S. *An Introduction to the Law of Contract*. Oxford: Oxford University Press, 1989.

Balkin, Jack M. " 'Wrong the Day It Was Decided' ": *Lochner* and Constitutional Historicism." *Boston University Law Review* 85 (2005): 677–725.

Banner, Stuart. *American Property: A History of How, Why, and What We Own*. Cambridge, MA: Harvard University Press, 2011.

Beard, Charles A. *An Economic Interpretation of the Constitution of the United States*. New York: Macmillan, 1913.

Beaton, Benjamin J. "Walking the Federalist Tightrope: A National Policy of State Experimentation for Health Information Technology." *Columbia Law Review* 108 (2008): 1670–1717.

Bernstein, David E. "*Lochner v. New York*: A Centennial Retrospective." *Washington University Law Quarterly* 85 (2005): 1469–1528.

Bernstein, Richard J. *The Pragmatic Turn.* Cambridge: Polity, 2010.

Bickel, Alexander M. *The Least Dangerous Branch: The Supreme Court at the Bar of Politics.* New Haven, CT: Yale University Press, 1962.

Blackman, Josh. "The Constitutionality of Social Cost." *Harvard Journal of Law & Public Policy* 34 (2011): 951–1042.

Bohman, James. "Participation through Publics: Did Dewey Answer Lippman?" *Contemporary Pragmatism* 7 (2010): 49–68.

Boorstin, Daneil J. *The Mysterious Science of the Law.* Gloucester: Peter Smith, 1974.

Brauneis, Robert. " 'The Foundation of Our "Regulatory Takings" Jurisprudence': The Myth and Meaning of Justice Holmes' Opinion in *Pennsylvania Coal Co. v. Mahon.*" *Yale Law Journal* 106 (1996): 613–702.

———. "Treanor's *Mahon.*" *Georgetown Law Journal* 86 (1998): 907–32.

Breyer, Stephen. *Active Liberty: Interpreting Our Democratic Constitution.* New York: Vintage, 2005).

Butler, Brian E. "Addendum to Law, Pragmatism and Constitutional interpretation: Information Production and Posner's Experimentalist Jurisprudence." *Pragmatism Today* 4 (2013): 209–14.

———. "Aesthetics in American Law." *Legal Studies Forum* 27 (2003): 201–20.

———. "Democracy and Justice: Political and Legal Thought." In *Historical Essays in 20th Century American Philosophy*, edited by Richard Hull and John Shook, 371–407. Charlottesville, VA: Philosophy Documentation Center, 2015.

———. "Democracy and Law: Situating Law within John Dewey's Democratic Vision." *Etica & Politica* 12 (2010): 256–80.

———, ed. *Democratic Experimentalism.* Amsterdam: Rodopi, 2012.

———. "Dews, Dworks, and Poses Decide Lochner." *Contemporary Pragmatism* 7 (2010): 15–44.

———. "From Sociable Contract Theory to Sociable Contract Theory." *Contemporary Pragmatism* 11 (2014): 1–17.

———. "Law as a Democratic Means: The Pragmatic Jurisprudence of Democratic Experimentalism." *Contemporary Pragmatism* 9 (2012): 241–354.

———. "Legal Pragmatism: Banal or Beneficial as a Jurisprudential Position?" *Essays in Philosophy* 3 (2002): unpaginated. http://commons.pacificu.edu/cgi/view content.cgi?article=1050&context=eip.

———. "Metaphysical Philosophers and the 'Practical Statesmanship' of Supreme Court Justices in *NFIB v. Sebelius.*" In *The Affordable Care Act Decision: Philosophical and Legal Implications*, edited by Fritz Allhoff and Mark Hall, 42–54. New York: Routledge, 2014.

———. "Obama's Pragmatism in International Relations: Appropriate or Appropriation?" In *Philosophical Pragmatism and International Relations: Essays for a Bold New World*, edited by Shane J. Ralston, 159–76.

———. "Pragmatism, Democratic Experimentalism and Law." In *Pragmatism, Law, and Language*, edited by Graham Hubbs and Douglas Lind, 205–23. New York: Routledge, 2014.

Chemerinsky, Erwin. *The Case Against the Supreme Court*. New York: Viking, 2014.

Chipman, Nathaniel. *Sketches of the Principles of Government*. Rutland, VT, 1793.

Chirelstein, Marvin A. *Concepts and Case Analysis in the Law of Contracts*. Westbury, NY: Foundation, 1990.

Coase, R. H. *The Firm, the Market, and the Law*. Chicago: University of Chicago Press, 1988.

Cohen, Amy J. "Producing Publics: Dewey, Democratic Experimentalism, and the Idea of Communication." *Contemporary Pragmatism* 9 (2012): 143–57.

Cornell, Saul. "Originalism on Trial: The Use and Abuse of History in *District of Columbia v. Heller*." *Ohio State Law Journal* 69 (2008): 625–40.

Cunliffe, M. *The Right to Property: A Theme in American History*. Leicester: Leicester University Press, 1973.

Damico, Alfonso J. *Individualism and Community: The Social and Political Thought of John Dewey*. Gainesville: University Presses of Florida, 1978.

Dewey, John. *The Early Works, Volume 4: 1882—1898, Early Essays and the Study of Ethics, A Syllabus, 1893–1894*, edited by Jo Ann Boydston. Carbondale: Southern Illinois University Press, 1971.

———. *The Middle Works*. Vol. 7, *1899—1924, Essays, Books Reviews, Encyclopedia Articles in the 1912–1914 Period, and Interest and Effort in Education*, edited by Jo Ann Boydston. Carbondale: Southern Illinois University Press, 1979.

———. *The Middle Works*. Vol. 10, *1899—1924, Journal Articles, Essays, and Miscellany Published in the 1916–1917 Period*, edited by Jo Ann Boydston. Carbondale: Southern Illinois University Press, 1980.

———. *The Later Works*. Vol. 2, *1925—1953, 1925–1927, Essays, Reviews, Miscellany, and the Public and Its Problems*, edited by Jo Ann Boydston. Carbondale: Southern Illinois University Press, 1984.

———. *The Later Works*. Vol. 3, *1925—1953, 1927–1928, Essays, Reviews, Miscellany, and "Impressions of Soviet Russia,"* edited by Jo Ann Boydston. Carbondale: Southern Illinois University Press, 1984.

———. *The Later Works*. Vol. 11, *1935–1937, Essays and Liberalism and Social Action*, edited by Jo Ann Boydston. Carbondale: Southern Illinois University Press, 1987.

———. *The Later Works*. Vol. 12, *1938, Logic: The Theory of Inquiry*, edited by Jo Ann Boydston. Carbondale: Southern Illinois University Press, 1986.

———. *The Later Works*. Vol. 13, *1938–1939, Experience and Education, Freedom and Culture, Theory of Valuation, and Essays*, edited by Jo Ann Boydston. Carbondale: Southern Illinois University Press, 1988.

———. *The Later Works*. Vol. 14, *1925—1953, 1939—1941, Essays, Reviews, and Miscellany*, edited by Jo Ann Boydston. Carbondale: Southern Illinois University Press, 1988.

———. *The Later Works*. Vol. 17, *1925—1953, 1885—1953, Miscellaneous Writings*, edited by Jo Ann Boydston. Carbondale: Southern Illinois University Press, 1990.

Dorf, Michael. "Legal Indeterminacy and Institutional Design." *New York University Law Review* 78 (2003): 875–981.

Dorf, Michael, and Charles Sabel. "A Constitution of Democratic Experimentalism." *Columbia Law Review* 98 (1998): 267–473.

———. "Drug Treatment Courts and Emergent Experimentalist Government." *Vanderbilt Law Review* 53 (2000): 831–83.

Du Bois, W. E. B. *Writings*. New York: Library of America, 1986.

Dworkin, Ronald. *Freedom's Law*. Cambridge, MA: Harvard University Press, 1996.

———. *Is Democracy Possible Here?* Princeton, NJ: Princeton University Press, 2008.

———. *Law's Empire*. Cambridge, MA: Harvard University Press, 1986.

———. *Taking Rights Seriously*. Cambridge, MA: Harvard University Press, 1978.

Eberlin, Burkhard. "Experimentalist Governance in the European Energy Sector." In *Experimentalist Governance in the European Union: Towards a New Architecture*, edited by Charles F. Sabel and Jonathan Zeitlin, 61–68. Oxford: Oxford University Press, 2010.

Elshtain, Jean Bethke. *Democracy on Trial*. New York: Basic Books, 1995.

Ely, John Hart. *Democracy and Distrust: A Theory of Judicial Review*. Cambridge, MA: Harvard University Press, 1980.

Epstein, Richard A. "*Citizens United v. FEC*: The Constitutional Right that Big Corporations Should Have but Do Not Want." *Harvard Journal of Law & Public Policy* 34 (2011): 639–61.

———. *The Classical Liberal Constitution*. Cambridge, MA: Harvard University Press, 2014.

———. *Design for Liberty: Private Property, Public Administration, and the Rule of Law*. Cambridge, MA: Harvard University Press, 2011.

———. "*Pennsylvania Coal v. Mahon*: The Erratic Takings Jurisprudence of Justice Holmes." *Georgetown Law Journal* 86 (1998): 875–905.

———. "A Structural Interpretation of the Second Amendment: Why *Heller* Is (Probably) Wrong on Originalist Grounds." *Syracuse Law Review* 59 (2008): 171–83.

———. *Supreme Neglect: How to Revive Constitutional Protection of Private Property*. Oxford: Oxford University Press, 2008.

———. *Takings: Private Property and the Power of Eminent Domain*. Cambridge, MA: Harvard University Press, 2011.

Fischel, William A. *Regulatory Takings: Law, Economics, and Politics*. Cambridge, MA: Harvard University Press, 1995.

Ford, Christie. "New Governance in the Teeth of Human Frailty: Lessons from Financial Regulation." *Wisconsin Law Review* 2010 (2010): 441–87.

Fung, Archon, and Erik Olin Wright. "Thinking about Empowered Participatory Governance." In *Deepening Democracy: Institutional Innovations in Empowered Participatory Governance*, edited by Archon Fung and Erik Olin Wright, 3–44. London: Verso, 2003.

Gillman, Howard. *The Constitution Besieged: The Rise and Demise of Lochner Era Police Powers Jurisprudence.* Durham, NC: Duke University Press, 1993.

Gilmore, Grant. *The Ages of American Law.* New Haven, CT: Yale University Press, 1977.

———. *The Death of Contract.* Columbus: Ohio State University Press, 1974.

Gilson, Ronald J., Charles F. Sabel and Robert E. Scott. "Braiding: The Interaction of Formal and Informal Contracting in Theory, Practice, and Doctrine." *Columbia Law Review* 110 (2010): 1377–1447.

———. "Contracting for Innovation: Vertical Disintegration and Interfirm Collaboration." *Columbia Law Review* 109 (2009): 431–502.

Goodnow, Frank J. *Social Reform and the Constitution.* New York: Macmillan, 1911.

Gough, J. W. *The Social Contract: A Critical Study of Its Development.* Oxford: Oxford University Press, 1957.

Graham, Mary. *Democracy by Disclosure: The Rise of Technopopulism.* Washington, DC: Brookings Institution Press, 2002.

Green, Judith M. *Pragmatism and Social Hope: Deepening Democracy in Global Contexts.* New York: Columbia University Press, 2008.

Grey, Thomas C. "The Disintegration of Property." In *Nomos XXII: Property*, edited by J. Roland Pennock and John W. Chapman, 69–85. New York: New York University Press, 1980.

———. "What Good Is Legal Pragmatism?" In *Pragmatism in Law and Society*, edited by Michael Brint and William Weaver, 9–27. Boulder, CO: Westview, 1991.

Heller, Michael. *The Gridlock Economy: How Too Much Ownership Wrecks Markets, Stops Innovation, and Costs Lives.* New York: Basic Books, 2008.

Hirschl, Ran. *Towards Juristocracy: The Origins and Consequences of the New Constitutionalism.* Cambridge, MA: Harvard University Press, 2004.

Holmes, Oliver Wendell, Jr. *The Common Law.* Boston: Little, Brown, and Company, 1881.

Hook, Sidney. *John Dewey: An Intellectual Portrait.* Westport, CT: Greenwood, 1971.

———. *Paradoxes of Freedom.* Buffalo, NY: Prometheus, 1987.

Issacharoff, Samuel. "Pragmatic Originalism?" *New York University Journal of Law & Liberty* 4 (2009): 517–32.

Karlan, Pamala S. "Citizen's Deflected: Electoral Integrity and Political Reform." In Robert C. Post, *Citizens Divided*, 141–51. Cambridge, MA: Harvard University Press, 2014.

Kellogg, Frederic R. *Oliver Wendell Holmes, Jr., Legal Theory, and Judicial Restraint.* Cambridge: Cambridge University Press, 2007.

Kens, Paul. *Lochner v. New York: Economic Regulation on Trial.* Lawrence: University Press of Kansas, 1998.

Klein, Alana. "Judging as Nudging: New Governance Approaches for the Enforcement of Constitutional Social and Economic Rights." *Columbia Human Rights Law Review* 39 (2008): 351–422.

Kluger, Richard. *Simple Justice: The History of Brown v. Board of Education and Black America's Struggle for Equality*. New York: Vintage, 2004.

Knight, Jack, and James Johnson. *The Priority of Democracy: The Political Consequences of Pragmatism*. New York: Russell Sage Foundation, 2011.

Lessig, Lawrence. "Out-Posting Post." In Robert C. Post, *Citizens Divided*, 97–105. Cambridge, MA: Harvard University Press, 2014.

Levi, Edward H. *An Introduction to Legal Reasoning*. Chicago: University of Chicago Press, 1949.

———. *Point of View: Talks on Education*. Chicago: University of Chicago Press, 1969.

Little, Rory K. "*Heller* and Constitutional Interpretation: Originalism's Last Gasp." *Hastings Law Journal* 60 (2009): 1415–1430.

Llewellyn, Karl N. *The Bramble Bush*. Oxford: Oxford University Press, 2008.

Lund, Nelson. "The Second Amendment, *Heller*, and Originalist Jurisprudence." *UCLA Law Review* 56 (2009): 1343–1376.

MacGilvray, Erick. "Dewey's Public." *Contemporary Pragmatism* 7 (2010): 31–47.

MacNeil, Ian R. *The New Social Contract: An Inquiry into Modern Contractual Relations*. New Haven, CT: Yale University Press, 1980.

Magee, Michael. *Emancipating Pragmatism: Emerson, Jazz and Experimental Writing*. Tuscaloosa: University of Alabama Press, 2004.

Maitra. Keya. "Ambedkar and the Constitution of India: A Deweyan Experiment." *Contemporary Pragmatism* 9 (2012): 301–20.

Mansbridge, Jane. "Practice-Thought-Practice." In *Deepening Democracy: Institutional innovations in Empowered Participatory Governance*, edited by Archon Fung and Erik Olin Wright, 175–99. London: Verso, 2003.

Marnell, William H. *Man-Made Morals: Four Philosophies that Shaped America*. New York: Anchor, 1966.

Menand, Louis. *The Metaphysical Club*. New York: Farrar, Straus and Giroux, 2001.

Michelman, Frank I. "Legitimacy, Strict Scrutiny, and the Case against the Supreme Court." In Robert C. Post, *Citizens Divided*, 106–24. Cambridge, MA: Harvard University Press, 2014.

———. "Property, Utility, and Fairness: Comments on the Ethical Foundations of 'Just Compensation' Law." *Harvard Law Review* 80 (1967): 1165–258.

Minow, Martha, and Elizabeth Spelman. "In Context." *Southern California Law Review* 63 (1990): 1597–1652.

Misak, Cheryl. *The American Pragmatists*. Oxford: Oxford University Press, 2013.

Morris, Charles. *The Pragmatic Movement in American Philosophy*. New York: George Braziller, 1970.

Nedelsky, Jennifer. *Private Property and the Limits of American Constitutionalism: The Madisonian Framework and Its Legacy*. Chicago: University of Chicago Press, 1990.

NeJaime, Douglas. "When New Governance Fails." *Ohio State Law Journal* 70 (2009): 323–99.

Pappas, Gregory Fernando. *John Dewey's Ethics: Democracy as Experience.* Bloomington: Indiana University Press, 2008.

———. "What Would John Dewey Say about Deliberative Democracy and Democratic Experimentalism?" *Contemporary Pragmatism* 9 (2012): 57–74.

Parker, Richard D. *"Here, the People Rule": A Constitutional Populist Manifesto.* Cambridge, MA: Harvard University Press, 1998.

Peirce, Charles Sanders. *The Essential Peirce.* Edited by Nathan Houser and Christian Kloesel. Bloomington: Indiana University Press, 1992.

Posner, Richard A. "In Defense of Looseness." *New Republic*, August 27, 2008. Accessed January 12, 2015. https://newrepublic.com/article/62124/defense-looseness.

———. *The Essential Holmes.* Chicago: University of Chicago Press, 1992.

———. *How Judges Think.* Cambridge, MA: Harvard University Press, 2008.

———. *Law, Pragmatism, and Democracy.* Cambridge, MA: Harvard University Press, 2005.

———. *Reflections on Judging.* Cambridge, MA: Harvard University Press, 2013.

Post, Robert C. *Citizens Divided.* Cambridge, MA: Harvard University Press, 2014.

Putnam, Hilary. "Pragmatism and Moral Objectivity." In *Words and Life,* edited by James Conant. Cambridge, MA: Harvard University Press, 1994.

———. "A Reconsideration of Deweyan Democracy." In *Pragmatism in Law and Society,* edited by M. Brint and W. Weavers. Boulder, CO: Westview, 1991.

———. *Renewing Philosophy.* Cambridge, MA: Harvard University Press, 1992.

Rawls, John. *Collected Papers.* Cambridge, MA: Harvard University Press, 1999.

———. *The Law of Peoples.* Cambridge, MA: Harvard University Press, 1999.

———. *A Theory of Justice.* Cambridge, MA: Harvard University Press, 1971.

Reich, Charles A. "The New Property." *Yale Law Journal* 73 (1964): 733–87.

Rescher, Nicholas. *Realistic Pragmatism: An Introduction to Pragmatic Philosophy.* New York: State University of New York Press, 2000.

Richardson, Henry S. *Democratic Autonomy: Public Reasoning about the Ends of Policy.* Oxford: Oxford University Press, 2002.

Robinson, Edward Steven. *Law and the Lawyers.* New York: Macmillan, 1935.

Rogers, Melvin L. *The Undiscovered Dewey: Religion, Morality, and the Ethos of Democracy.* New York: Columbia University Press, 2009.

Rose, Carol M. *"Mahon* Reconstructed: Why the Takings Issue Is Still a Muddle." *Southern California Law Review* 57 (1984): 561–99.

Rosenberg, Gerald N. *The Hollow Hope: Can Courts Bring about Social Change?* Chicago: University of Chicago Press, 2008.

Sabel, Charles. "Dewey, Democracy, and Democratic Experimentalism." *Contemporary Pragmatism* 9 (2012): 35–55.

Sandel, Michael J. *Democracy's Discontent: America in Search of a Public Philosophy.* Cambridge, MA: Harvard University Press, 1996.

Sax, Joseph L. "Takings and the Police Power." *Yale Law Journal* 74 (1964): 36–76.

Scalia, Antonin. *A Matter of Interpretation*. Princeton, NJ: Princeton University Press, 1997.

———. "The Rule of Law as a Law of Rules." *University of Chicago Law Review* 56 (1989): 1175–188.

Schlegel, John Henry. *American Legal Realism and Empirical Social Science*. Chapel Hill: University of North Carolina Press, 1995.

Schulkin, Jay. *Naturalism and Pragmatism*. New York: Palgrave Macmillan, 2012.

Seigfried, Charlene Haddock. *Pragmatism and Feminism: Reweaving the Social Fabric*. Chicago: University of Chicago Press, 1996.

Shalin, Dmitri N. *Pragmatism & Democracy: Studies in History, Social Theory, and Progressive Politics*. New Brunswick, NJ: Transaction, 2011.

Sherry, Suzanna. "Property Is the New Privacy: The Coming Constitutional Revolution." *Harvard Law Review* 128 (2015): 1452–1476.

Shook, John R. *Dewey's Social Philosophy: Democracy as Education*. New York: Palgrave Macmillan, 2014.

Siegal, Reva B. "*Heller* and Originalism's Dead Hand—in Theory and Practice." *UCLA Law Review* 56 (2009): 1399–1424.

Simon, William H. "Afterward—Part II: New Governance Anxiety: A Deweyan Response." *Wisconsin Law Review* 2010 (2010): 727–36.

———. "Solving Problems vs. Claiming Rights: The Pragmatist Challenge to Legal Liberalism." *William & Mary Law Review* 46 (2004): 127–212.

———. "Toyota Jurisprudence: Legal Theory and Rolling Rule Regimes." In *Law and New Governance in the EU and the US*, edited by Grianne de Burca and Joanne Scott, 37–64. Oxford: Hart, 2006.

Stern, Mark Joseph. "Judge Posner's Gay Marriage Opinion Is a Witty, Deeply Moral Masterpiece." *Slate*, September 5, 2014. Accessed January 10, 2015. http://www.slate.com/blogs/outward/2014/09/05/judge_richard_posner_s_gay _marriage_opinion_is_witty_moral_and_brilliant.html.

———. "Listen to a Conservative Judge Brutally Destroy Arguments against Gay Marriage." *Slate*, August 27, 2014. Accessed January 10, 2015. http://www.slate .com/blogs/outward/2014/08/27/listen_to_judge_richard_posner_destroy_arguments _against_gay_marriage.html.

Strauss, David A. "Why Was *Lochner* Wrong?" *University of Chicago Law Review* 70 (2003): 373–86.

Sullivan, Michael. *Legal Pragmatism: Community, Rights and Democracy*. Bloomington: Indiana University Press, 2007.

Sunstein, Cass. *Designing Democracy: What Constitutions Do*. Oxford: Oxford University Press, 2001.

———. "Incompletely Theorized Agreements." *Harvard Law Review* 108 (1995): 1733–1772.

———. *Infotopia: How Many Minds Produce Knowledge*. Oxford: Oxford University Press, 2006.

———. *"Lochner's* Legacy." *Columbia Law Review* 87 (1987): 873–919.

———. *Radicals in Robes: Why Extreme Right-Wing Courts Are Wrong for America.* New York: Basic Books, 2005.

———. *Republic.com 2.0.* Cambridge: Cambridge University Press, 2007.

Super, David A. "Laboratories of Destitution: Democratic Experimentalism and the Failure of Antipoverty Law." *University of Pennsylvania Law Review* 157 (2009): 541–616.

Tan, Sor-Hoon. *Confucian Democracy: A Deweyan Reconstruction.* Albany: State University of New York Press, 2004.

Thaler, Richard H., and Cass R. Sunstein. *Nudge: Improving Decisions about Health, Wealth, and Happiness.* New Haven, CT: Yale University Press, 2008.

Treanor, William Michael. "Jam for Justice Holmes: Reassessing the Significance of *Mahon.*" *Georgetown Law Journal* 86 (1998): 813–74.

Tribe, Lawrence. *American Constitutional Law.* New York: Foundation Press, 1988.

———. "Dividing *Citizens United*: The Case v. The Controversy." Paper presented at a First Amendment law and corporate law conference held at Harvard Law School on November 7, 2014.

Tribe, Lawrence and Joshua Matz. *Uncertain Justice: The Roberts Court and the Constitution.* New York: Henry Holt, 2014.

Tufts, James H. *The Ethics of Cooperation.* Boston: Houghton Mifflin, 1918.

———. *Our Democracy: Its Origins and Its Tasks.* New York: Henry Holt, 1917.

Tushnet, Mark. "*Heller* and the Critique of Judgment." *Supreme Court Review* 2009 (2008): 61–87.

———. "*Heller* and the New Originalism." *Ohio State Law Journal* 69 (2008): 609–24.

———. *The New Constitutional Order.* Princeton, NJ: Princeton University Press, 2003.

———. *Taking the Constitution Away from the Courts.* Princeton, NJ: Princeton University Press, 1999.

Unger, Roberto Mangabeira. *Democracy Realized: The Progressive Alternative.* London: Verso, 1998.

———. *What Should Legal Analysis Become?* London: Verso, 1996.

Urbinati, Nadia. "Free Speech as the Citizen's Right." In Robert C. Post, *Citizens Divided,* 125–40. Cambridge, MA: Harvard University Press, 2014.

Waldron, Jeremy. *The Dignity of Legislation.* Cambridge: Cambridge University Press, 1999.

———. *The Rule of Law and the Measure of Property.* Cambridge: Cambridge University Press, 2012.

Wechsler, Herbert. "Toward Neutral Principles of Constitutional Law." *Harvard Law Review* 73 (1959): 1–35.

West, Cornel. *Democracy Matters: Winning the Fight against Imperialism.* New York: Penguin, 2004.

Westbrook, Robert. *John Dewey and American Democracy.* Ithaca, NY: Cornell University Press, 1991.

Index

Ackerman, Bruce, 109
Adair v. United States, 6
Addams, Jane, 21, 175
Adkins v. Children's Hospital, 110
Ages of American Law, The (Gilmore), 187
Alden v. Maine, 6
Alito, Samuel (justice), 162, 174, 177, 180
Allgeyer v. Louisiana, 6, 112
American Constitutional Law (Tribe), 106, 111
American Express v. Italian Colors Restaurant, 6
Ansell, Christopher, 40–42
"Anthropology and the Law" (Dewey), 32
Arizona Free Enterprise Club's Freedom Club PAC v. Bennett, 6
Arnold, Thurman, W., 4, 36
Arthur, John, 170. See also *Obergefell v. Hodges*
Ashcroft v. al-Kidd, 6
Atiyah, P. S., 185–86
Atkin v. Kansas, 112
AT&T Mobility v. Conception, 6
Austin, John, 31–32
"Austin's Theory of Sovereignty" (Dewey), 31
Austin v. Michigan Chamber of Commerce, 129–30, 132, 136
authority (method of pragmatic inquiry), 99; as described by Charles Sanders Peirce, 15–16, 20, 62, 79, 161, 204. *See also* Peirce, Charles Sanders; pragmatic; pragmatism

A.L.A. Schecter Poultry Corp. v. United States, 6
"a priori" (method of pragmatic inquiry), 15–17, 20, 34, 79, 123, 161, 204. *See also* Peirce, Charles Sanders; pragmatic; pragmatism

Bakeshop Act, 106, 109–11, 113, 115, 122
Bakke. See *Regents of the University of California v. Bakke*
Balkin, Jack, 109
Baskin v. Bogan, 49–50, 174, 178, 180–81, 202–3
Beachfront Management Act, 90, 93
Beard, Charles A., 8
Becker, Gary, 133, 142, 146
Becker-Posner Blog, 133
behavioral economics, 37
Belotti, 140
benchmarking, 44–45, 47, 192; and *Brown*, 155, 161, 167; as information-producing, 66, 71, 74–75, 122–23
Berea College v. Kentucky, 5
Bernstein, David, 111, 120, 125
Bickel, Alexander, M., 9
Bill of Rights, 169
Bipartisan Campaign Reform Act of 2002 (BCRA), 129–30, 137
Blackmun, Harry (justice), 91–92
Blackstone, William, 54, 72–73, 100
Board of Trustees of University of Alabama v. Garrett, 6
Bogan v. Scott-Harris, 6
Boorstin, Daniel J., 100

Bowers v. Hardwick, 169
Bramble Bush, The (Llewellyn), 3
Brandeis, Louis D., 36, 77, 80, 82–83, 92, 159
Bratz v. Bollinger, 157
Brennan, William J., 84
Breuer, Marcel, 84
Breyer, Stephen (justice), 52–53, 55, 62, 70, 165–68
bright-line rules, 13; and *Heller*, 54, 67, 70; and *Lochner*, 115, 123; and *Mahon*, 78, 202; and *Moore v. Madigan*, 74–75; in regulatory takings cases, 91, 93, 96, 98, 102, 104
Briscoe v. LaHue, 6
Brown v. Board of Education, 1, 151–66, 168, 176–77, 180–82, 203
Brown v. Board of Education 2, 155–56
Bryan County, Oklahoma v. Brown, 6
Buck, Carrie, 5. See also *Buck v. Bell*
Buck v. Bell, 5, 7
Bush v. Gore, 6

Cambridge Metaphysical Club, 15
campaign finance, 129; and *Citizens United*, 131, 133, 138–44, 146, 148–49, 170
Carter v. Carter Coal Company, 6
Case against the Supreme Court, The (Chemerinsky), 5, 200
Chemerinsky, Erwin, 5–8, 10–12, 22, 200; and *Citizens United*, 132–33, 147–48; and judicial review, 151, 156
Circuit City v. Adams, 6
"Citizens Deflected: Electoral Integrity and Political Reform" (Karlan), 142
Citizens Divided (Post), 137–38
Citizens United, 1, 6, 128–44 *passim*, 146, 149, 203
Civil Rights Cases of 1883, 157
Clinton, Hillary, 129
Coase, Ronald, 195. See also Coase theorem
Coase theorem, 94
Collected Papers (Rawls), 184
Columbia v. Heller, 48, 50–55, 59, 67–73, 202
Commentaries (Blackstone), 100
common-law, 56, 69; and contract law, 186; and *Lochner*, 107, 110, 125, 127–28; and regulatory takings jurisprudence, 87, 91–92, 95, 98–100
Common Law, The (Holmes), 186

Congress (United States), 44–45, 52, 66; and campaign finance legislation, 130–31, 134, 137, 149
conservative foundationalist constitutional theory, 77–78, 122
conservativism: as a legal stance, 38, 77–78, 126, 157, 177; as a political stance, 2, 54, 116, 135. *See also* conservative foundationalist constitutional theory; formalism; originalism; politics
Constitution (of the United States), 10–12, 19, 22, 143–44; and contract theory, 182, 198–99; fetishism/idolatry of, 12, 26; limits of, 9, 13; meaning of, 136; moral readings of, 117–20, 137; in originalist methodology, 51, 54, 56–57, 68, 70; protections within, 170; purpose of, 7–8, 12–13, 20, 135; and regulatory takings jurisprudence, 99, 100, 102; and the right to marriage, 168, 171–72
constitutional law (in the United States), 167, 180–83, 204; antiprecedent in, 108, 111, 128, 132; in contemporary thought and practice, 1, 8, 10–12, 31–32, 36–37, 48; democratic conception of, 1–4, 10, 14, 21–23, 76–78, 114–17, 128, 135–36, 200; and politics, 63; standard conceptions of, 2–3, 15, 22–23, 48, 50; theory, 9, 48
constitutional populism, 8, 10–11, 13–14, 200
contract, 183–98 *passim*, 204; discrete, 196–97; law of, 183, 186, 191
"Contracting for Innovation: Vertical Disintegration and Interfirm Collaboration" (Gilson, Sabel, and Scott), 191
cooperation, 182, 190, 195
Coppage v. Kansas, 6
Corbin, Arthur, 186
Courts of Appeals (United States), 171
"cruel and unusual punishment," 5
Cumming v. Board of Education, 5

Death of Contract, The (Gilmore), 186
DeBoer, April, 170. See also *Obergefell v. Hodges*
Debs v. United States, 5
"The Decision that Threatens Democracy" (Dworkin), 135
Declaration of Independence, 14

DeKoe, Ijpe, 170. See also *Obergefell v. Hodges*
democracy, 1, 12–15, 20–21, 125, 140; and agency, 40–41; a priori theories of, 28, 128; and change, 23–26; corporate, 130, 148; cultural, 23–26, 121; discursive, 138–39; "elite," 26–27, 35, 48; and institutions, 38–42, 44–47, 121; and judicial supremacy, 116–18; political, 23–27, 30–33, 39, 44, 143–44, 211n12; and the rule of law, 58–59, 67; social, 31, 160–61. See also democratic experimentalism; democratic process; Deweyan democracy; jurisprudence of democratic experimentalism
democratic experimentalism, 2, 4, 21, 23, 36–50 *passim*, 200–204; and *Brown*, 155–56, 160; as information-producing, 65–67, 71–72, 74, 76–79; and *Lochner*, 104–6, 115; and *Obergefell*, 174, 176–77; as a political practice, 121; rights in, 126; and social contract theory, 182–83. See also democracy; jurisprudence of democratic experimentalism
democratic process, 133, 180; and the Constitution, 7–8, 182; Court's position within, 11, 118, 129, 203; under democratic experimentalism, 21–23, 25, 37–38, 45, 47; as information-producing, 71–72; obstruction of, 120, 174, 176, 178. See also democracy
Dennis v. United States, 5
Designing Democracy (Sunstein), 37
Dewey, John, 1, 4, 60, 65, 68, 78; and democracy, 14, 18–36 *passim*, 40–48, 120–21, 161, 201 (*see also* democracy; Deweyan democracy); and the law, 27–36 *passim*, 40–41, 45, 104–6, 175; and the public, 27, 33, 41, 159. See also specific titles
Deweyan democracy, 4, 18, 23, 176, 181–82. See also democracy; Dewey, John
Deweyan pragmatism, 65, 146, 200. See also Dewey, John; pragmatic; pragmatism
discrimination, 5, 9, 101, 163, 178–79, 203
"Distributive Justice: Some Addenda" (Rawls), 184
District Courts (United States), 171
DOMA (Defense of Marriage Act), 169
Dorf, Michael, 4, 21, 43–47, 201
Dred Scott v. Sandford, 5, 102–3, 111
Du Bois, W. E. B., 168

due process, 108, 113, 152, 174. *See also* Due Process Clause
Due Process Clause, 55, 87, 106–7, 126, 169–70, 172–73, 181. *See also* due process
Dworkin, Ronald, 9, 22, 50, 62, 201, 203; on *Citizen's United*, 134–37, 147; on *Lochner*, 105, 115–22

Eberlin, Burkhard, 156
Economic Interpretation of the Constitution of the United States, An (Beard), 8
electioneering communications, 129–30, 147
electoral integrity, 142, 146–48
Eleventh Amendment, 63
Ely, John Hart, 9
"Empowered Participatory Governance" (Fung and Wright), 155
Epstein, Richard, 9, 22, 55, 77–79; and *Citizens United*, 133–35, 139, 144, 146; and *Lochner*, 108, 110–11, 115, 125–26; and regulatory takings jurisprudence, 77–79, 93–105 *passim*, 116, 121, 202–3
equal protection, 57–58, 62, 152–55, 178, 180–81. *See also* Equal Protection Clause
Equal Protection Clause, 5, 56–57. *See also* equal protection
Ethics (Dewey), 120
Ethics of Cooperation, The (Tufts), 182
experimental intelligence, 27, 33, 47
experimental method (of pragmatic inquiry). *See* scientific method (of pragmatic inquiry)

fallibilism, 183, 197, 199
Fifteenth Amendment, 157
Fifth Amendment, 63, 84, 86
First Amendment, 63, 86; and *Citizens United*, 129–31, 133–34, 136–41, 143–46, 148
First National Bank of Boston v. Belloti, 140
Fisher v. University of Texas at Austin, 5, 142
"Fixation of Belief, The" (Peirce), 15
Florida Prepaid v. College Savings Bank, 6
Ford, Franklin, 103
formalism, 38, 48, 79, 101, 142, 202; after *Brown*, 157–58, 160, 162–63, 166–68, 177; and contract law, 186–88; as information-excluding, 51, 55, 79, 101; and *Lochner*, 106, 125

Fourteenth Amendment: and *Brown*, 152–53, 155, 157; and *Lochner*, 106, 108, 112, 114–15, 120, 122, 124; and *Obergefell*, 164, 168–69, 173; and regulatory takings jurisprudence, 78, 86. *See also* due process; Due Process Clause
Frankfurter, Felix (justice), 156
"Free Speech as the Citizen's Right" (Urbinati), 142
Frohwerk v. United States, 5
Fung, Archon, 155

Garcetti v. Ceballos, 6
Gillman, Howard, 109–10, 120, 125
Gilmore, Grant, 183, 186–88, 195–96, 204
Gilson, Ronald J., 183, 191–93, 195–97, 204
Ginsburg, Ruth Bader (justice), 165
Gong Lum v. Rice, 5
Goodnow, Frank J., 182
Goodridge v. Department of Public Health, 169
governance mechanism, 192, 195–96, 198

Hamdi v. Rumsfeld, 5
Hammer v. Dagenhart, 6
Harlan, John Marshall (justice): and *Brown*, 153, 160, 164; and *Lochner*, 105–6, 113–15, 119, 121, 123–24, 203; and regulatory takings jurisprudence, 88
Hart, H. L. A., 39
Heller, Dick Anthony, 51. See also *Columbia v. Heller*
"Here, the People Rule": A Constitutional Populist Manifesto* (Parker), 11
Hirschl, Ran, 10–12
Holder v. Humanitarian Law Project, 5
Holmes, Oliver Wendell, Jr., 5, 15, 28, 36, 137; and contract law, 186–87; and *Lochner*, 114–15, 119–21, 124–25, 172, 175; regulatory takings jurisprudence of, 77–90 *passim*, 92–94, 97, 100–106, 202–3; and *Virginia v. West Virginia*, 156
Hook, Sidney, 14
Hope v. Pelzer, 6

Imbler v. Pachtman, 6
information production, 48, 50, 65–69, 72–76, 122–23, 155
inquiry: interest balancing, 53; pragmatic method of, 15–19, 21, 28, 33, 43–44. *See also* pragmatic; pragmatism

Introduction to the Law of Contract (Atiyah), 185
Issacharoff, Samuel, 53

J. A. Croson v. City of Richmond, 5
Jacobson v. Massachusetts, 112
James, William, 36, 126
Johnson, James, 38–39, 42
judicial activism, 13, 54, 68, 108–9, 126; and *Brown*, 156, 161; and *Obergefell*, 181
judicial decision-making: and *Citizens United*, 136, 149; and information production, 49–50, 57, 59–63, 64–65, 69, 72; and regulatory takings jurisprudence, 78–79, 99
judicial review, 9–11, 13, 46, 151, 174, 209n1; and *Lochner*, 105, 107–9, 115–17, 125
judicial supremacy, 10, 59, 144, 151, 156, 174; in the interpretation of constitutional law, 4, 9, 12–14, 116, 169, 200
jurisprudence of democratic experimentalism, 199, 201–3; and *Brown*, 161, 167–68, 178; and *Citizens United*, 144–46, 149, 151–52; and *Lochner*, 121–29; and *Obergefell*, 181–82. *See also* democratic experimentalism
justice: theory of, 183–85, 197, 203

Karlan, Pamela S., 142, 146
Kay v. Board of Higher Education of the City of New York (1940), 30
Kellogg, Frederic R., 78, 103
Kennedy, Anthony (justice): and *Citizens United*, 131, 135, 144, 147–48; and *Obergefell*, 177–78; and *Parents Involved*, 162, 164–65, 167–71
Kens, Paul, 108
Keystone Bituminous v. DeBenedictus, 87, 89
Kimel v. Florida Board of Regents, 6
Kluger, Richard, 156–59, 161
Knight, Jack, 38–39, 42
Knoxville Iron Co. v. Harbison, 112
Kohler Act, 79–80, 82–83, 87–89, 94
Korematsu v. United States, 5
Kostura, Thomas, 170. See also *Obergefell v. Hodges*
Kramer, Larry, D., 12–14, 47

Landmark Act, 85
Langdell, Christopher Columbus, 186
law: as constructed set of social practices, 2, 35–36; as "democratic means," 4, 20–23,

40–43, 45–48, 79, 123, 201, 204; as "natural type," 2, 33–38, 107, 125, 127; as profession, 3, 59
"The Law of Peoples" (Rawls), 184
Lawrence v. Texas, 169
"learning by monitoring," 44–45, 47, 66
Ledbetter v. Goodyear Tire and Rubber Co., Inc., 6
"legalism," 59–66, 68–71, 75, 157
Levi, Edward, 204
liberalism (political stance), 2, 27, 54, 116, 118. *See also* politics
Liberalism and Social Action (Dewey), 121
libertarianism, 143, 149
Llewellyn, Karl N., 3
Lochner v. New York, 1, 6; as antiprecedent, 87, 92, 97–99, 149, 172–76, 182; Epstein's evaluation of, 103, 134; Holmes's dissent in, 77–81; legacy of, 105–28 *passim*, 202–3
Lucas v. South Carolina Coastal Council, 1, 91, 93, 100, 102–3, 202

MacNeil, Ian R., 183, 188–91, 193, 196, 204
Mansbridge, Jane, 156
Marnell, William, 108
Marshall, John (chief justice), 54, 87
Matz, Joshua, 162
McClesky v. Kemp, 5
McConnell v. Federal Election Commission, 136
McDonald v. City of Chicago, 55, 72, 74
McLaurin v. Oklahoma State Regents, 154
Michelman, Frank, 142, 145
Miller v. Schoene, 53, 88, 107
Milliken v. Bradley, 157
Mills, John Stuart, 173
Mireles v. Waco, 6
Misak, Cheryl, 18–19
Missouri Pacific Railway Company v. Nebraska, 103
Mobile v. Bolden, 5
Moore v. Madigan, 48, 50, 72–75
Mugler v. Kansas, 88, 221n10
Munn v. Illinois, 87, 221n10
Mutual Pharmaceutical v. Bartlett, 6
"My Philosophy of Law" (Dewey), 33

NAACP, 158–60, 166
National Federation of Independent Business v. Sebelius, 6
Nedelsky, Jennifer, 110, 120, 125

"The New Property" (Reich), 100
New Social Contract: An Inquiry into Modern Contractual Relations, The (MacNeil), 188
New York v. United States, 6
Nudge (Thaler and Sunstein), 101

Obergefell, James, 170. See also *Obergefell v. Hodges*
Obergefell v. Hodges, 1, 9, 50, 105, 203; as positive precedent, 151–52, 168, 172, 174–76, 178, 180–81
originalism, 71, 154; and Scalia, 48, 50–62, 68, 145, 173, 201

Pappas, Gregory, 24
Parents Involved in Community Schools v. Seattle School District No. 1, 5, 161–62, 166–68
Parker, Richard D., 11–12
Peckham, Rufus Wheeler (justice), 98, 105, 111–13, 115, 118–19, 121–23
Peirce, Charles Sanders, 1, 4, 15–20, 75, 104, 200; pragmatic methodology of, 25, 29–30, 34, 43, 62, 78–79, 123, 161, 204
Penn Central Transportation Co. v. New York City, 83–86, 89–90
Pennsylvania Coal Co. v. Mahon, 1, 202; and regulatory takings, 77–80, 82–83, 85–90, 92–94, 103–4
People Themselves: Popular Constitutionalism and Judicial Review, The (Kramer), 12
personhood (definition of), 34–35
Plessy v. Ferguson, 5, 111, 152–53, 157, 164–68, 203
Pliva, Inc. v. Mensing, 6
pluralism, 24, 27, 31–32, 36, 45, 47–48
police powers of the state, 96–97, 101–3, 110–14, 120–22, 134, 152
Political Action Committee (PAC), 130
politics, 63–64, 135, 137. *See also* conservativism; liberalism
popular constitutionalism. *See* constitutional populism
positivism, 31–32, 39
Posner, Richard, 36, 120, 167; and *Baskin v. Bogan*, 49–50, 174, 178–81, 202–3; and *Citizens United*, 133, 147; and *Heller*, 54–55; and information production, 59–65, 68–70; and *Moore v. Madigan*, 48, 72, 74–77

Post, Robert C., 137–42, 144, 148, 203
pragmatic, 35, 43–44, 58, 73, 79; canon, 15; critique, 14; ideals, 1; institutions, 41–42; jurisprudence, 50, 63–65, 68–71, 124; "maxim," 18–19, 21, 46; methodology, 15–21, 25, 34. *See also* Dewey, John; pragmatism
pragmatism, 4, 15, 42, 44, 126, 200; critiques of, 118. *See also* Dewey, John; pragmatic
Pragmatism (James), 126
Pragmatist Democracy: Evolutionary Learning as Public Philosophy (Ansell), 40
Prigg v. Pennysylvania, 5
Prinz v. United States, 6
Priority of Democracy: The Political Consequences of Pragmatism, The (Knight and Johnson), 38
property, 98; law of, 100, 102, 104, 221n10, 223n84. *See also* regulatory takings
Pruneyard Shopping Center v. Robins, 86, 100, 104
"Psychology and Justice" (Dewey), 29
Putnam, Hilary, 18–19, 25

race, 5–6, 8; and *Brown*, 152, 153, 159–68
Railroad Retirement Board v. Alton R. Co., 6
Rawls, John, 15, 22, 182–85, 195, 197, 203
Red Lion Broadcasting Co. v. Federal Communications Commission, 140
Regents of the University of California v. Bakke, 157
regulatory takings, 77–78, 83–104 *passim*, 202
Rehnquist, William (chief justice), 85–86, 89
Reich, Charles A., 100
rights, 8–9, 45, 116, 126; to bear arms, 50–53, 56, 72–73; to bodily integrity, 5; civil, 122; of contract, 101, 112, 122, 125; economic, 128; to free speech, 86, 100, 137, 143, 148 (*see also* First Amendment); of individual liberty, 95–96, 112, 118; to marriage, 168, 170–72, 176, 178 (*see also* same-sex marriage); of minorities, 7, 10, 153; to petition, 86; of self-defense, 52, 72–73. *See also* Bill of Rights; property
Roberts, John (chief justice), 60–61, 105; and *Citizens United*, 131, 135, 143; and *Obergefell*, 171–73, 175–77, 180, 202–3; and *Parents Involved*, 162–67
Robinson, Edward Steven, 4, 36
Romer v. Evans, 169
Rose, Carol M., 100

Rowse, Jayne, 170. See also *Obergefell v. Hodges*
"rule of law," 14, 187; and democratic experimentalism, 34, 36, 38–39, 47–48, 121; "as a law of rules," 57–60, 68, 123, 148
Russell, Bertrand, 30

Sabel, Charles F., 4, 21, 43–47, 126, 183, 201; and contract law, 191–93, 195–97, 204
same-sex marriage, 49–50, 72, 151, 168–79 *passim*, 203. See also *Citizens United*
Scalia, Antonin: and *Citizens United*, 129, 131, 134–35, 145; and *Obergefell*, 173, 176; and originalism, 48, 50–52, 55–61, 65–71, 75, 201–2; and *Parents Involved*, 162; and regulatory takings, 78, 89, 91, 100, 102–3
Schenk v. United States, 5
scientific method (of pragmatic inquiry), 17–18, 20, 25, 75, 79, 201. *See also* pragmatic; pragmatism
Scott, Robert E., 183, 191–93, 195–97, 204
Second Amendment, 50–55, 63, 72–74, 202. *See also* rights: to bear arms
segregation, 160, 162–67. *See also* race
"separate but equal," 152–54, 157–58, 160, 167, 181, 203. See also *Brown v. Board of Education*; discrimination; race; segregation
Shelby County, Alabama v. Holder, 6
Shelton, R. G., 5
Shook, John, 24
Siegal, Reva, 54
Simon, William, 4, 42–43, 126
Simple Justice: The History of Brown v. Board of Education and Black America's Struggle for Equality (Kluger), 156
simultaneous engineering, 44–45, 66, 192
Slaughter-House Cases, 5, 157
"sociable contract theory," 182–83, 195, 197–99, 203–4
social contract theory, 182–85, 195–96, 198, 203
social Darwinism, 108, 110
"Social Realities *versus* Police Court Fictions" (Dewey), 30
Social Reform and the Constitution (Goodnow), 182
Souls of Black Folk, The (Du Bois), 168
Souter, David (justice), 165
sovereignty, 31–32, 41, 45, 52, 55–57

speech, 132–34, 137, 139; corporate, 129, 131, 135, 136, 140, 146, 149; political, 128–31, 143–45, 147
Spencer, Herbert, 34, 109, 114, 121
stare decisis, 58
Stern, Mark Joseph, 49–50
Stevens, John Paul (justice), 52–55, 70; and *Citizens United*, 131–34, 136, 145–47, 149; and *Parents Involved*, 165, 167–68; regulatory takings jurisprudence of, 87–88, 92–93
Strauss, David, 109, 126
"strict construction school," 62
strict scrutiny, 142, 145, 162, 164–67
Subsidence Act (1966), 88–89
Sullivan, Michael, 18–19
Sunstein, Cass, 37–39, 42, 101, 110, 125, 201
Supreme Court (of the United States): antiprecedents of, 182, 200, 203; and the Constitution, 56–57 (*see also* Constitution); critiques of, 4–6, 9–11, 53–55, 125, 132–33, 141–42, 200; and democracy, 14, 149, 161 (*see also* democracy); and democratic experimentalism, 2, 70–72 (*see also* democratic experimentalism); *Lochner*-era, 109–10, 127; proper function of, 6–10, 20, 115–19, 125, 143–44, 156; takings jurisprudence of, 83–87, 91–94, 99, 104. *See also* specific cases and justices
Supreme Judicial Court of Massachusetts, 169
Supreme Neglect: How to Revive Constitutional Protection for Private Property (Epstein), 110
Swann v. Charlotte-Mecklenburg Board of Education, 165
Sweatt v. Painter, 154

Takings: Private Property and the Power of Eminent Domain (Epstein), 110
"Takings Clause," 78, 86, 90, 93, 95–96, 98–99. *See also* regulatory takings
Taking the Constitution Away from the Courts (Tushnet), 13
"tenacity"(method of pragmatic inquiry), 15–16, 20, 79, 99, 204. *See also* pragmatic; pragmatism

Thaler, Richard H., 101
Theory of Justice (Rawls), 15, 182–83
Thirteenth Amendment, 157
Thomas, Clarence (justice), 131, 162, 164, 167, 173, 176–77
Tillman Act of 1907, 132, 136
"Toward Neutral Principles of Constitutional Law," 157
Towards Juristocracy (Hirschl), 10
"Toyota Democracy" (Simon), 42
Tribe, Lawrence, 106–9, 111, 162; on *Citizens United*, 142, 144, 149–50; on *Lochner*, 120, 125, 175
Tufts, James, H., 23, 160, 182
Tushnet, Mark, 13, 48, 53, 78
"tyranny of the majority," 4, 7–12, 21, 59, 67–68, 200
Tyson & Bro. v. Banton, 102

Unger, Roberto, 37–39, 42, 201
United States v. Apel, 6
United States v. E.C. Knight Co., 6
United States v. Lopez, 6
United States v. Morrison, 6
United States v. Windsor, 169
Urbinati, Nadia, 142, 148

Van de Kamp v. Goldstein, 6
Vanetta, Seth, 126
Virginia v. West Virginia, 156

Waldron, Jeremy, 100, 103
Wal-mart Stores v. Dukes, 6
Warren, Earl (chief justice), 153–55, 177, 180
Warren Court, the, 6, 9, 157
Washington v. Davis, 5
Weschler, Herbert, 157, 159
Westbrook, Robert, 27
West Coast Hotel v. Parrish, 106, 110, 120
"Why Was *Lochner* Wrong?" (Strauss), 109
Williams, Ann Claire (Seventh Circuit), 75, 219n97
Williston, Samuel, 186–87, 197
Wright, Erik Olin, 155